# Hispanic (LGT) Masculinities in Transition

# MASCULINITY STUDIES

Literary and Cultural Representations

Josep M. Armengol and Àngels Carabí
*General Editors*

Vol. 4

---

This book is a volume in a Peter Lang monograph series.
Every title is peer reviewed and meets
the highest quality standards for content and production.

---

PETER LANG
New York • Washington, D.C./Baltimore • Bern
Frankfurt • Berlin • Brussels • Vienna • Oxford

# Hispanic (LGT) Masculinities in Transition



EDITED BY
Rafael M. Mérida-Jiménez

PETER LANG
New York • Washington, D.C./Baltimore • Bern
Frankfurt • Berlin • Brussels • Vienna • Oxford

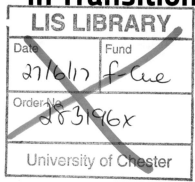

**Library of Congress Cataloging-in-Publication Data**

Hispanic (LGT) masculinities in transition / edited by Rafael M. Mérida-Jiménez.
pages cm. — (Masculinity studies: literary and cultural representations; v. 4)
Includes bibliographical references.
1. Masculinity in literature. 2. Homosexuality in literature.
3. Spanish literature—20th century—History and criticism.
4. Masculinity in motion pictures. 5. Homosexuality in motion pictures.
6. Motion pictures—Spain—History and criticism.
I. Mérida Jiménez, Rafael M., editor of compilation.
PQ6073.H65H58 860.9'353—dc23 2014013265
ISBN 978-1-4331-2410-5 (hardcover)
ISBN 978-1-4539-1365-9 (e-book)
ISSN 2161-2692

Bibliographic information published by **Die Deutsche Nationalbibliothek**.
**Die Deutsche Nationalbibliothek** lists this publication in the "Deutsche Nationalbibliografie"; detailed bibliographic data are available on the Internet at http://dnb.d-nb.de/.

The paper in this book meets the guidelines for permanence and durability of the Committee on Production Guidelines for Book Longevity of the Council of Library Resources.


29 Broadway, 18th floor, New York, NY 10006
www.peterlang.com



Printed in Germany

# CONTENTS

# EDITOR'S NOTE

This volume aims to offer a whole of different approaches around the plurality of lesbian, gay, and trans masculinities in Spain during the 1970s and 1980s. The end of the Francoist dictatorship (1975) and the reappearance of the democratic freedom suspended after the Civil War (1936–1939) determined the historical period known as the Transition. Multiple political, social, and sexual tensions characterized that time and turned it into a topic that has been object of study of the interdisciplinary research project entitled "Representaciones culturales de las sexualidades marginadas en España (1970–1995)" ["Cultural Representations of Marginalized Sexualities in Spain (1970–1995)"], FEM 2011-24064, funded by the Spanish Ministry of Economy and Competitiveness.

It is important to recall, among the publications of this international group of researchers, the seventeenth issue of *Lectora: Revista de dones i textualitat*, published in 2012—focused on Hispanic literatures and LGTBQ studies—or the contributions to the book *Minorías sexuales en España (1970–1995): Textos y representaciones* (Barcelona: Icaria, 2013), among many others. As the supervisor of the team, I would deeply thank all its members for their generosity and interest during the last three years. In addition, I must thank José L. Ramos-Rebollo for his invaluable help during the preparation of this volume, which could have never been completed without his unremitting support and dedication.

Rafael M. Mérida-Jiménez
*Serra Húnter Associate Professor of Hispanic Studies*
*Universitat de Lleida/Centre Dona i Literatura*

# INTRODUCTION

## Hispanic/Masculinities/Transition: An Introduction

Dieter Ingenschay
*Humboldt-Universität zu Berlin*

If masculinity studies have succeeded in challenging the social sciences and humanities since the 1980s, this has been due to important scholars—such as Raewyn Connell, George Mosse, Pierre Bourdieu, Michael S. Kimmel, and others—and their groundbreaking studies, and to the same degree to the unforeseen advances in women's studies.[1] It was Simone de Beauvoir's insight that the "unmarked" gender had ceased to be automatically male. She argued that being a man was not simply the "normal case" and that men were not the "first sex" any longer in the second half of the twentieth century. Being conscious about what masculinity studies owe to feminism, Rachel Adams and David Savran have asked rather polemically whether "masculinity studies represent a beneficial extension of feminist analysis or does it represent a hijacking of feminism?" (Adams and Savran 7). By now, over a decade later, hardly anyone will question the rightful existence of masculinity studies as an autonomous discipline, and the above mentioned pioneers' work has been extended all over the world by numerous theoretical studies and has been completed by a huge number of locally determined empirical investigations. These have made inquiries into many urgent issues of historical or contemporary political, social, and cultural life. One of the most influential notions when studying the impact of men has probably been Connell's notion of *hegemonic masculinity* (Connell *Gender* and *Masculinities*), inspired, as are large parts of gender studies on the whole, by Michel Foucault, a concept which aims at the very heart of the practice of gender inequalities, i.e., to the subordination of women by men (Gracia Trujillo's essay in this volume further investigates Connell's thesis from a new and consequent angle). Recently, voices can be heard that warn against a demonization of masculinity, against blaming men for all evil in the world, as if fascism, colonialism, imperialism, dictatorship, and injustice were simply masculine qualities, hence reducing questions of power and hegemony to a mere problem of testosterone. Masculinity studies have shown that not only women are men's victims, but rather that male power constellations suppress men as well.

That the rapes of homosexuals in Franco's prisons are a perfect paradigm of hegemonic masculinity is one of the insights of Juan Vicente Aliaga's article in this book ("Demasculinizing: Challenging Hegemonic Masculinity in Spanish Art and Culture"), in which he goes back to the repressive climate of the 1970s, created by the anti-gay *Ley de Peligrosidad y Rehabilitación Social* (Law of Social Dangerousness and Social Rehabilitation), amended in August 1970, exacerbating the former law against *vagos y maleantes* ("vagrants and wasters") and extending it to large parts of the (mainly male) Spanish homosexual community. While early forms of "transgressive" masculinities (often taking the form of transvestism) emerged in Spain during the 1970s and 1980s, Aliaga focuses on more recent activist groups challenging and questioning gender binarism in the 1990s.

The significant break between the 1970s and 1980s on the one hand and the 1990s on the other is treated in almost all of the articles in the volume the reader has in hand. Taken as a whole, they reflect the fundamental changes that masculinities underwent towards the end of the twentieth century in Spain since Franco's death in November 1975. Its interdisciplinary approach and international authors make a significant contribution to the field of historical masculinity studies—a particularly important task–as cultural discourse in Spain suffered from a remarkably late discovery of feminism in general, and masculinity and queer subjects in particular. Nevertheless, feminist and gay movements had appeared shortly after Franco's death, first the Catalonian FAGC, as Kerman Calvo, a specialist in comparative research on gay movements, shows in his article for this volume ("Sexual Movements Without Sex? Sex-Talk in the Spanish Gay Liberation Movement"). Calvo distinguishes radical from revolutionary movements, uncovers their Marxist foundations as well as the lack of historical models in Spain (as opposed to, say, Jeffrey Weeks's views on the British nineteenth century). In fact, the same could be said about my own field, and from my personal perspective as a German scholar of Hispanic literatures and cultures: Lorca's role in the cultural archeology of Spanish homosexuality is quite different from that of Wilde, Gide, Proust, or Thomas Mann in their respective countries. That France (and not the Anglo-American world) was the "constant source of inspiration and guidance," as Calvo confirms, corresponds to my own experience (as an early reader of Guy Hocquenghem and an occasional visitor of the Sunday tea dance at *Arcadie* in Rue du Château d'eau in Paris in the 1970s).

Calvo wonders "why a sexual movement did think so little about sex," and calls this generation "boring" (here my own experience differs from his analysis). Again, he notes that Spain was rather late (in comparison to Western democracies) due to the stigmatization of gays and lesbians under Franco, and he expounds the controversies between extreme-leftist organisations and bourgeois ones, and between "queens" and masculine gays. All this contributes to a complex archive of gay life and its accelerated development in the last decades of the twentieth century (which can be completed by Gracia Trujillo's description of the lesbian movement in her contribution to this book).

Thinking back to those years, I feel Calvo is right. It took quite a long time until the Spanish academia opened itself to LGT issues. The first books in this field were Spanish translations from French (Hocquenghem, whose *Homosexualidad y sociedad represiva* was published in Argentina as early as 1974) or from English (such as Steiner and Boyers). I perfectly remember the initial craven steps of what we used to proudly call *Gay and Lesbian Studies* within Spanish academia, and when María Ángeles Toda with her colleagues of the University of Seville published a special pink issue of *Stylistica. Revista Internacional de Estudios Estilísticos y Culturales* on homosexual culture in 1995 and 1996 (a time when, according to Gracia Trujillo, the Sociology Departments were the only institutions at the Spanish universities to admit gender relevant questions). Four years before, Óscar Guasch had presented his socio-anthropological text *La sociedad rosa* with a large second chapter dedicated to the rudimental homosexual life during the decades of the Dictatorship and to introducing the difference between a "pre-gay model" and post-Franco present with an emerging gay infrastructure. As for my research field, cultural and literary studies, the first surveys came from abroad: Paul J. Smith's *Laws of Desire* (1992), Emilie L. Bergmann's and Paul J. Smith's *¿Entiendes? Queer Readings, Hispanic Writings* (1995), Alfredo Martínez-Expósito's *Los escribas furiosos,* published in the U.S. (1998), or *Hispanisms and Homosexualities*, by Sylvia Molloy and Robert McKee Irwin (1998), to mention only a few groundbreaking studies.

Guasch's essay in this volume ("Bodily, Gender, and Identity Projects in Spain: From the Transvestite to the Transsexual," co-authored by Jordi Mas) recalls the origin of the "new" gay movement in transvestite culture according to the model of the *loca latina* prevailing in the mid 1970s—and not only in Spain, but also in large parts of the Americas–as we can learn from Puig and Donoso as well as the rebellious "queens" of Christopher Street. Guasch defines the transvestite for the Spanish context as a liminal being that "personifies the social reality of the period," whereas the transsexual "presents a body integrated into the standard codes of gender classification." Guasch and Mas consider transsexualization as a late modern process of a rationalization of certain modern forms of gender dissidence, which they relate to the homophobic and transphobic Francoist society. Under this perspective, Spain, where "trans" phenomena were a prominent film subject in the 1970s and 1980s, becomes a special case of Western ethnocentrism, and the authors complain about the erroneous inclusion of transvestites among the categories of homosexualities in early research on this subject.

The state of LGT studies has improved considerably over the last years in Spain, thanks to the work of researchers such as Fernando Villaamil, Fernando Olmeda, Jordi Petit, Javier Ugarte, or others, included in this volume, like Alberto Mira, Juan Vicente Aliaga, Rafael M. Mérida-Jiménez, and Óscar Guasch. All of them have essentially contributed to the debate, and I could add some "non-Hispanic" specialists such as Brad Epps, Christopher Perriam, or Paul J. Smith. Gay men's history up to the mid-twentieth century has been explored by Richard Cleminson and Francisco Vázquez (2007). The field of masculinity studies *sensu stricto* was opened by *Nuevas masculinidades*, published by Marta Segarra and Àngels Carabí (2000), and *Debating Masculinity* (2009), edited by Josep M. Armengol and Carabí (2009), reaching the current debate with Armengol's *Queering Iberia* (2012). Yet there is still much research to be done, and these interdisciplinary essays respond to some of the fundamental questions at stake. Spain has remained "different," as the old Francoist slogan suggested, for a long period even after the death of the *Caudillo*, for three reasons: the long Dictatorship with its repressive politics in all gender questions, the ongoing influence of the Catholic Church and its fundamentalist male representatives, who are yet to give up either their controversial views against female self-determination or against queer people's civil rights, and finally the widespread *machismo* in parts of the population.

The title of this volume, *Hispanic (LGT) Masculinities in Transition*, requires a double comment. First, the term "Hispanic" could refer, as it so often has, to both Latin American and Peninsular phenomena. This was the case in many publications on gay or queer culture, from Smith's and

Bergman's *¿Entiendes?* to the books of David D. Foster and Roberto Reis (1996) or Susanna Chávez-Silberman and Librada Hernández (2000). Although still nowadays some studies cover geographically and socially these two distinct regions (the last book I know in this respect is *Deseos, juegos, camuflaje. Los estudios de género y queer y las literaturas hispánicas de la Edad Media a la Ilustración*, edited by Tobias Brandenberger and Henriette Partzsch in 2011), Latin American studies took a different road, advanced faster (under the influence of Anglophone postmodern and postcolonial theory), and produced a large number of academic debates on masculinities (Valdés and Olavarría; Helfrich; Guttman; Hernández; Ströbele and Wollrad). This has been the case especially since the foundation of the *Organización Multidisciplinaria Latinoamericana de Estudios de Masculinidades* (OMLEM, "Interdisciplinary Organisation for Masculinity Studies"), which publishes the review *Masculinidad(es)*, and of interdisciplinary networks (such as the *Red Iberoamericana y Africana de Masculinidades* [RIAM, "Iberoamerican and African Network for Masculinities"] headed by the Cuban historian Julio César González Pagés). To these, one must add many fundamental studies of Latin American gay or queer literature and culture (Balderston and Guy; Melhuus and Stølen; Foster and Reis; Balderston; Foster; Ingenschay; Millington; Kulawik; Peluffo and Sánchez Prado). The authors of the present book are in fact *Hispanic*, as they come from different Spanish, Latin American, and European cultural and academic contexts, yet the subject in question is (almost exclusively) the Spanish peninsula and its special situation under post-dictatorial conditions. There are only two exceptions which are not really exceptions, as Elena Madrigal includes one Mexican novel among her corpus of novels with lesbian protagonists, and Jorge Luis Peralta writes about two Argentinean activists, even if he focuses on their Spanish exile.

The second part of the title requiring explanation is the notion of *transition*, which apparently refers to the political *transición*—the period between Franco's death and the (however problematic) consolidation of the young democracy in the 1980s; a highly contested period in today's discussions (below I shall comment on a second meaning of masculinity *in Transition*). Some Spanish intellectuals emphasized the enormous success of the Spanish society in its progress towards democracy at the end of the twentieth century, and some of the authors of these collected essays take this position, for example Rafael M. Mérida-Jiménez ("From Stage to Screen: *Flor de Otoño*'s Transitional Impersonations"), when he characterizes the

Transition as a "fortunate political transition process […] that led to a system of civic freedoms." At the same time, he points to the "lights and the shadows that bring this political transition." In fact, one cannot deny that the exemplarity of the democratic transition was rather a quite relative one, that the undeniable achievements are outweighed by a significant lack of historical responsibility (called amnesia by critics such as Joan Ramon Resina [2000] or Teresa Vilarós [1998]), and the exclusive bet on a neoliberal and still quite centralist system. It is a fact that Spanish society had to wait more than thirty years for a *Ley de memoria histórica* ("Historical Memory Law") to ban—still cautiously—fascist and dictatorial symbols from the public sphere in 2007. Still, many questions remain open—the destiny of Franco's monumental Mausoleum in the Valle de los Caídos is only one of them. On the other hand, as far as homosexuality (as one possible manifestation of queerness) is concerned, Spain has meanwhile taken the role of a forerunner in the Western world. No other country in the world saw within half a century a similar revolutionary change from social and political prosecution, exacerbated by the above mentioned Law of Social Dangerousness and Social Rehabilitation in 1970, to the full civil rights of same-sex marriage and adoption of children by gay and lesbian couples granted by the Law 13/2005. Thus, the focus of these essays on the development of civil rights for LGT (respectively LBGTI) people is hardly surprising.

I have promised to comment shortly on a second aspect implied in the key notion of *transition. Masculinities in Transition* may not only allude historically to the early post-Franco years, but in a systematic perspective to the fact that socially constructed notions of gender are always "in transition," "on the move," and never static. Stable masculinity is fictional, as Tod Reeser has pointed out in *Masculinities in Theory* (2010), and masculinity in itself is "hybrid" rather than uniform.

Elena Madrigal-Rodríguez ("Undressing Masculinity: Male Dress and Accoutrements in Four Female Spanish Characters") recurs to Reeser's "hybrid" masculinity, and in particular to Judith Halberstam's notion of "female masculinity," when she analyzes four Hispanic novels with lesbian characters, among them the successful *Beatriz y los cuerpos celestes* by Lucía Etxebarria and one Mexican text, Susana Guzner's *La insensata geometría*. Referring to Julia Kristeva, Elena Madrigal-Rodríguez states that without a phallic affirmation, these characters would not have been able to express their singularity.

I briefly mentioned Rafael M. Mérida-Jiménez's comment on the ambiguity of the *transición*; he illustrates this referring to the significant changes that occurred during the decade of the 1970s with a rich variety of "trans"-masculine/feminine forms (and a focus on sex reassignment surgeries), as thematized in Spanish films such as *El transexual* (1977) by José Lara or *Cambio de sexo* (1977) by Vicente Aranda (which features Bibí Andersen and Victoria Abril before they became Almodóvar stars). His main point of interest is a comparison between José María Rodríguez Méndez's conservative and homophobic play *Flor de Otoño: Una historia del Barrio Chino*, written in the late Franco era, and the festive filmic version by Pedro Olea, *Un hombre llamado Flor de Otoño* (1978). The protagonist is a young lawyer who starts acting in a transvestite performance of a seedy bar in Barcelona's red-light district. The comparison between both versions gives evidence to the transformations of the discourse on sexual otherness in the 1970s and shows the central importance of "trans"-phenomena in Spanish cinema and society.

The role of film as a seismographic medium for social change also interests other authors in this volume. Alberto Mira, a well-known specialist in the cultural history of homosexuality in Spain in general and in Hispanic film in particular, writes about what he calls the "queer pastoral" ("Queer Pastoral: Rural Homoeroticism on Film during the Early Years of the Spanish Transition"). Mainly focusing on movie productions of the period between 1977 and 1982, his observation on Gonzalo Suárez's *Parranda*, on Ventura Pons's "queer *sainete*" *El vicari d'Olot*, or *Ocaña. Retrato intermitente* refutes the simple equation of Francoist culture as rural and republican or post-Francoist as metropolitan, as films like Pedro Lazaga's *La ciudad no es para mí* (1966) had suggested.

There is another new and important contribution to the study of the cinema of the Spanish Transition in Alberto Martínez-Expósito's article on the legendary director Eloy de la Iglesia ("Embodiments of Class and Nation in Eloy de la Iglesia's Gay Films"), in which he focuses on *Los novios búlgaros* (2003), the director's special version of Eduardo Mendicutti's witty novel in which he reacts to the fall of the iron curtain and the arrival of young immigrants from Eastern Europe. This document of the "post-materialist society" of the Aznar years, in which Madrid converted itself to a gay Mecca, differs from de la Iglesia's preceeding "gay" movies such as *Los placeres ocultos* (1977) or *El diputado* (1978), showing the cultural axioms of the *transición*. Martínez-Expósito characterizes de la Iglesia as a Marxist and anti-academicist director with *auteur* awareness.

From movie to theatre: Richard Cleminson and Carlos Pons ("Female Masculinity on Stage: *Young Man!* and the Subversion of Gender Roles") present the Catalan DeNada Dance Theatre which moved to the UK in 2005 and describe in detail the ways in which this group succeeds in queering ballet. One of these is the (re)production of camp images of Spanishness that play with the Almodovarian legacy, with *jamón*, *sangría*, and *toros* on one hand, and are, on the other hand, bound in a dense intertextuality to elements known from Lorca and many others, namely death and machismo. They do not only examine gender stereotypes, but also their more subtle secret codes, and they propose a dialogue on gender perceptions to the audience.

I am happy to see that, among the essays in the present volume, one takes a comparative perspective on the years of the *transición* in Spain and the situation in Argentina, where the process of overcoming the dark era of military dictatorship has culminated paradigmatically in full civil rights for LGT and queer persons. Jorge Luis Peralta ("*Machos* or *divinas*? A Quandary in Argentinean and Spanish Gay Activism") investigates the discussion of masculinity in political life and literary production of two gay activists, Héctor Anabitarte Rivas and Ricardo Lorenzo Sanz, who left Argentina for Spain when the generals took over. The issues that arise from the representation of homosexuality in Manuel Puig's *El beso de la mujer araña*—the stereotypes of the effeminate homosexual and the politically conscious heterosexual revolutionary—reappear in the discussions about "sexual roles" in their key texts (published in the late 1970s and early 1980s). They show that their positions on "masculinity" and "femininity" changed over the years, in accordance with the tensions and contradictions that the emerging Argentinean and Spanish gay communities were experiencing. In almost all collective volumes on queer and gender issues, the reader is left to lament the rather modest contributions on lesbian perspectives. In her theoretically well-grounded article ("Butches Excluded: Female Masculinities and Their [non] Representations in Spain"), Gracia Trujillo argues (with J. Halberstam) that the notion of "female masculinity," which makes of "masculinity" an "umbrella term," may be more useful than "lesbian" for researchers doing intercultural comparisons of queer communities. When looking back on the part lesbian life played in the years of the *transición*, she situates herself among the great variety of feminist debates of the early 1990s, when Monique Wittig postulated that lesbians are not women (as she considered "woman" a political category). Her suggestive application of the (Anglophone) theoretical discourse of "radical" feminism (quoting Gayle Rubin and Biddy Martin, Teresa de Lauretis and Judith Butler, and many others) to the specific conditions of the Spanish "fores" (forums) of the 1990s and to the spontaneous actions of lesbian groups such as LSD (with rapidly changing contents to that abbreviation) in Madrid shows the lack of a sexual language from which Spanish queer discourse suffered particularly at the time, when "masculine" lesbians were the target of social and political hostility. Whereas (male) gays considered the derogation of the Law of Social Dangerousness and Social Rehabilitation (in 1979) a political victory which allowed them a more visible socialization and an active part in the growing gay leisure industry, lesbians—even the relatively visible "butch" persons—felt they had to go on with their fight for a proper representation and against homo and lesbophobia.

I hope the reader will take the same delight as I did when reading these essays. Historically, these are articles on the *transición*, reveal that lesbian, gay, and transgender theory and practice have contributed in essential ways to the positive results of this process, even if they could not avoid nor even diminish its negative side-effects, its neoliberalism, historical amnesia, and economic crisis. While this temporal framework provides the collection with a strong inner coherence, the variety of theoretical aspects and the abundance of interesting empirical material change from one essay to the next. This works to engage the reader to participate in all the details of this archive, of this retrospective that looks back on a decisive span of recent Spanish history with its transnational and transcultural coordinates.

## Notes

1 This chapter was conducted as part of the research project entitled "Representaciones culturales de las sexualidades marginadas en España (1970–1995)" ["Cultural representations of marginalized sexualities in Spain (1970–1995)"], FEM2011–24064, funded by the Spanish Ministerio de Economía y Competitividad.

## Bibliography

Adams, Rachel, and David Savran. Ed. *The Masculinity Studies Reader*. Malden: Blackwell, 2002. Print.

Armengol, Josep M. Ed. *Queering Iberia: Iberian Masculinities at the Margins*. New York: Peter Lang, 2012. Print.

———, and Àngels Carabí. Ed. *Debating Masculinity*. Harriman: Men's Studies P, 2009. Print.

Balderston, Daniel, and Donna Guy. Ed. *Sex and Sexuality in Latin America*. New York: NYU P, 1995. Print.

Balderston, Daniel. *El deseo, enorme cicatriz luminosa. Ensayos sobre homosexualidades latinoamericanas*. Buenos Aires: Beatriz Viterbo, 2004. Print.

Bergmann, Emilie L., and Paul J. Smith. Ed. *¿Entiendes? Queer Readings, Hispanic Writings*. Durham: Duke UP, 1995. Print.

Brandenberger, Tobias, and Henriette Partzsch. Ed. *Deseos, juegos, camuflaje. Los estudios de género y queer y las literaturas hispánicas (de la Edad Media a la Ilustración)*. Frankfurt am Main: Vervuert, 2011. Print.

Carabí, Àngels, and Marta Segarra. Ed. *Nuevas masculinidades*. Barcelona: Icaria, 2000. Print.

Chávez-Silberman, Susana, and Librada Hernández. Ed. *Reading and Writing the Ambiente. Queer Sexualitites in Latino, Latin American, and Spanish Culture*. Madison: The U of Wisconsin P, 2000. Print.

Cleminson, Richard, and Francisco Vázquez García. *'Los invisibles': A History of Male Homosexuality in Spain 1850–1940*. Cardiff: U of Wales P, 2007. Print.

Connell, Robert W. *Gender and Power: Society, the Person and Sexual Politics*. Stanford: Stanford UP, 1987. Print.

———. *Masculinities*. Cambridge. 2005 ed. Berkely: U of California P, 1995. Print.

Foster, David W. *Gay and Lesbian Themes in Latin American Writing*. Austin: U of Texas P, 1991. Print.

Foster, David W., and Roberto Reis. *Bodies and Biases: Sexualities in Hispanic Cultures and Literature*. Minneapolis: U of Minnesota P, 1996. Print.

Guasch, Óscar. *La sociedad rosa*. Barcelona: Anagrama, 1991. Print.

Guttman, Matthew C. *Changing Men and Masculinities in Latin America*. Durham: Duke UP, 2003. Print.

Halberstam, Judith. *Female Masculinity*. Durham: Duke UP, 2004. Print.

Helfrich, Silke. Ed. *Género, feminismo y masculinidad en América Latina*. El Salvador: Heinrich Böll, 2001. Print.

Hernández, Óscar Misael. "Estudios sobre masculinidades. Aportes desde América Latina." *Revista de Antropología Experimental* 7 (2007): 153–160. Print.

Ingenschay, Dieter. Ed. *Desde aceras opuestas. La literatura/cultura gay y lesbiana en América Latina*. Frankfurt am Main: Vervuert; Madrid: Iberoamericana 2006. Print.

Kimmel, Michael S. *Changing Men. New Directions in research on Men and Masculinity*. Newbury Park: Sage Publications, 1987. Print.

———. *Misframing Men: The Politics of Contemporary Masculinities*. New Brunswick: Rutgers UP, 2010. Print.

Kulawik, Krysztof. *Travestismo lingüístico. En enmascaramiento de la identidad sexual en la narrativa latinoamericana neobarroca*. Frankfurt am Main: Vervuert; Madrid: Iberoamericana, 2009. Print.

Martínez-Expósito, Alfredo. *Los escribas furiosos. Configuraciones homoeróticas en la narrativa española*. New Orleans: The U of the South P, 1998. Print.

Melhuus, Marit, and Kristi Stølen. Ed. *Machos, Mistresses, Madonnas: Con-testing the Power of Latin American Gender Imagery*. London: Verso, 1996. Print.

Millington, Mark. *Hombres in/visibles. La representación de la masculinidad en la ficción latinoamericana*. Bogotá: Fondo de Cultura económica, 2007. Print.

Molloy, Sylvia, and Robert McKee Irwin. Ed. *Hispanisms and Homosexualities*. Durham: Duke UP, 1998. Print.

Mosse, George L. *The Image of Man: The Creation of Modern Masculinity*. Oxford: Oxford UP, 1996. Print.

Peluffo, Ana, and Ignacio M. Sánchez Prado. Ed. *Entre hombres. Masculinidades del siglo XIX en América Latina.* Frankfurt am Main: Vervuert; Madrid: Iberoamericana, 2010. Print.

Reeser, Todd. *Masculinities in Theory.* Chichester: Wiley-Blackwell, 2010. Print.

Resina, Joan Ramon. Ed. *Disremembering the Dictatorship. The Politics of Memory in the Spanish Transition to Democracy.* Amsterdam: Rodopi, 2000. Print.

Smith, Paul J. *Laws of Desire: Questions of Homosexuality in Spanish Writing and Film 1960–1990.* Oxford: Clarendon P, 1992. Print.

Steiner, George, and Robert Boyers. *Homosexualidad, literatura y política.* Madrid: Alianza, 1985. Print.

Ströbele-Gregor, Juliane, and Dörte Wollrad. Ed. *Espacios de género.* Buenos Aires: Fundación Foro Nueva Sociedad, 2013. Print.

Valdés, Teresa, and José Olavarría. Ed. *Masculinidad/es. Poder y crisis.* Santiago de Chile: Isis Internacional, 1997. Print.

Vilarós, Teresa. *El mono del desencanto. Una crítica cultural de la transición española (1973–1993).* Madrid: Siglo XXI, 1998. Print.

# CHAPTER 1

## Sexual Movements Without Sex? Sex-Talk in the Spanish Gay Liberation Movement

Kerman Calvo

*Universidad de Salamanca*

The fight for the rights of sexual minorities in Spain was initiated by a generation of activists that campaigned for "liberation."[1] We might call them "gay" liberationists, although politically this generation often talked about themselves as "homosexuals." Most of them were men, as lesbians in Spain mostly marched within the women's movement until the late 1980s. Homosexual/gay liberationists worked in so-called "liberation fronts;" they felt the most at home when engaging with discourses that connected their cause with revolutionary ideas about social change, cultural transformation and personal redefinition. These pioneering activists explicitly aligned with a generation of protesters in France, the United Kingdom or the United States, acclaimed for having successfully challenged the regulatory frameworks of sexual behavior that were so fiercely established in post-war western Europe and the United States.

Gay liberation, however, was not the same everywhere. A review of several historical experiences reveals that gay liberation during late 1960s and early 1970s indeed took one of two forms (Marotta). In some cases, the emphasis rested with the personal and cultural dimension of sexual liberation; in others, the economic and political aspects took the lead. I call the former "radical" and the latter "revolutionary" liberation. The revolutionary model was more popular in France and Spain, while radical liberation defined better the ideas and claims of "gay liberation fronts" in Great Britain or the United States.[2]

Subtle, but important, differences in the attribution of blame and, also, in the definition of strategies distinguished both types. Both shared an emphasis with oppression (Altman; Teal 28). As Valocchi puts it (68), in doing so campaigners analyzed the ways in which various institutions as well as the dominant culture stigmatized, marginalized, or discriminated against lesbians and gays. However, while radical liberationists—clearly drawing on feminist thinking—underscored the role of moral systems and social codes as sources of oppression, revolutionary liberation blamed capitalism. Moreover, radicals and revolutionaries formulated different recipes for future action. Whereas radicals went little beyond consciousness—raising activities—an effort designed to "teach homosexual men and lesbians the politics of being liberated persons" (Licata 179)—revolutionaries believed that political and economic transformation had to precede cultural and social transformation. So, while radical liberation encompassed the formulation of a strategy of cultural change, revolutionary liberation impelled an understanding of activism as a "vanguard" activity, relentlessly political and always aimed at eroding the foundations of the capitalist system.

Distinguishing radical and revolutionary helps understand how campaigners thought about sex during the early years of the lesbian and gay movement in Spain. Revolutionary gay liberation was not for sex; radical gay liberation was. It is true that Spanish (and French) liberationists did think about sexuality; for instance, they deeply believed in the idea of the universality of homosexual desire, arguing for a people's open acceptance of one's homosexual impulses. Body rights were also often claimed. "Raw" sex, however, was not appreciated. Spanish (following French) revolutionary liberation yielded against a nonpolitical form of human behavior that blinded individuals to their oppression. Revolutionary gay liberation was also against the commercial subcultures, the porn industry and, one dares to say, pure sexual freedom. To give an example; a French pamphlet called in the early 1970s the attention to the oppression of "those who make love exclusively for pleasure and not for production of an industrial army reserve" (quoted in Fillieule and Duyvendak 189). Similarly, and according to the recollections of a leading personality in the Spanish gay liberation movement, the regular participants in the meeting of the FAGC (*Front d'Alliberament Gai de Catalunya*—the gay liberation front of Catalonia) viewed sexuality as "linked to the interests of the ruling class" (Fluvià, "Apéndice" 487).

The question, hence, is not one about how Spanish gay liberationists talked and thought about male gay sexualities; rather, a stronger case can be found to wonder about why a sexual movement did think so little about sex. Drawing on a wide array of archive material, and also on conversations with pioneering activists, this chapter argues about a generational explanation to this puzzle. Spanish early activists had learned how to be political in the very contentious "revolutionary left" (izquierda revolucionaria, in Spanish); this commonly refers to a Marxist-inspired form of political participation that contested not only Francoism, but also much of what was settled during the

Spanish process of transition towards democracy. The alliance with the revolutionary left imposed heavy restrictions to liquid representations of non-politicised sexualities, as they appeared associated with expressions of apathy, disengagement and lack of pure democratic orientation. Most of the enormous gap between gay liberation militants and the urban population of gay and lesbians is explained, thus, by a problem of divergent priorities: while the later wanted better and safer chances to actually engage in sexual activities, the former pushed for a confrontational political agenda that gave priority to short-term political chance rather than to the satisfaction of long-term individual personal problems.

I shall proceed as follows. Firstly, I discuss the key ideas of gay liberation as understood in the Spanish context. Secondly, I argue that the association with revolutionary understandings of gay liberation resulted in a large gulf between political and apolitical homosexuals. Acknowledging the consequences of these tensions, the chapter then proceeds to explain why the first generation of gay activists in Spain was so "boring," opting for skewing any serious discussions of the cultural, psychological or recreational dimensions of sexuality to focus, instead, in trying to change the law.

## Spanish Revolutionary Homosexual Liberation

In the opinion of Jeffrey Weeks ("Introduction" 5), gay liberation was extremely useful to "pull previous experiences together, give them a theoretical structure and some sense of history." Indeed, rather than a single idea, the symbolizing around the liberation of gays and lesbians represents what political sociologists define as a "master frame" (Snow and Benford). I prefer to use the idea of collective cognitive maps, a concept that both stresses the collective character of the system of ideas (something that the idea of master frame does not always do) and place the basic element of cognition at the forefront of the analysis. Collective cognitive maps can be, then, held to be complex system of beliefs, assumptions and proposals for action that condense and simplify reality. In that process, cognitive maps effect a transformation in the definition of certain social conditions, redefining as unjust what was previously seen as unfortunate. They also attribute causality and sketch a general line of action.

Note the essential connection between cognitive maps and strategies: collective cognitive maps delimit the repertoire of possible actions of participants, rendering from the very start some courses of action possible and some others impossible. Space constraints prevent a full presentation of that part of the argument here; it will suffice to say that the peculiar political profile of the Spanish gay liberation movement, i.e. its claim-making, action repertoire or decisions on alliances and bargaining, owed much to the cognitive frames of the first generation of activists. Political strategizing was not an automatic response to new political opportunities; much of what Spanish gay liberationists did vis-à-vis policy makers, other movements and the press was a logic consequence of their ideas (Calvo and Trujillo; Calvo, "Building"); and, therefore, it is possible to believe that, should the structure of opportunities have been different, they would have acted in a similar way.

The Barcelona-based FAGC publicly defined itself as a "group with a revolutionary spirit." It aimed at a landslide reshaping of power relations in society (FAGC 4). As introduced above, a reference to sexuality was the prologue for much of the movement's ideological production: Spanish liberation groups, in the lines of American, French or British liberationists, insisted on calling for a de-stigmatization of homosexuality. It was acknowledged that for homosexuals to mobilize on behalf of their interests, the ethos of "normality" associated to the subordination of homosexuals had to be dispelled.[3] However, Spanish gay liberationists did not linger much further in these thoughts; much to the contrary, they quickly jumped to discuss what to do about that, forgetting about sex along the way. Radical liberationists, in challenging certain dangerous binaries (female/male, heterosexual/homosexual, public/private) fostered, instead, a much broader discussion of sex and sexuality and also about their intersections with politics and culture (Epstein 40).

Revolutionary liberation blamed the "bourgeoisie" for the design of a certain set of social, economic, and cultural mechanisms of oppression. Building on the broad concern of radical liberation with the perpetuation of patriarchy and similar social structures of domination, "French-style homosexual liberation" moved forward and charged against the owners of the capitalist system. Firstly, the capitalist system was presented as an aggressive mechanism that reacted violently against threats. As the Basque EHGAM (*Euskal Herriko Gay Askapen Mugimendua*—gay liberation movement of the Basque Country) put it (3), "the capitalist system opposes with the strongest determination anything that puts its system of exploitation under threat." Secondly, and more importantly, sexual liberation in general and homosexual liberation in particular, was held to represent a central threat to the capitalist order. Thus, behind the relentless insistence on arguing that "the capitalist order fights homosexuality to protect its value system" (EHGAM, 1981: 1), laid a Marxist-inspired definition of power relations. In this, both the oppression of women and the definition of sexuality in reproductive terms were considered instrumental mechanisms of oppression (FAGC). Both things guaranteed, in the short term, an endless reservoir of exploitable workers and, in the longer term, the consolidation of the value system that normalized exploitation and domination. In other words, in the pursuit of their interests, so the argument went, the ruling classes had designed a set of basic social norms that, despite the appearances, only aimed to preserve the economic structure of society. The idea that sexual liberation could destroy the capitalist order became something close to a mantra, a steering idea to build a comprehensive ideational system. As the juvenile section of the PCE (*Partido Comunista de España,* Spanish Communist Party) claimed in 1981: "the historical partnership between the gay movement and the worker's movement demonstrates the existence of a kind of socialism that is very well aware of the role of sexual liberation in the erosion of the pillars of the capitalist system" (Herrero Brasas 334).

**Abandoning Homosexuals to Their Lives**

For Spanish gay liberationists, sexual liberation was not an end on its own. Much on the contrary, it was merely a step in the fulfillment of a grander aspiration. For instance, in a founding document, the Madrid-based FLHOC (*Frente de Liberación Homosexual de Castilla*—homosexual liberation front of Castilla) (2) stipulated that for sexual liberation to be achieved, the "destruction of the social order of the bourgeoisie and a change in the structures that sustain oppression and perpetuate the repressive and sexist bias of our societies" must be achieved. Armand de Fluvià argued in 1981: "The gay movement, in its revolutionary quest to prompt a definition of sexuality detached from the sexual codes of the bourgeoisie, should aim at a total change in social relations" (*Egin*). Also in Barcelona, a group of particularly contentious activists wrote: "our reality as homosexuals is only a departing point towards a larger critique, never an end point on its own right."[4]

It is obvious that much emphasis was to be placed in the "hard" elements of societal and political involvement; namely, confrontation, protest, challenge, hard work, intellectual integrity. Neither time nor energies were found, however, to engage with "softer," but pressing questions nonetheless about identity, the self, and the meaning of coming out as a homosexual person in a democratic Spain. These were tasks that were to be resolved outside the realm of political involvement at a later stage, in new urban territories and in a host of sub-cultural commercial institutions mostly thought for the needs of gay men (Villaamil and Jociles).

Instead of engaging with sex-talk, gay liberation militants thought about families and ghettos (Quita, "Próxima reorganización" n. pag.; Fluvià, "El movimiento" 162; FAGC, 11). As well as considering the family the cause of the subordination of women to men, revolutionary homosexual liberation viewed family relations as the intermediate link between the exploitative interests of the bourgeoisie and the perpetuation of oppression. The Basque organization EHGAM summarized the concern about the family in starkly clear terms: "The family is the vehicle that the system uses to make up the individual's mind, making him or her assume the system is their own and, therefore, pre-empting any future dissent" (EHGAM 2). Thus, "down with the patriarchal family" soon became one of the leading mobilizing messages. Equally important to homosexual liberation appeared to be the destruction of the ghettos. In dismantling (oppressive) community practices, Spanish liberationists intended to apply the Marxist-inspired principle that condemned social categorization as essentially unjust. The critique of ghettos was justified on a threefold rational. Firstly, by creating the illusion of freedom, ghettos fostered demobilization and apathy. Secondly, they privatized homosexuality, adding to the generalized impression that homosexuality belonged to the realm of the private. Thirdly, the spatial concentration of gays and lesbians did not represent a natural phenomenon. More to the contrary, ghettos—and by extension the very notion of gay identity—were an artifact used by the ruling class to perpetuate homosexual oppression and segregation from society. A generous quotation from a position paper elaborated by the gay caucus of the PCE illustrates this question nicely:

> The categorization of homosexuality as a distinctive form of social behavior and as a different "community" carries the brunt of sexual and homosexual oppression, which is suffered not only by homosexuals but also by the entire social fabric. Homosexual males and lesbians do not belong to a different category of people; their distinctive sexual practices are neither the source of a distinctive personality, nor the basis for a different identity. Every aspect of the so-called "gay sub-culture" is the outcome of stigmatization and appears as a logical response of a minority that is under threat. In spite of that, neither the culture nor the members of the group can be defined as parts of a single group. (PCE 5).

This leads us to one of the most noticeable idiosyncrasies of the Spanish case: in this country, more than in any other western country, homosexual liberation involved a conscious "desexualisation" of gay collective protest. Whereas American or British homosexual liberationists cared about the implications of liberationist principles in the common lives of gays and lesbians, in Spain the homosexual liberation movement lacked an applied theorization of sexual liberation. Unlike in France, (as mentioned above the best example of European revolutionary gay liberation politics), where according to historical testimonies activism cohabited with a free expression of sexual impulses (see Fillieule and Duyvendack), activism in Spain did not seek to guide "down to earth" homosexuals as to how to live and cope with a shifting social and political environment. Questions about sexual experiences and the life-cycle, sexual diseases or sexual stigma were sidelined to find, instead, the energies and time to focus on the short-term (and very urgent) political, rights-related needs of homosexual peoples. Moreover, one could safely contend that politicized homosexual activists in Spain of those years virtually despised their non-politicized peers. What might have been the reason for this? That those without a fully developed political consciousness could be too eager to fall into the trap of the so-called "golden cage" (the ghetto).[5] Uninterested in, and deeply opposed to community building, the strategy of Spanish homosexual liberation fronts stressed the similarities between homosexual liberation and other revolutionary movements, working to generate political consciousness among the homosexual population. It needs to be stressed that this was a decision with profound consequences for later developments in LGTB politics in the country: subsequent generations of activism worked very hard to elaborate a discourse that common gay and lesbians could see as necessary and meaningful in the ages of AIDS and the commercialization and globalization of personal identities.

American gay liberation impelled the creation of gay communes; in France the periodical meetings of homosexual liberation activists often "degenerated" into collective sexual activity. Spanish groups, however, in embracing a Marxist-inspired understanding of collective protest basically "abandoned the homosexual to his life" (*Egin* n. pag.). This is inextricably linked to the widening of an enormous gap between politicized and non-politicized homosexuals that, in very many ways, has survived until recent times.

## Boyfriends, Gay Bar, Militancy, and Franco

In the democratic countries of the west, the birth of an autonomous homosexual liberation movement took root in the previous consolidation of homosexual commercial subcultures after the Second World War (Jivani; Levine). In the United States, by the mid 1950s the gay bar had become the centrepiece of a complex network of social interaction devoted, in the first place, to the provision of sex, and, later on, emotional support. This should not surprise anyone: as Achilles (176) explained it, bars were leisure-driven institutions, flexible to provide an agile response to constant police harassment. Also, they could guarantee a degree of segregation and anonymity.

The loyalty of bar-goers with their patrons was a decisive element for the formation of collective identities in countries such as the United States or the United Kingdom: thanks to these loyalties, stable social networks of people were formed (Achilles 180). More to the point, by hosting the collective response to police abuse, bars aided in the consolidation of a shared consciousness among bar-goers. The crowds around particular bars fought together, and they suffered the consequences together as well (Achilles 178). As D'Emilio (33) masterly puts it gay bars were "seedbeds for a collective consciousness that might one day flower politically." Very interestingly, Portuondo (97) makes a very similar claim in relation to the formation of a revolutionary consciousness among Spanish university students during the 1960s: it was the concerted and recurrent fight against the police what knitted revolutionary students together.

Of course not everyone who participated in the subculture joined the generation of Stonewall. A number of intervening factors must be taken into account to link participation and consciousness acquisition. Generally speaking, "those who had least to lose by being defiantly open" were more prepared to embrace the new consciousness (Weeks, *Coming Out* 191). Age, the intensity by which people participated in the subculture, the number and severity of the confrontations with the police, and also the connections with other protest movements were key variables in this respect. Men in drags have been at the forefront of the pioneering gay liberation events in most countries. However, on the whole, it is commonly accepted that, in places like the United States, Great Britain and even France to some extent, the homosexual liberation movement originated in the commercial subculture.

In Spain, what we might deem as the process of "consciousness acquisition" could not take place in the framework of a thriving homosexual subculture. As it is very well known by now, a blend of economic and intellectual underdevelopment, and the moral supremacy of the Catholic Church cooperated in solidifying a Spanish dictatorial sexual regime where homosexuality was blatantly stigmatized (Guasch, "Social Stereotypes"). Never ignoring that the development of the homosexual subculture in other countries suffered from external hostility (see for instance Jivani for the British case), the intensity of the threat was what set the Spanish case apart. Homosexuality was very early constructed by Francoist ideologists as an attack to the national identity, a "tumor" within an otherwise harmonious social fabric (Fuentes; Monferrer); accordingly, since 1954 a number of legal reforms were introduced so that homosexuality could be punished in all fronts. The national newspaper *El País*, argued in 1978 that Spanish law on homosexuality was the "toughest and most repressive in Western Europe" (*El País*, "Génesis" n. pag.).

All this left Spanish homosexuals with three very dismal options. In the first place, they could become effeminate "queens" (Guasch, *La sociedad* and "Social Stereotypes"). Óscar Guasch's thesis is that social categorization based on sexual orientation is a relatively recent phenomenon in Spain. Particularly in rural areas, sexual regimes well until the late 1960s drew on basic gender roles to distinguish between "top," masculine men and "bottom," passive, submissive, effeminate queens. Male sexual behavior that did not involve being sexuality "taken" by another man was relatively acceptable, particularly in environments of a very low supply of women. Applying the same rules, very camp men that took a sweet, sensible, funny, and unchallenging role found some social pace and comfort, provided they did not aim at social recognition or appreciation of their sexual and life style choices. In short, as Michael Pollack points out, there was some room in this sexual regime for homosexuals that accepted to "display the grotesque identity—funny, folkloric, extremely effeminate, passive, submissive—that the heterosexual majority assume all homosexuals possess" (Guasch *La sociedad* 60). The "queen" ("la loca"), as recently argued in Melero's recent analysis of film production during the 1970s, achieves some degree of social peace (at best patronizing pity) by relinquishing the masculine elements of his identity (Melero).

In the second place, they could shelter into denial and iron-clawed invisibility. Lastly, of course, they could join the prisons' population by virtue of the arbitrary implementation of Francoist legislation against social deviants (Monferrer and Calvo). Consequently, the possibilities for the institutionalization of a commercial homosexual subculture were extremely limited. Confined to marginal areas in downtown Barcelona and Madrid, only but a few cabaret-style places welcomed gay patrons. Even a smaller number were exclusively devoted to a homosexual clientele.[6] And, as Armand de Fluvià recollects, attending them was extremely risky: "The few of us who attended the scarce gay bars in Barcelona were perennially fearful of the police, who dispossessed those that it captured from their ID cards and/or took them to the police stations for long sessions of verbal and physical abuse. And if you were foolish enough to keep an address book with you, they used it to have the time of their lives, calling everyone on the list—(heterosexual) partners, family, employers, telling them that you had been caught at a queer bar" (Herrero Brasas 297).

Unable to offer a permanent refuge against external hostility, the Spanish gay bar became an extreme solution in the pursuit of sex. Bars were either difficult to find, dangerous to visit, or simply non-existent. As a matter of fact, most of the gay male population found no other alternative than to resort to street flirting (*ligue callejero*) and to interact with other homosexuals in non-institutionalised spaces, such as parks, theatres, etc. Considering this, a different route had to be taken if a gay and lesbian movement was to have a solid ground. The birth of the Spanish gay movement is embedded in the process of generational formation that gave way to what I have elsewhere called the "generation of homosexual militants" (Calvo *Pursuing*). Indeed, the genesis of this social movement has to be read as a combination of two basic factors: on the one hand, the formation of a political consciousness among a pool of committed homosexuals who, after years of experience as militants in the extreme-left, were ready to engage in "gay-specific" collective action; on the other hand, a process of regime change that altered the structure of political opportunities and, in doing so, created opportunities for mobilization. Militancy in extreme-leftist parties permitted homosexuals to interact with one another on a permanent basis and, as a consequence, give shape to primary social networks around friendship and comradeship. Reflecting on the themes of this volume, one could see in this particular pattern of socialization a view of (gay) masculine identities as artificially pushed as far as possible from the universe of the "queens." When deployed at the political sphere, Spanish gay activists might have adopted views about their identities that emphasized traditional male values, such as rigor, seriousness, strength and efficacy.

### (Gay) Freedom Fighters

Regular social interaction among male homosexuals (let alone among female homosexuals) was extremely difficult during up to the 1960s. This was so not only because the homosexual subculture was badly institutionalized, but also because membership in organizations other than those explicitly sponsored by the regime was banned. However, the strengthening of internal political contestation during that decade lowered somehow the costs of joining clandestine political organizations. Growing conflicts in the workplace forced the dictatorial regime to somehow tolerate the clandestine trade unions (Fishman). This made syndicalism a plausible alternative for politicized people. Also, the 1960s witnessed the consolidation of the Spanish Communist Party (PCE) as the force of resistance *par excellence.* Increasing numbers of young people joined the (then illegal) communist party during those years, pulled in by the need to collaborate in the pursuit of democracy. Moreover, the 1960s made it possible for growing numbers of people to secretly join other kind of political groups, namely revolutionary leftist parties and nationalist organizations (in Catalonia and the Basque Country mainly).

While the bulk of those prepared to put out a fight against Francoism joined the PCE, homosexuals mostly joined the revolutionary left—foremost of all the Trotskyism-inspired LCR ("Liga Comunista Revolucionaria"—communist revolutionary league).[7] Although my evidence is not strong in this respect, it appears that some homosexuals could have also joined the Catalonian nationalist movement and the Basque separatist movement. There are good reasons to understand why so many homosexuals opted for the more revolutionary political organizations. To begin with, the PCE was perceived as a deeply homophobic party, largely at ease with the Stalinist view that defined homosexuality as yet another manifestation of the poor moral stature of the bourgeoisie. A similar thing happened in France, where the French Communist Party also held clearly antigay views during the 1970s (Fillieule and Duyvendak 190). Equally worrying were the homophobic inclinations of prominent socialist leaders, such as Enrique Tierno Galván (later to become Mayor of Madrid): he became (in)famous for his bitter opposition to the public release of a film in 1978 called *El diputado* (*The Congressman*). The film, which told the story of a bisexual leftist Congressman who was blackmailed after having an affair with a young boy, was widely assumed to be inspired on the real story of a politician that belonged to Mr. Tierno's own political party (Aguilar et al. 178).

In comparison, militancy in revolutionary leftist parties permitted homosexuals to interact with their peers on a more regular basis. These parties built on strategic needs (the acquisition of a distinctive profile), and structural factors (a very young membership) to craft a leftist discourse that made clear room for a host of new "postmaterialist" issues, such as feminism or environmentalism. The sway of feminist ideas in the ideology of revolutionary leftist parties created the conditions for a relatively smooth integration of homosexual liberation. Revolutionary leftist parties hosted the formation of networks of homosexuals. In a context where attending gay bars was extremely dangerous, and where private sociability networks were difficult to find (and even more so to be accessed), the relatively stable environment of meetings and actions of protest permitted formerly isolated individuals to network with one another on a permanent basis. By doing so, the possibility emerged to talk about sexual orientation in public, in some cases for the first time ever. Pedro Moreno, a member of the first generation of homosexual activists in Spain, and, therefore, a privileged observer of the inception of Spanish homosexual liberation, emphasized the fundamental importance of this seemingly innocuous fact:

> For us, the simple decision of disclosing our homosexuality was terribly revolutionary, and wonderfully liberating. Gay talk was not something that we could often do. Some people went to the bars, and others became part of secret circles where homosexuals could interact on a more or less regular basis. But, well, bars were dangerous and accessing those networks was not always easy, particularly if you were not rich, young, or both! So, at the end, getting embroiled with the revolutionary left was a liberating experience.[8]

Not only militancy in revolutionary leftist parties offered homosexuals the chance to interact with one another; it also exposed them to different ways of understanding the world. Note that the pool of homosexuals that joined the revolutionary left had only very vague references about how to be publicly political, let alone about how to be politically "gay." Certainly, "the questioning of the traditional family and the institution of marriage, the liberation of sexual relations [and] the demand of equality for women in all spheres" were recurrent features in the conversation within revolutionary leftist circles (Portuondo 98). But little else. With very few exceptions, those with an emerging gay political consciousness defined their political knowledge at that time as "insufficient," "very poor," "incomplete" or "non existent at all." Pedro Moreno's answer is again the most illuminative of these answers:

> We knew that we had a problem, that something was wrong with the state of affairs, this is why we did what we did [joining the revolutionary left]… However, before joining these parties, we had no clue about what the solution could be (…) an open community of "faggots"?, for God's sake, we could not even think of that. Then the people we were working with introduced us to basic Marxist ideas, to the credo of the feminist movement, and, of course, we became revolutionary.

Why homosexual leftist militants assimilated revolutionary ideas so earnestly is thus not difficult to see. In the first place, they were evidently predisposed to embrace extremist recipes for action. Acutely aware of the scope of Francoist repression, only an explosive program for change could satisfy the anxieties of a group that was profoundly stigmatized. Secondly, most of them simply had no alternative intellectual response. Despite the fact that a minority of Catalonian homosexuals followed with endless curiosity the unfolding of events in France, Britain, and the United States, (and hence were able to understand the differences between the homophile movement and gay liberationists), knowledge about gay liberation outbursts in the world was is short supply among most homosexual militants. Thirdly, Marxist ideas sounded very good at the time, being an example of the kind of ideas that everyone wanted to replicate due to their sheer brightness. Note as well that clandestine activism promoted an iron-like solidarity among participants, which invariably involved consensus about ideas.

By 1973, when a group called the "Movimiento Español de Liberación Homosexual" (MELH, Spanish Movement for Homosexual Liberation) started to do some work, virtually every homosexual who had joined the revolutionary left was equipped to define his or her personal problematic as an instance of capitalist malicious use of sexual identities. Key ideas such as exploitation, domination, oppression, and liberation were already in their armory. However, with the exception of the few recipients of *Arcadie*, the newsletter and pamphlet of the French homosexual community at the time, no one had heard about homosexual liberation. In spite of the fact that the ideas of second wave feminism had already broken the iron curtain of Francoist's censorship, Spanish homosexuals still remained immune to the empowering slogans of American and French homosexual liberationists.[9]

## Conclusion

The deep intellectual underpinnings of a political generation are an extremely powerful inspiration for preference formation and decision making. That does not rule out alternative explanations completely: beyond the sheer transformation spawned by the engendering of the transition process, the early configuration of the structure of alliances fostered the ongoing collaboration between the homosexual liberation movement and the most committed sponsor of revolutionary politics in the country: namely, the revolutionary left. Also, the striking similarities between the Spanish and the French cases suggest that the French model was a constant source of inspiration and guidance.

The definition of the Spanish homosexual liberation movement as a revolutionary force cannot be merely approached as a question of rational adjustment to a shifting landscape, or as an example of a successful process of cross-national diffusion of ideas. Spanish homosexual militants did not have to wait until the offer to set a revolutionary partnership came: they had knocked at the doors of these parties already. Similarly, it should not be forgotten that, to a large extent, it was an already thriving Spanish liberationist movement who sponsored the circulation of French ideas on homosexual liberation. As Adam et al. put it, "we should not overlook the possibility that some countries share characteristics, and these common characteristics color the national movements in the same direction" (368). The particularities of the Spanish social and political context restricted the role of the commercial subculture as a sponsor for the engendering of a political generation of activism. A history of repression, a justified fear of police crackdown, and a sexual regime that defined homosexuality as a deviance and a pathology prevented gay bars from performing this role. Nevertheless, the same idiosyncrasies of the Spanish context opened up an unexpected route for the networking of homosexual people and for the development of a political consciousness around their common sexual orientation: it was militancy in the extreme-left which made the process of consciousness acquisition possible. This kind of militancy allowed for sustained interaction, provided a more or less secure and permissive environment for the disclosure of sexual orientation, and exposed militants to ideas coming from abroad. At this stage, however, this did not result in a diversification of masculine identities. In spite of the leading role of transgender males in the pioneering gay liberation protest events, activists pushed themselves far from dominant ideas about queerness. A liberated homosexual male was a political creature, a strong man that was to play no part in the amusement of an homophobic society.

All this, of course, had unexpected consequences. Sex talk, a seemingly obvious dimension for the organization of collective identities in a social movement by people with a common "sexual" orientation was heavily disassociated with the daily activities of Spanish "homosexual militants." It is, thus, difficult to discuss how male sexualities were represented by politicized homosexual in Spain during the transition towards democracy. Sexuality was viewed as an enemy of political consciousness; a weakness that could help the owners of the sexual regime to continue with their oppression of alternative sexualities.

It is perhaps fair to acknowledge the unique and not at all easy decisions that homosexual militants had to make. Pushing for homosexual "rights" seemed an obvious priority. However, the role of ideas should not be overlooked: Spanish homosexual militants were badly equipped to reconcile political strategizing and the need to elaborate new discourses on life-styles, health, affection, desire and body practices. There were already out there: but still quite some time was needed for everyone to rehearse new social practices that could integrate the daily needs of "ordinary" homosexuals with the obligations of human rights recognition of sexual citizenship building.

## Notes

1 This chapter was conducted as part of the research project entitled "Representaciones culturales de las sexualidades marginadas en España (1970–1995)" ["Cultural representations of marginalized sexualities in Spain (1970–1995)"], FEM2011—24064, funded by the Spanish Ministerio de Economía y Competitividad.

2 This distinction is to be taken at the level of broad analytical categories, of course; in all countries the labels revolutionary and radical were often used as equivalents, particularly at the level of mass media.

3 The Basque group EHGAM and the Barcelona-based FAGC, together with other groups in other cities made an effort to justify mobilization on the basis of enduring oppression (EHGAM, 1981; FAGC, 1977). See López Romo (2008) for a careful historical reconstruction of activism in the Basque country. The FAGC complemented this analysis in several articles published in *debat Gai,* its own magazine. These included a relatively well-known article titled: "*Sobre el machismo y la liberación gai: elementos para un debate*" (about *machismo* and homosexual liberation: some elements for a debate), published in *debat Gai,* #2 (1978: 12).

4 These words were published on behalf of a short-lived group in Barcelona that was born after internal tensions within the FAGC. The ideas and statements of the so-called Platform of Radical Gay Groups of Catalonia were displayed in its own publication,

titled *La Pluma*. The arguments of this particular quotation were published in the magazine's first issue: *La Pluma*, #0 (1978: 1).

5 This was argued in the article above quoted called "Sobre el machismo y la liberación gai: elementos para un debate" (1978: 16).

6 Some sources suggest that the subculture in Barcelona was more developed and more permissive than in Madrid. See, for instance Viladrich's recreation of the imaginary diary of a Communist Homosexual Militant (Viladrich, 1977: 45).

7 In Catalonia many activists were particularly close to PSUC (Partit Socialista Unificat de Catalunya), the Catalonian branch of the PCE.

8 Pedro Moreno, personal interview.

9 The MELH became a focal point for the dissemination of foreign ideas. Particularly attentive to developments taking place in nearby France, the growing understanding between the MELH and homosexuals affiliated to the Catalonian revolutionary left resulted in the formation of a cadre of knowledgeable soon-to-be homosexual militants that was ready to seize any opportunity that could arose to organise autonomous forms of homosexual activism. *Aghois*, the MELH's periodical bulletin, counted on the collaboration of well-known leftist catalonian intellectuals. By 1973 *Aghois* was sent to more than one hundred addressed in Barcelona only. Eighteen issues were edited between 1972 and 1974.

## Bibliography

Adam, Barry, Jan W. Duyvendak, and André Krouwel. "Gay and Lesbian Movements Beyond Borders? National Imprints of a Worldwide Movement." *The Global Emergence of Gay and Lesbian Politics. National Imprints of a Worldwide Movement.* Ed. Barry Adam, Jan W. Duyvendak, and André Krouwel. Philadelphia: Temple UP, 1999. 344–371. Print.

Achilles, Nancy. "The Development of the Homosexual Bar As an Institution." *Social Perspectives in Lesbian and Gay Studies*. Ed. Peter M. Nardi, and Beth E. Schneider. New York: Routledge, 1998. 175–82. Print.

Aguilar, Carlos, Dolores Devesa et al. *Conocer a Eloy de La Iglesia.* San Sebastián: Filmoteca Vasco-Euskadiko Filmategia, 1996. Print.

Altman, Dennis. *Homosexual: Oppression and Liberation.* 1993 ed. New York: New York UP, 1971. Print.

Calvo, Kerman. *Pursuing Membership in the Polity. The Spanish Lesbian and Gay Movement in Comparative Perspective*. Madrid: Instituto Juan March, 2005. Print.

———. "Building Reciprocal Relations between Lesbian and Gay Organizations and the State." *The Lesbian and Gay Movement and the State: Comparative Insights into a Transformed Relationship.* Ed. Manon Tremblay, David Paternotte, and Carol Johnson, Farnham: Ashgate, 2011. 167–181. Print.

——— and Gracia Trujillo. "Fighting for Love Rights: Demands and Strategies of the LGBT Movement in Spain." *Sexualities: Studies in Culture and Society* 14 (2011): 562–580. Print.

D'Emilio, John. *Sexual Politics. Sexual Communities*. Chicago: U of Chicago P, 1983. Print.

*El País*. "Génesis y reivindicaciones de los grupos homosexuales españoles." *El País* 25 June 1978: N. pag. <http://goo.gl/FI5INL>. 16 Dec. 2013.

*Egin*. "Interview with Armand de Fluvià." *Egin* 27 June 1981: N. pag. Print.

EHGAM. "El movimiento gay y el movimiento obrero y popular." N. p., n. p. 1981. TS.

Epstein, Steven. "Gay and Lesbian Movements in the United States. Dilemmas of Identity, Diversity, and Political Strategy." The *Global Emergence of Gay and Lesbian Politics:*

*National Imprints of a Worldwide Movement*. Ed. Barry Adam, Jan W. Duyvendak, and André Krouwel. Philadelphia: Temple UP, 1999. 30–81. Print.

FAGC. Front d'Alliberament Gai de Catalunya (FAGC). *Manifest*, N. p., n. p. 1977. TS.

Fillieule, Olivie, and Jan Willem Duyvendak. "Gay and Lesbian Activism in France. Between Integration and Community-Oriented Movements." *The Global Emergence of Gay and Lesbian Politics. National Imprints of a Worldwide Movement*. Ed. Barry Adam, Jan Willem Duyvendak, and André Krouwel. Philadelphia: Temple UP, 1999. 184–213. Print.

Fishman, Robert. *Working-Class Organisation and the Return to Democracy in Spain*. Ithaca: Cornell UP, 1990. Print.

FLHOC. "Origen de la opresión homosexual. Situación actual. Declaración de objetivos. Plataforma Reivindicativa." 1978. TS.

Fluvià, Armand de. "Apéndice sobre el caso español." *Homosexuales masculinos: sus problemas y adaptación*. Ed. Martín Weinberg and Colin Williams. Barcelona: Fontanella, 1977. 466–482. Print.

———. "El movimiento homosexual en el estado español." *El homosexual ante la sociedad enferma*. Ed. José Ramón Enríquez. Barcelona: Tusquets. 1978. 149–167. Print.

Fuentes, Pablo. "Autoridad y desviación sexual en la España franquista." *Gesto* 2001: 16. Print.

Guasch, Óscar. *La sociedad rosa*. Barcelona: Anagrama, 1991. Print.

———. "Social Stereotypes and Masculine Homosexualities: The Spanish Case." *Sexualities* 14 (2001): 526–543. Print.

Herrero Brasas, José Antonio. *La sociedad gay. Una invisible minoría*. Madrid: Foca, 2001. Print.

Jivani, Alkarim. *It's Not Unusual: A History of Lesbian and Gay Britain in the Twentieth Century*. London: M. O'Mara Books; London: BBC, 1997. Print.

Levine, Mauren. "Gay Ghetto." *Social Perspectives in Lesbian and Gay Studies*. Ed. Peter M. Nardi and Beth E. Schneider. New York: Routledge, 1998. 194–207. Print.

Licata, Salvatore. "Homosexual Rights Movement in the United States: A Traditionally Overlooked Area." *Journal of Homosexuality* 6 (1981): 161–89. Print.

López Romo, Raúl. *Del gueto a la calle. El movimiento gay y lesbiano en el País Vasco y Navarra*. Bilbao: Gakoa, 2008. Print.

Marotta, Toby. *The Politics of Homosexuality*. Boston: Houghton Mifflin, 1981. Print.

Melero, Alejandro. "Hormones and Silk. Gay Men in the Spanish Film Comedies of the Transition to Democracy (1976–1981)." *Journal of Homosexuality* 60 (2013): 1450–1474. Print.

Monferrer, Jordi. "La construcción de la protesta en el movimiento gay español: la ley de peligrosidad social (1970) como factor precipitante de la acción colectiva." *Revista española de investigaciones sociológicas* 102 (2003): 171–203. Print.

——— and Kerman Calvo. "Homosexualidad y peligrosidad social." *El Mundo* 30 Sep. 2001: N. pag. Print.

PCE. "El PCE y la cuestión homosexual" [The Spanish Communist Party and the Homosexual Issue]. N.p, n.d. 1986. Discourse.

Portuondo, Ernesto. "Forja de rebeldes: una aproximación a los orígenes de las vanguardias militantes del radicalismo de izquierdas en la segunda mitad de los sesenta: el movimiento estudiantil (1964–1970)." *El proyecto radical. Auge y declive de la izquierda revolucionaria en España (1964–1992)*. Ed. José Manuel Roca. Madrid: Los libros de la catarata, 1994. 91–123. Print.

Quita, Alfons. "Próxima reorganización de los homosexuales catalanes." *El País* 16 May 1979: n. pag. <http://goo.gl/TImGzH> 16 Dec. 2013.

Snow, David, and Robert D. Benford. "Master Frames and Cycles of Protest." *Frontiers in Social Movement Theory*. Ed. Aldon D. Morris and Carol McClurg Mueller. New Haven: Yale UP, 1992. 133–56. Print.

Teal, Donn. *The Gay Militant: How Gay Liberation Began in American, 1969–1971*. 1995 Reprint. New York: St Martin's P, 1971. Print.

Valocchi, Steve. "Riding the Crest of a Protest Wave? Collective Action Frames in the Gay Liberation Movement, 1969–1973." *Mobilization* 4 (1999): 59–73. Print.

Viladrich, Jordi. *Anotaciones al Diario de un homosexual comunista*. Madrid: Mirasierra, 1977. Print.

Villaamil, Fernado and Maribel Jociles. "Risk and Community: The Impact of HIV among Gays in Madrid. The Case of Sex Clubs." *Sexualities: Studies in Culture and Society* 14 (2011): 580–596. Print.

Weeks, Jeffrey. *Coming Out: Homosexual Politics in Britain From the Nineteenth Century to the Present*. 1990 ed. London: Quartet Books, 1977. Print.

———. "Introduction to the 1993 Printing." *Homosexual: Oppression and Liberation.* New York: New York UP, 1993. 1–15. Print.

# CHAPTER 2

# Butches Excluded: Female Masculinities and Their (non) Representations in Spain

Gracia Trujillo
*Universidad de Castilla-La Mancha*

> By allowing ourselves to be portrayed as the good deviant, the respectable deviant, we lose more than we will ever gain. We lose the complexity of our lives, and we lose what for me has been a lifelong lesson: you do not betray your comrades when the scapegoating begins.
>
> Joan Nestlé, *A Restricted Country*, 123.

> What place does the butch occupy in the history of our feminisms, in its commemorative archives?[1]
>
> valeria flores, *Interruqciones*, 204.

## Masculinities without Men

During the last decades, research has analyzed and documented a diversity of masculinities which emerge in specific contexts (Connell 1995, Connell & Messerschmidt 2005, Cortés 2001).[2] In her pioneer work *Masculinities* (1995), the sociologist Raewyn Connell argued that there are many different masculinities, each associated with different positions of power. Furthermore, that power relations of gender operate between groups of men as well as between men and women (and among women too). Masculinities are "configurations of practices that are accomplished in social interaction and, therefore, can differ according to the gender relations in a particular social setting" (Connell & Messerschmidt 836). Despite this multiplicity, masculinities do not align all at the same level, as we know, but they form into a hierarchy. Occupying the highest position is what Connell called hegemonic masculinity: "the configuration of gender practice which embodies the currently accepted answer to the problem of the legitimacy of patriarchy, which guarantees (or is taken to guarantee) the dominant position of men and subordination of women" (Connell 77). Accordingly to this, hegemonic masculinity has been constructed, in the Western world, mostly as a process of differentiation and negation of *others*, namely women and gay men. Connell also emphasizes the key idea that the relationship between hegemonic masculinity, subordinated masculinity, and femininity is a historically mobile relation. What follows these ideas is that both femininity (understood as passivity or weakness) and desire among men should be negated or erased from public sphere (Cortés).

However, as Connell and Messerschmitt argue, the concept of hegemonic masculinity does not equate to a model of social reproduction; these authors point out the need to recognize social struggles in which subordinated or non normative masculinities might (and they do) influence dominant forms. Not only that, but also hegemonic masculinity depend totally on minority or alternative masculinities, just as it happens with heterosexuality, that needs sexual deviants to exist (Sedgwick). Connell also underlines the importance of considering how the axis of class, race, and ethnicity intervene in the articulation of the opposition between hegemonic and subordinated masculinities. The hegemonic masculinity is male, middle class, white… and heterosexual. Thus far, what we see is that the majority of researchers have analyzed masculinities, and how they are constructed in particular historical and cultural settings, associated with (biological) men. Masculinity is related to strength, cultural and political power, privilege, legitimacy, and representation; that is why men protect it and keep it for themselves. But what about *masculine* women? Where are the subjects assigned "women" at birth who have masculine looks and/or perform different forms of masculinities in that picture?

A key reference for our analysis is Judith/Jack Halberstam's *Female Masculinity*. As this author has pointed out, scholars have absolutely shown no interest in masculinity without men, and, as s/he argues, if we want to find points at which masculinity really transgresses its boundaries, we need to locate instances of masculinity that do not directly concern (biological) men. In other words, if our aim is to understand masculinity we need to analyze *female masculinity*, that is, masculinity as it is embodied and lived by women, and not the hegemonic one. Far from being an imitation of heterosexual or homosexual masculinity, but rather a creation of *other* gender expressions, female masculinity is crucial to understand how masculinity is constructed. Halberstam also warns us that the suppression of female masculinities allows for (hegemonic) male masculinity to stand unchallenged as the bearer of gender stability and gender deviance: "female masculinities are framed as the rejected scraps of dominant masculinity in order that male masculinity may appear to be the real thing" (Halberstam, *Female*, 1).

I agree with Halberstam when s/he argues that "female masculinity" can be a more useful term than "lesbian" for researchers doing intercultural comparisons of queer communities, precisely because it is a term marked by gender and role playing, and not so much an identity.[3] It can work, as Halberstam suggests, as "an umbrella term to describe a wide variety of practices of gender crossing" ("Introducción" 11).[4] However, this kind of research is missing: women with a masculine look are definitely not the favorites of heteropatriarchy, which most of the time results in lack of funding for working on these issues, among other things. Writing from and about the Latin American context, valeria flores also criticizes the very few studies existing on female masculinities. The variety and complexities of non hegemonic masculinities and its contextual conditions are not being analyzed. For all these reasons, it would be not only interesting but also necessary to do such analysis in a near future.

In fact, what I will try to show in this chapter relates to Spain but, in my estimation, could be applied to other Western European countries such as Portugal, Italy or France, among others. In these pages, I analyze female masculinities and their representations, comparing the decades of 1970s, 1980s, and 1990s, when queer feminist activisms radically changed sexual dissidents' images from those previously held by lesbian feminisms. At this point, one might wonder why look at political groups while analyzing representations. The answer has to do with their efforts to create alternative and defiant images of other sexualities, bodies, and identities. But also due to the fact that, as Lazy pointed out, to understand feminist art from the 1970s on, "we need to look outside the art world because the initial impetus came from the wider world of political action" (264).[5]

The arguments that I defend in this piece are, on the one hand, that this outstanding change in sexual representations in the Spanish case was possible thanks to the generational change, to activists' travels, and to the contagion and mutual interaction with multiple and diverse queer activist groups in France, England, and the US, among others. On the other hand in spite of this fact and the sexualization of images and discourses carried out by queer feminist groups, representations of female masculinities needed to wait longer. In other words, even the more radical (queer) groups did not dare to display images of butches and drag kings until the end of the 1990s.[6] The article tries therefore to explain why and how this absence, these silences, and invisibilities exist in the Spanish case, which I think, as I mentioned before, does not differ much from other European countries.

The article draws on extensive field work carried out in Spain, including a revision of the so-called "movement literature." Pamphlets, non-published ideological texts, internal notes and, *zines* edited and published by lesbian feminist and queer groups themselves have been analyzed, together with press articles. The theoretical framework is an interdisciplinary one, which I think is a much needed one to analyze sexuality and gender issues, and masculinities in particular, as Connell defends; it includes both sociology of gender and sexuality, and feminist and queer theories and practices. Being a historian myself who did her doctoral thesis in a sociology department (the only place at my University in Madrid where, during the mid 1990s, some courses on gender issues were offered) and who now teaches sociology, my attempt to use a "queer methodology" has meant an effort to combine historical studies, sociological analyses, archive work, discourse analysis, and observatory participation.[7] This kind of methodology is also a way to question not only the barriers between knowledge areas but also conventional academic methods (that, among other things, reinforce the former ones), and the gaps between theory and political practice, Academia(s), and activisms: queer feminism is not just a "topic" studied here but the movement which I also belong to.

## Of Silence and Invisibility. Coming Out from a Dictatorship

The first attempts to organize sexual protests in Spain were framed in the terms of "gay" liberation as it was understood in France, Great Britain, and North America. The transition from dictatorship to democracy was a period of social and political euphoria for the possibility of achieving lost freedoms and rights under Franco's fascist regime (1939–1975). It offered new opportunities for social mobilization, which, in the case of non heterosexuals, resulted in the creation of the so-called Homosexual Liberation Fronts; the term "fronts" echoed Marxist ideas on collective organization. These groups were organized in the main cities of the country, Madrid and Barcelona, but also in Bilbao, Valencia or Seville (Fluvià and Petit).

The gay and lesbian liberation movement was essentially a radical ideology that called for combative mass mobilization (Adam and Altman). It described itself also as a revolutionary force (Fluvià), embedding a discourse on sexual politics in larger narratives about class struggle. The homosexual liberation movement defended the use of non-hierarchical forms of organization and direct democracy. The function ascribed to mobilization was also revolutionary: the key ideas that emerged at that time called for a classless society, the fading of the family and the elimination of all those structures that maintain and feed (hetero) sexism and *machismo*. Lesbian autonomous groups were created within the movement as early as 1977, sharing with their gay colleagues the fight against a series of urgent social and legal discriminations based on a different sexual option (Trujillo, *Deseo*). The first protest march was organized in Barcelona in 1977, when lesbian and gay groups had not yet been legalized.

One of the key ideological elements of these Homosexual Fronts was the critique of the existence of a homosexual identity. As it can be read in an internal political document, "this is a right to differ what we reject. It is nothing but a mere formal acceptation, with no value, for where there is difference there is oppression."[8] Difference in relation to the majority was precisely one of the controversial issues in these organizations. There were several ideological positions about the public image that was to be displayed by the movement to the society and the media. The defence of the gay *pluma* ("camp") or the so-called *locas* was carried out by one sector and rejected by another one that saw it as an expression of the homosexual difference they did not share.[9] The former supported that transvestites and trans people occupied positions at the front of the marches, in what constituted a defence and a celebration of that difference, together with the need to achieve increased levels of visibility of "other" sexual minorities.[10]

In the case of lesbians, there was, in general, a rejection of masculine looks (among politicized dykes and also among straight feminists, as it would happen later on within feminist organizations). In the active years of the transition to democracy, libertarian ideology was the protest frame in the fronts, where lesbian and gay men mobilized together, and it influenced to a great degree the configuration of lesbian identity with its critique of social labelling and the existence of a homosexual identity (understood, as explained before, as difference). Lesbian political groups, however, defended the need to name themselves as such, although images of masculine lesbians, or lesbians with *pluma*, were not elaborated or used by these groups. The context of control, repression, and social and political hostility in general was too tough to be able to expose themselves like that.

An important turning point for the gay and lesbian movement was the repeal of the Law of Social Dangerousness and Social Rehabilitation in 1979, a piece of legislation that had been used by Francoist law makers to criminalize, persecute, and put homosexuals into jail. Lesbians and gay males, however, had different perceptions as to the implications of the law on their daily lives. While gays saw the repeal as a political victory that was also going to have a direct impact on their lives in terms of (more visible) socialization and leisure options, lesbians considered that it was another step on the fight against homo and lesbophobia, but not as something that would make a noticeable difference in their personal—and more invisible—lives the day after. As I mentioned earlier, I think that this invisibility and absence of images of masculine women in general, and lesbians in particular, was due to the vigilance and control mechanisms acting on gender roles and sexual morality in the end of the dictatorship.

As shown in other work (Calvo and Trujillo), the "pendulum swing" from radicalism to more moderate understandings of activism is mediated by domestic factors that shape the speed, intensity, and consequences of internal ideological conflicts. A historical approach to sexual protest politics in Spain quickly reveals the radical visions of sexual politics, which started up in the 1970s, have always been popular among grass roots and activists. While in the end, a large section of the Spanish lesbian, gay, transsexual, and bisexual (LGTB) movement has succumbed to moderation and institutionalization, radical ideas and forms of action survived longer than in other western countries, always representing an active challenge to the mainstream.

## Butches Are Not "Women"

The configuration of collective identities is a central aspect in social movements' lives because, among other functions, it serves to affirm common interests among members of a social group in opposition to dominant ones (Taylor and Wittier). However, the definition of a political subject is not an easy process that is carried out as if identities just reflected essential differences among people before mobilization (Stein). Identity constructions and reconstructions are quite the opposite: contingent, changeable elements, the result of dilemmas, debates, and (most of the time, hard) discussions within political groups. In Spain, as it has happened in many other contexts, such as the US one, we can find conflicts and tensions between straight feminists and lesbians (and gender queers in general). Nevertheless, these processes have, in each case, a socio-historical background and different elements or peculiarities that need to be explored in every concrete context. This is what I am trying to do here with the Spanish case.

Following the chronological line, at the end of the 1970s the majority of lesbians started to abandon the Liberation Fronts. From the beginning of the 1980s onwards, these activists began to defend that they were *mujeres antes que nada* ("women before any other thing"), and thus, give priority to their gender identity rather than to the sexual one (Trujillo, *Deseo*, 95). Their place was within the feminist movement, so they joined the fight for women's rights (abortion, divorce, equal rights in jobs and education, among others) and intended to establish a dialogue about sexuality and lesbianism with their straight political colleagues. Lesbian feminism sought to transform women's organizations, so that their debates and demands could be routinely included as another aspect of feminist politics.

A minority of them, however, insisted on securing political autonomy to focus on their own issues. There were also exceptions to this identity configuration that considered gender more important than sexuality. The Feminist Lesbians from Barcelona or those from Bilbao named themselves "lesbians" first and foremost; the term "feminist" came afterwards. This debate about the order of both terms might seem trivial nowadays, but it was crucial. Lesbians who were very active politically in those years have recognized that they invested a countless number of hours in these debates, not without tensions, splits within activist groups, and so on. Putting "lesbians" before "feminist" was a political statement, a strategy to make visible that (non hetero) sexual identities also mattered. It was their way to distance themselves from the main stream of the movement, represented by the Collective of Lesbian Feminists of Madrid, which by that time centered nearly all its mobilizing energy and discourses on the main feminist issues.[11] The paradox we find in this constellation of organized political groups under the label of "lesbian feminism" is that while lesbianism is a sexual identity, there is a significant lack of sexual language in the discourses of lesbian feminists, and an also incredible absence of lesbian sexual images. That is why the groups that named themselves Feminist Lesbians (following that specific order) not only included in their agendas lesbian demands, but also questioned the silence and contention of feminists in general and lesbian feminists in particular on sexual themes, debating issues such as sexual practices among dykes, butch and femme role playing and relationships, the use of pornography, and many others.

As it was to be expected, the political decision of prioritizing gender over sexuality had an important effect on the representations displayed by groups and, more concretely, on the avoidance of showing sexual images and dykes with masculine *pluma*. These organizations usually showed timid images of (feminine, in the majority of the cases, or, quite exceptionally, androgynous) women hugging or kissing, many of them "imported" from other countries, such as Great Britain or the US. This had to do, on the one hand, with the tensions already mentioned with some sectors of the feminist movement, and on the other hand, with the understandable fear of coming out publicly as a lesbian during those difficult years. It is quite well known that one of the classic attacks to feminism was (and still is today) the derogatory affirmation that "all feminists are lesbians." In fact, lesbians were a majority in the feminist ranks. In this context, representation of lesbians portrayed women to women images, real ones (that is, feminine), and not the ones playing with or questioning their gender.

When analyzing the dilemmas around the definition of political identities that activists have to face, we cannot forget that sexual identities are stigmatized, that is, they are associated with a deviation, anomaly or a socially undesirable attribute. Definitions of butch and femme desires and relationships, for example, depart from a distorted image or a *spoiled* one, to use Goffman's term. Fight against that stigmatization imposed from outside, is one of the engines of sexual protest (Altman). As Foucault pointed out, the Church, the Medicine, and the Law have all historically produced discourses that respectively identify non straight subjects as sinners, sick people, and criminals. Not to mention the media and its use of mockery and negative imagery and stereotypes about lesbians, gay men, transvestites, and transgenders. Lesbian political organizations (and artists) have actively sought to make lesbianism and other sexualities visible in their/our own terms, desirable, legitimate, and powerful. Nevertheless, identity as representational strategy can give non "normal," stigmatized subjects power, but can be dangerous at the same time. More concretely, stereotypes are usually considered a pejorative form of representation, as they are used to reduce a group's heterogeneity to a few individuals who seem to follow a certain profile. An interesting issue here is that the stereotype of the butch (*camionera, marimacho* or *bollera* in Spanish) makes lesbianism visible, but in non (classical) lesbian terms. In other words, butches cause lesbianism to be read in masculine codes, and it has been argued that by doing so, they collaborate with the widespread notion that lesbians are not or cannot be feminine.

Butches are one of the "repulsive" stereotypes. They represent what Esther Newton called *stigma* when talking about drag queens. Masculine women, or those subjects assigned "women" at birth who perform masculinity with their (socially considered "masculine") way of dressing, their gestures, haircuts, attitudes, and codes, are less tolerated than feminine lesbians, who at least fit into what is expected from a proper "woman": they are feminine (without being exaggerated), not sexualized, and powerful (without being virile). Butches and gender queers (drag kings, tranny bois, transgenders…) are perceived as a pathological sign of a wrong identification, as subjects who aspire to be men and have a power that is always out of their reach (Halberstam, *Female*). There exists a lot of social, cultural, and political prohibitions against female masculinity: it is seen as a threat to issues like maternity, and it questions, overall, heteropatriarchy. Masculine women are socially punished for having and enjoying a non appropriate self-image. These punishments are carried out through silencing, lack of (non stereotypical) representation, stigma, and verbal and physical violences. However, although stereotypes can work as an insult and as a negative form of representation, they can also be recognized by the subjects involved in them so that they become strategic tools. Butches, transgenders, faggots, and other deviant sexualities can exceed the limits of stereotypical representation and distort those representation systems that depend on negative images of non straight people.[12] As Halberstam shows (*Female* 181), masculinity in black women or Latinas can be a place in which dominant forms of power can be recognized with subversive and even revolutionary results.

There are different silences and forms of invisibility in relation to lesbian bodies and sexualities (sometimes coming from feminism itself). While there are lesbians who feel surrounded by silence, others feel too exposed or hyper-visible (Halberstam, *Female*). The latter ones are the butches. They give visibility to lesbianism, and not only that: masculine dykes are *both* very visible and are read as hyper-sexual. valeria flores has recently written on butches (*chongas* or *marimachos*) in the Latin American context, warning that "we expose ourselves to an optical plus that reinforces the process of social and cultural stigmatization, given the visibility of our desire" (191). The identity of the (sexual) butch does not represent an imposed male identity on a female body, but the destabilization of the way in which these terms are presented in the erotic game. And, as Rubin ("Of Catamites") explains, there are a lot of ways of being a butch, of adopting and changing many of the available codes of masculinity.

As we know, there has been a traditional feminist distrust of masculinity (associated with patriarchal power), and, although much less analyzed, on female masculinity. Butches were (and are) visible and excluded (like transvestites and *locas*) and not tolerated, for they look like men, and because their images had a sexual element that was highly disturbing in the 1980s debates within feminism.[13] We should also not forget the class distance here. As French queer theorist Marie Hélène Bourcier (*Queer zones*) has explained, historical silences of lesbian masculinities have to do both with class prejudices and with their questioning of the concordance of the dominant sex-gender system. Precisely, and thanks to that, masculine attitudes and looks in female bodies have an enormous erotic potential that can be displayed in a huge variety of forms in the sexual game (Hollinbaugh and Moraga). Butch-femme images sexualize lesbianism and, as Butler argues, are not "an uncritical appropriation of sex-role stereotyping from within the practice of heterosexuality [...] The relation between the 'imitation' and the 'original' is, I think, more complicated than that critique [the one coming from the feminist theory] generally allows" (*Gender Trouble* 175). In my view, the exclusion of butches has to do, therefore, with both the feminist rejection of masculinity in general and female masculinity in particular (together with feminist lesbophobia), and the contention and desexualization of feminist images.

As Taylor and Wittier point out, lesbian feminist discourse re-evaluated lesbianism as a part of feminism. At the end of the 1980s, Spanish lesbians had relative success in raising awareness among the larger feminist movement. However, the price they had to pay, in my opinion, was too high: they postponed the battle for their own demands, discourses, and representations, which, in turn, made the gap between lesbian political organizations and the scene much wider (Trujillo, *Deseo*). Not only that, but also lesbian feminism repressed a lesbian radical politics throughout the 1980s, which was reflected in their discourses and in the concealment of lesbian desires and sexualities. As valeria flores argues, "in this sense, the whole of visual images constructed by feminism shapes our perception of the subjects who can be represented and the ones who are left outside from the sphere of vision and legibility" (204). By the end of that decade, gay groups showed signs of fatigue, being challenged, and eventually surpassed, by a host of moderate, reformist groups that started to spring up during the second half of the 1980s. And for lesbian feminists, the more they were prepared to think on (lesbian) sexual terms, the more they felt inclined to find new ways of collaboration with a "lesbian and gay" movement, which was starting to get organized by that time. The category "woman," which worked as a closet for lesbians during many years, began then to be questioned by queer (feminist) groups.[14]

Female masculinities constitute an appropriation and change of concepts. Butches and transgenders question both the categories "woman" and "lesbian," showing their limits and exclusions. One of the things to analyze is whether they are actually considered "women," whether they feel included in the category or do not care or want to be part of it in anyway. The essential reference here is French theorist Monique Wittig, who defended, already in 1978, the revolutionary idea of "lesbians are not women," in her groundbreaking work *The Straight Mind*. "Woman" (and "man"), as Wittig argued, is a political category that needs to be destroyed, an unhistorical term produced by heterosexual economic and thought systems: as such, it only makes sense within it. Wittig breaks with the hierarchical binaries woman *versus* man, which renders impossible the existence of the third category, "lesbian," excluding her, just as the rest of the non straight subjects. If being a woman is to be defined in opposition to being a man, lesbians are out of that relation: they therefore are the "non women." The figure of the lesbian in Wittig is actually a runaway from gender and heteronormativity. They/we live an "internal exile within feminism, an escape from the class 'women' (flores 188). In brief, if lesbians are not women, butches are even less, they do not fit in the category at all; as most, they are *other* women (Trujillo, "Y no, no somos").

In the early 1990s, conflicts in relation to lesbianism within the feminist movement, the unbearable contention of lesbian sexualities and lives and the exclusion of butches carried out by lesbian feminist groups ended up in a total change of direction, a coup d'état led by a new generation of activists that demanded the specificity, legitimacy, and visibility of other sexual desires, bodies, and identities. Anne Marie Smith wrote, in relation to the British case that "some of the more serious threats to the establishment of a visible lesbian presence as a sexual one do not come from the 'State' but from 'our own' community" (211). Arlene Stein, in turn, pointed out how "intimate communities" become sometimes "exclusion communities." Gayle Rubin also reflected, in a piece entitled "Of Catamites and Kings: Reflections on Butch, Gender and Boundaries" (1992), the need to build up an inclusive community. One of the key issues here is that processes of identity construction can have a mobilizing and cohesion effect and, at the same time, be a limitation to it (Gamson). Lesbians, along with trans people and *other women* (such as sexual workers or migrants), opened up an escape route from the limits built up around the unitary and homogeneous feminist identity, "the Woman." This identity was put into question by subjects who were being expelled to the margins. During the 1990s, lesbian feminism was displaced by several different queer discourses that shared emphasis on the need to talk about it and make visible other sexualities and bodies, and its intersections with other elements such as class, ethnicity or age. In this process, these groups were influenced by the repertoire of ideas and experiences imported from other LGTB and queer movements from Western European countries and from North America.

## Queer or the Language of Desire(s)

In the 1990s, radical ideas from the 1970s were recuperated and adapted by the queer movement. Queer activism shares with the liberation movement of the 1970s the belief in the need of a transformation or social liberation on a broad scale (Jagose, 1996). Perhaps, in spite of representing a small section of a broader movement, queer activisms have had—and still do have—a relevant impact as far as discourses, representations, and actions that are concerned (Trujillo, "Del sujeto"). Queer political practices began in communities such as the *chicanas*, black lesbians, working class gays, HIV positive, and "sexual rebels" (Seidman 106). These groups, among others, started to question, as I mentioned before, their exclusion from a dominant culture and from a white and middle class gay movement (Stein, Phelan, and Seidman), just as it happened with the feminist movement. In the US, lesbians who rebelled against the purity standards of the feminist movement (mainly S/M lesbians and butch-femme couples), led the so-called pro-sex stream, together with sexually "liberated" heterosexuals and women who were close to radical feminism (Rubin, "The Leather" and "Thinking Sex").

In Spain, queer anger started to get organized in response to the AIDS crisis and the increasing homophobia that accompanied it (Llamas). Another important element to understand the beginning of the queer movement was the search by a new generation of lesbian activists for other spaces, discourses, and representations far from a male dominated gay and lesbian movement or the often unsympathetic Spanish feminist movement (Trujillo, "Del sujeto"). The Madrid-based group *La Radical Gai* ("Gay Radicals"), the first Spanish (male) queer group (it was set up in 1991), sought to display an alternative view to the increasingly resonant principles of pragmatism within gays groups, using parody and provocation as tools against silence and homophobia. Two years later, in 1993, LSD, the first lesbian queer group was created in Madrid. LSD would stand for "Lesbians Without Doubt" or "Lesbians Sweating Desire" or "Lesbians Going out on Sundays"... and other variants. They played with their name—the only non altered word was "Lesbian," which was a strategic (and fun) way to show that sexual identities are something that are to be redefined, changeable, and negotiable (as they would say, "choose and change"). Like activists declared, "we define ourselves through our actions and proposals."[15] By constantly modifying the name, they were questioning, in a very original and creative way, the idea of that identities are fixed and homogenous elements, while showing the possibility of negotiating their assigned meanings (Butler, "Acerca"). LSD was also the first lesbian organization that defended the idea of "difference": "I am queer. I am not straight and I do not want my relationships to be legitimated by the straight world. I am queer, I am different."[16]

Queer activism emphasizes, as Lisa Duggan explains, the need to carry out actions that take into account historical and local contexts. They search to establish a collaborative network with the rest of the organizations that question the traditional (sexist, racist, and homophobic) dynamics in the spaces where they participate or gather in: squatters, feminists, some neighbours groups, and people who refuse to join the military service (*insumisos*), as well as other collectives. They resist gender and sexual heterosexist norms and renounce to participate in the circuits of the traditional "main politics" (Bourcier, "Foucault," 14–15). The aim is to carry out micro politics from the margins, from autonomous activisms; to mobilize together they only need to share common political goals, not a homogeneous identity. The political demands of queer activism spin around social transformation, opposite to a moderate LGTB movement centered in the institutional sphere and on civil rights strategies. In Stein's and Plummer's words, they focus on the "politics of carnival, transgression and parody which leads to deconstruction, decentering, revisionist readings and an anti-assimilationist politics" (181). These aims and strategies, traditionally considered "cultural," are, at the same time, political (in fact, they can be very effective, politically speaking). Our (abject) bodies are already political, "battlegrounds," as lesbian artist Barbara Kruger once called them.[17]

Identity discourses displayed by queer lesbians put sexuality on the front line and started naming a *different* political subject who rebels against silences and timid and fearful representations and ideas about bodies, desires, sexual practices... that comes from both lesbian feminism, centered in women's demands, and a gay and lesbian movement that, immersed in the institutionalization process, defended a conciliatory and normalizing discourse of sexual diversity. In society and media in general, lesbians have been traditionally represented as hypersexual (in mainstream porno for straight guys, for example) and, at the same time, completely non sexual. Queer activists underlined the need to create their own images and discourses to confront the contention and invisibility that neither named nor talked about their (sexual, but not only) experiences and practices they were living as lesbians: "We ourselves create our own representations with our own bodies, our own images."[18] During those years, in Spain, new ideas and strategies (like the "in your face" actions) started to be discussed and put into practice thanks to diffusion (Giugni) and learning processes within movements (Adam). Spanish activists established a series of contacts and connections, both on an individual and a collective level, with organizations from the US, France, and England, such as ACT UP (Paris), Lesbian Avengers, Radical Furies or Queer Nation from the US, or the British group OutRage, to name but a few.

As Gamson explains, queer groups in the 1990s were influenced by feminist theories and political practices, constructivist sociology and history, and poststructuralist philosophy. Most of these references were written by authors (some of them part of activist groups) who, although departing from feminist positions, defend that feminism is not a sufficient corpus (even puritan many times) while analyzing sexuality. Rubin ("Thinking sex") had already warned that sexuality issues needed a separate analysis from those related to gender. Queer theory was, as De Lauretis put it, another discursive horizon, a different way to think about sexuality. LSD activists translated, analyzed, and debated works by (post) feminists such as Donna Haraway, Judith Butler, and Eve Kosofsky Sedgwick, among many others. There was, and it still continues, a very productive exchange between political theories and practices among queer groups and circles, a reflection of the attempt to blur the frontiers between these two spheres.

A key issue here is that queer lesbian identities go beyond sexual preference. Their discourses are defined not only by the sexual dimension but also by other variables like class, race, ethnicity, age… "where sexuality, we insist, is another element of our lesbian identity, maybe the one that has made us talk the most, and maybe, paradoxically, the one that has made us silent the most."[19] According to this idea, queer lesbian activists do not defend strict lesbian politics but a transversal activism to the different oppressions. As Biddy Martin argues, queer does not mean so much in an identity but a critical interrogation of identities, spaces of complex interactions of different variables. In this sense, butches vary in the way they relate with their female bodies, and forms of masculinities are in turn shaped by experiences and expectations related to class, race, ethnicity, religion, occupation, age, subculture, and individual personality (Rubin, "Thinking sex").

Picking up the issue of representation again, for queer lesbians (and trans people and gays), the critique to integration, normalization, and respectability, as an element that supports traditional gender roles, plays a key role (Aliaga and Cortés). That is why images created by these groups are highly subversive, critical, and do not look for "tolerance" to difference at all. In the context of the AIDS crisis, queers rebelled against feminist silences and those from society in general (including, of course, the medical system) about lesbian sexual practices, organizing safe sex workshops and related campaigns. If we think about visibility and the different ideas associated to it, in the case of queer groups what we see is that they defend a double strategy. On the one side, a hyper visible one, that is, a vindication of the pride of being different, not normal, as a form of protest; on the other hand, they choose the escape, to not identify themselves, and avoid control by society. However, as it has been shown earlier, butch lesbians and transgenders cannot or do not want to pass or hide anything. While writing this piece and looking for images of butches and of masculine dykes displayed by queer groups in general, I realized something that I had not come across earlier: although their images were, during the 1990s, really creative, powerful, and sexually transgressive, they did not get further and show masculine codes on bodies assigned as female ones, on dyke bodies. More time was still needed to do so, something that says quite a lot not about these groups but mostly about the society they had to confront, with its anxieties and fears regarding control of gender and sexuality norms. In the 1990s there were—and many still persist—an amazing number and forms of punishments, silences, and violences for bodies, sexual practices, and identities that questioned those norms, had to face.

Why was it that difficult? Why is it so complicated to think about masculinity as a code, as a repertoire of behaviors, that should be available to *any* body? Because, as Halberstam points out

> …female masculinity within queer sexual discourse allows for the disruption of even flows of gender and anatomy, sexuality and identity, sexual practice and performativity. It reveals a variety of queer genders, such as stone butchness, that challenge once and for all the stability and accuracy of binary sex-gender systems. (*Female* 139).

## Some Final Notes

As I have explained in the preceding pages, in Spain, the radical change in sexual iconography from those previous representations of lesbian feminist groups was possible in the 1990s thanks to generational change, activists' travels, and the contacts and exchanges with several queer activist groups in other contexts, both in Europe and North America. Also, I have argued that, in spite of this impressive change and the sexualization of representations carried out by queer feminist groups, images of butches needed to wait longer. We cannot find images of butches, drag kings, and other forms of queer masculinities in female bodies, created and displayed by queer political groups until the end of the 1990s.

Today, in current media and culture we see queer genders (butch-femme relationships, among others) portrayed as a working class phenomenon or, in the US, also associated with women of color. Nowadays, after all the feminist and queer theoretical works and activisms on the streets for at least a couple of decades (Córdoba and Grupo de Trabajo Queer), a noticeable resistance against gender queers can still be found within white and middle class educated (gay and) lesbians. I think that artists like Cabello and Carceller, who worked with images of butches in the second half of the 1990s, benefitted, as the rest did, from all these previous (and contemporary) queer activist energies and ideas.[20]

An analysis like this one, which talks about representations of female masculinities with no images available, paradoxically functions in the end as an archive: it is a compilation of the tracks, failures, deviances, and violences from the bio-political project of sex and gender. More than an analysis of the representations, this finally turned out to be an analysis of the geographies of invisibilities, silences, erasures… of butches. "Masculinity," as Halberstam warns us, "of course, is what we make it; it has important relations to maleness, increasingly interesting relations to transsexual maleness and a historical debt to lesbian butchness" (*Female* 144).

To conclude, I would like to add that now that we are starting to analyze and debate "new" masculinities, what is clear is that alternatives or non hegemonic ones need to be anti-sexist, non homophobic, and anti-racist, if we are really talking about changing *anything* here. Otherwise, we would be just reinforcing that "everything must change so that everything can stay the same," like the famous line of Lampedusa's *Il Gatopardo* goes.

## Notes

1 My translation from the original in Spanish, like the rest from valeria flores' work in this chapter.

2 This chapter was conducted as part of the research project entitled "Representaciones culturales de las sexualidades marginadas en España (1970–1995)" ["Cultural representations of marginalized sexualities in Spain (1970–1995)"], FEM2011—24064, funded by the Spanish Ministerio de Economía y Competitividad. The author would like to thank Kerman Calvo and Alexis Meyners for their valuable comments on an earlier version of this chapter.

3 This idea was included in the Introduction to the Spanish edition of *Female Masculinities* (8), where the author reflects on the need to carry out more intercultural studies on gender diversities among women.

4 My translation into English.

5 On this issue, see also Aliaga.

6 See Aliaga's chapter in this volume.

7 On queer methodologies, see Halberstam (*Female* 9–13).

8 "Perspectivas generales del Movimiento Gai." IV *Jornadas de la* COFHLEE (*Coordinadora de Frentes de Liberación Homosexual del Estado español*). Conference. País Valencià, 1–3 April, 1983.

9 See *Frente de Liberación Homosexual de Castilla.*

10 The *Coordinadora de Col·lectius d' Alliberament Gai* organized an alternative march (led by transvestites) in 1979 in Barcelona. See *Mundo Diario*, June 26th 1979, and *Tele/Express*, June 25th 1979. About this issue, see also Fluvià (72–73).

11 For an interesting analysis of these (very similar) tensions and conflicts in the US, see Mandy Merck, Naomi Segal, and Elizabeth Wright.

12 On this topic, see Muñoz.

13 On the parallelisms between the exclusion of butches and transvestites in the Latin American context, see Fernández.

14 See Calhoun.

15 See *Lesbianas Sin Duda, Non Grata* 0.

16 *Ibid.*

17 "Untitled (your body is a battleground)," poster designed by the artist Barbara Kruger for the march to Washington of the feminist and pro-choice movement, 1989.

18 See *Lesbianas Sin Duda, Non Grata* 1.

19 See *Lesbianas sin Duda, Non Grata* 0.

[20] These artists who are a couple and work together, made a video with the title *Bollos* (*Dykes*), in which they both eat *bollos* (pastries or bakery in Spanish) in 1996. Two years later, there was an exhibition called "*Transgenéricos*: representations and experiences about society, sexuality and genders in the contemporary Spanish art," held in Koldo Mitxelena Kulturunea, San Sebastián.

## Bibliography

Adam, Barry. *The Rise of the Gay and Lesbian Movement*. New York: Twayne, 1987. Print.

Aliaga, Juan Vicente, and José María Cortés. *Identidad y diferencia. Sobre la cultura gay en España*. Barcelona: Egales, 1997. Print.

Aliaga, Juan Vicente. *Arte y cuestiones de género: Una travesía del siglo XX*. San Sebastián: Nerea, 2004. Print.

Altman, Dennis. *Homosexuality: Oppression and Liberation*. 1993 ed. New York: New York UP, 1971. Print.

Bourcier, Marie-Hélène. "Foucault, ¿y después?…" *Reverso* 2 (2000): 9–19. Print.

———. *Queer zones, politique des identités sexuelles et des saviors*. Paris: Éditions Amsterdam, 2006. Print.

Butler, Judith. *Gender Trouble: Feminism and the Subversion of Identity*. New York: Routledge, 1990. Print.

———. "Acerca del término queer." *Cuerpos que importan. Sobre los límites materiales y discursivos del "sexo."* 2002 ed. Buenos Aires: Paidós, 1993. 313–339. Print.

Calhoun, Cheshire. "The Gender Closet: Lesbian Disappearance under the Sign 'Women'." *Feminist Studies* 21 (1995): 7–34. Print.

Calvo, Kerman and Gracia Trujillo. "Fighting for Love Rights: Demands and Strategies of the LGBT Movement in Spain." *Sexualities: Studies in Culture and Society* 14 (2011): 562–580. Print.

Connell, Raewyn. "Politics of Changing Men." *Socialist Review* 25 (1995): 135–139. Print.

———. *Masculinities*. Berkeley: U of California P, 1995. Print.

Connell, Raewyn and James W. Messerschmidt. "Hegemonic Masculinity: Rethinking the Concept." *Gender and Society* 6 (2005): 829–859. Print.

Córdoba, David, Javier Sáez and Paco Vidarte. *Teoría queer: Políticas bolleras, maricas, trans, mestizas*. Barcelona: Egales, 2005. Print.

Cortés, José Miguel. "Construyendo masculinidades." *Héroes caídos. Masculinidad y representación.* Castelló: Espai d'Art Contemporani de Castellò, 2001. Print.

De Lauretis, Teresa. "Queer Theory: Lesbian and Gay Sexualities." *Differences: A Journal of Feminist Cultural Studies* 3 (1991): 3–18. Print.

Duggan, Lisa. "Introduction." *Sex Wars: Sexual Dissent and Political Culture*. Ed. Lisa Duggan and Nan D. Hunter. New York: Routledge, 1995. 1–14. Print.

Fernández, Josefina. "Los cuerpos del feminismo." *Sexualidades migrantes. Género y transgénero*. Ed. Diana Maffia. Buenos Aires: Feminaria, 2009. 138–154. Print.

flores, valeria. *Interruqciones*. Neuquén: La Mondanga Dark, 2013. Print.

Fluvià, Armand de. "El movimiento homosexual en el Estado español." *El homosexual ante la sociedad enferma.* Ed. José Ramón Enríquez. Barcelona: Tusquets, 1978. 149–160. Print.

Foucault, Michel. *History of Sexuality. Volume I: An Introduction.* New York: Pantheon Books, 1978. Print.

*Frente de Liberación Homosexual de Castilla.* Ed. *Aquí el FLOHC* Summer 1981. N. pag. Print.

Gamson, Joshua. "Must Identity Movements Self-destruct? A Queer Dilemma." *Social Problems* 42 (1995): 390–406. Print.

Giugni, Marco G. "The Cross National Diffusion of Protest." *New Social Movements in Western Europe: A Comparative Analysis*. Ed. Hanspeter Kriesi, Ruud Koopmans, Jan Willem Duyvendak, and Marco G. Giugni. Minneapolis: U of Minnesota P, 1995. 181–206. Print.

Goffman, Erving. *Stigma. Notes on the Management of Spoiled Identity*. New Jersey: Penguin Books, 1963. Print.

Halberstam, Judith. *Female Masculinity*. Durham: Duke UP, 1998. Print.

———. "Introducción a la edición española." *Masculinidad femenina*. Barcelona: Egales, 2008. 7–17. Print.

Hollibaugh Amber, and Cherríe Moraga. "What We're Rollin around in Bed with: Sexual Silences in Feminism: A Conversation towards Ending Them." *The Persistent Desire: A Femme-Butch Reader*. Ed. Joan Nestlé. Boston: Alyson Publications, 1992. 243–253. Print.

Jagose, Annamarie. *Queer Theory: An Introduction*. New York: New York UP, 1996. Print.

Lazy, Susanne. "Affinities: Thoughts on an Incomplete History." *The Power of the Feminist Art: The American Movement of the 1970s: History and Impact*. Ed. N. Broude and M. D. Garrad. New York: Harry N. Abrams, 1994. 264–275. Print.

*Lesbianas Sin Duda*. Ed. *Non Grata* 0 (1994) and 1 (1995). N. pag. Print.

Llamas, Ricardo. Ed. *Construyendo sidentidades. Estudios desde el corazón de una pandemia*. Madrid: Siglo XXI, 1995. Print.

Martin, Biddy. "Lesbian Identity and Autobiographical Difference[s]." *The Lesbian and Gay Studies Reader*. Ed. Henry Abelove, Michéle Aina Barale, and David M. Halperin. New York: Routledge, 1993. 274–293. Print.

Merck, Mandy, Naomi Segal and Elizabeth Wright. Ed. *Coming Out of Feminism?* Massachusetts: Blackwell Publishers, 1998. Print.

Muñoz, José. *Disidentifications: Queers of Color and the Performance of Politics*. Minneapolis: U of Minnesota P, 1999. Print.

Nestle, Joan. *A Restricted Country*. Ithaca, NY: Firebrand Books, 1987. Print.

Newton, Esther. *Mother Camp: Female Impersonators in America*. Chicago: U of Chicago P, 1979. Print.

Petit, Jordi. "Gays y lesbianas: la experiencia de la Coordinadora gay y lesbiana." *Diez palabras clave sobre movimientos sociales*. Ed. José María Mardones. Estella: Verbo Divino, 1996. 293–325. Print.

Phelan, Shane. "(Be) Coming Out: Lesbian Identity and Politics." *Signs* 18 (1993): 765–90. Print.

Rubin, Gayle. "The Leather Menace: Comments on Politics and S/M." *Coming to Power: Writings and Graphics on Lesbian S/M*. Ed. SAMOIS. San Francisco: Alyson Publications, 1981. 194–229. Print.

———. "Thinking sex: Notes for a Radical Theory of the Politics of Sexuality." *Pleasure and Danger: Exploring Female Sexuality*. Ed. Carole Vance. Boston: Routledge, 1984. 267–319. Print.

———. "Of Catamites and Kings: Reflections on Butch, Gender and Boundaries." *The Persistent Desire: A Femme-Butch Reader*. Ed. Joan Nestlé. Boston: Alyson, 1992. 466–482. Print.

Sedgwick, Eve Kosofsky. *Epistemology of the Closet*. Berkeley: U of California P, 1990. Print.

Seidman, Steven. "Identity and Politics in a 'Postmodern' Gay Culture: Some Historical and Conceptual Notes." *Fear of a Queer Planet: Queer Politics and Social Theory*. Ed. Michael Warner. Minneapolis: U of Minnesota P, 1993. 105–142. Print.

Smith, Anne Marie. "Resisting the Erasure of Lesbian Sexuality: A Challenge for Queer Activism." *Modern Homosexualities: Fragments of Lesbian and Gay Experience*. Ed. Ken Plummer. London: Routledge, 1992. 200–213. Print.

Stein, Arlene. "Sisters and Queers: The Decentering of Lesbian Feminism." *Social Perspectives in Lesbian and Gay Studies.* Ed. Peter. M. Nardi and Beth E. Schneider. 1998 ed. London: Routledge, 1992. 553–563. Print.

Stein, Arlene, and Ken Plummer. "I Can't even Think Straight: Queer Theory and the Missing Sexual Revolution in Sociology." *Sociological Theory* 12 (1994): 178–187. Print.

Taylor, Verta and Nancy Whittier. "Collective Identity and Social Movement Communities. Lesbian Feminist Mobilization." *Frontiers in Social Movement Theory*. Ed. Aldon Morris and Carol McClurg Mueller. New Haven: Yale UP, 1992. 104–129. Print.

Trujillo, Gracia. *Deseo y resistencia. Treinta años de movilización lesbiana en el Estado español.* Barcelona: Egales, 2008. Print.

———. "Del sujeto político *la Mujer* a la agencia de *las (otras)* mujeres: el impacto de la crítica feminista queer en el feminismo del Estado español." *Política y Sociedad* 46 (2009): 161–172. Print.

———. "Y no, no somos mujeres. Legados e inspiraciones para los feminismos queer." *Las lesbianas (no) somos mujeres. En torno a Monique Wittig.* Ed. Beatriz Suárez Briones. Barcelona: Icaria, 2013. 185–211. Print.

Wittig, Monique. *The Straight Mind and Other Essays*. Boston: Beacon P, 1992. Print.

# CHAPTER 3

# Bodily, Gender, and Identity Projects in Spain: From the Transvestite to the Transsexual

Óscar Guasch
*Universitat de Barcelona*
&
Jordi Mas
*Universitat de Barcelona*

During the 1970s and 1980s a rapid process of political and institutional change took place in Spain (referred to as the Transition),[1] taking the country from a dying dictatorship toward a consolidated democracy (although certainly with room for improvement, socially and institutionally).[2] In this historical period, a range of social transformations, which had been initiated in the 1960s thanks to the gradual economic and cultural opening of Spain toward Europe, took root. From the very dark image of Spain portrayed in 1951 by Eugene Smith for *Life* magazine, there was a transition to a colorful, stereotypical Spain of beaches full of half-naked tourists eating paella. Some of these changes can be seen in the *destape* ("The Revealing"): a social trend in Spanish cinema that expressed the new social perceptions of the body through nudity (Ponce). After Franco's death, the Spain of the 1980s finally breathed the air of political freedom and began to understand the meaning of sexual freedom. In this context of rapid social and cultural transformation, ideas about gender and sexuality also underwent important changes.

This chapter reviews the socio-historical construction of the figure of the *transvestite* in Spain as a category to theorize and refer to transgenderism. It also explores its subsequent conversion into the figure of the *transsexual.* The shift from the transvestite to the transsexual was a historical process that took place in the medium-term and that established the hegemony of the medical category of the *transsexual* to refer to transgender realities, to the detriment of the concept of the *transvestite.* The study of this conceptual mutation is an instrument that helps us to better understand all of the changes that have affected gender and sexuality in the Spain of the last thirty years.

Throughout the 1980s and 1990s, the term used in Spain to refer to transgender realities was *transvestite.* As argued by Alberto Cardín (45–49), this category represents a problem of classification as the transvestite is a figure that violates standard systems in the cultural representation of gender. The *transvestite* is a social being on the boundaries of gender and creates both fear and desire simultaneously. Using the terminology that Victor Turner borrowed from Arnold Van Gennep, we could say that the *transvestite,* as an "effeminate man," is a liminal subject to the extent that he occupies an "inter-structural," ambiguous position, in relation to the (dichotomous) gender categories of Western societies (Mas). The *transvestite* is not a man, given that "his" appearance and mannerisms transgress the normative codes of virility; but "he" is not exactly a woman, given that he conserves the quintessential masculine attribute: a penis.

During the post-Franco period in Spain a sort of "parallelism" between two forms of liminality occurred: on the one hand, a political liminality (with the transition from a dictatorial state to a democratic one); and on the other, a transgender liminality embodied in the figure of the *transvestite.* In Picornell's opinion, "the image of the transvestite (always in the form of a man dressed as a woman) has become a recurring metaphor in the political transition from Franco's dictatorship to a new democratic state still in the process of defining itself" (Picornell 283). The *transvestite* personifies the social reality of the period, given that his image is a reflection of "the ambivalent process from the old to the new in the political and social panorama of the Spain of the transition" (Paredes 56). For her part, Robbins (140) points out that "the public parodying of jubilant sexuality in the drag shows of the 1970s and 1980s seemed like […] a celebratory funeral for the outdated repressions of national Catholicism" in Franco's Spain.

In the Spain of the Transition, both transgendered bodies and the political system were in the need of definition: there were both gender and political instability. Inter-structuralism is the shared essence of the *transvestite* and the Spain of the Transition. In contrast, the *transsexual* and democracy incarnate perfectly regulated corporeal and political realities. If the ambiguity of the *transvestite* challenges the duality of gender, the *transsexual* presents a body integrated into the standard codes of gender classification. Thanks to medical practices (hormone treatments and surgery), the *transsexual* obtains a body in accordance with one (and only one) of the two socially legitimate genders. In this way, both democracy and the *transsexual* represent desirable destinations in as much as they establish mechanisms of governance (political and of the body) capable of guaranteeing social order.

Rationalization processes are one of the most important mechanisms in the construction of modernity. They consist of a series of transformations in which science, with medicine in the lead, legitimizes new forms of organizing social control over dissidence and diversity. Generally, in these processes of rationalization, religious artifacts are replaced by scientific and medical ones. In this way, the commandment *you must not steal* gets transformed into *kleptomania* and the *possessed* become the *mentally ill,* while from the broad religious category of the sodomite, *sexual perversions* arise (Guasch *Héroes*). From this perspective, the transsexualization process can be understood as a late modern form of the process of rationalization of certain radical forms of gender dissidence (Núñez), which has the side-effect of reinforcing the current dichotomous sex/gender system.

The change from *transvestite* to *transsexual* involves diverse techno-political interventions that are carried out on concrete bodies through institutionalized medical processes. During the latter years of Franco and through the Transition, the *transvestite* was thought of as "a woman with a penis" or as "a man with breasts" and therefore there were subverted standard codes in the social classification of gender. Subsequently, the redefinition of the *transvestite* through the medical category of the *transsexual* would permit his/her normalized representation in the system of gender classification. As a result, the process of techno-medical feminization that the *transvestite* has gone through to become the *transsexual* is a special type of rationalization process. In this case, it is a process of the rationalization of gender.

One of the most common political strategies to legitimize rationalization processes is to naturalize the realities that one wants to regulate medically. This can be seen here, as the hegemonic medical perspective argues that "transsexuality is not a new phenomenon: it has existed since ancient times and in different cultures. The phenomenon of gender dysphoria has existed throughout all recorded history" (Díaz Morfa 83). Medicine conceives transsexuality as a sort of anthropological constant, which was treated incorrectly throughout history because societies did not have the necessary knowledge or technology. In contrast, for the social sciences, transsexuality is a historical phenomenon that emerged in a particular sociocultural context, that is: in the moment in which bio-medicine began to intervene in the bodies of individuals that reject the gender assigned to them at birth. As Billings and

Urban point out, before the work Harry Benjamin exercised its potent influence on the scientific community, therapy based on hormonal-surgical body reassignment generated misgivings among medical professionals. The majority favoured psycho-therapeutic treatment, which has as its objective that the patient ultimately accepts the gender identity he/she was assigned at birth. In this sense, from the psychoanalytic sphere, doctors that practiced sex change surgery were accused of collaborating with the castration desires of patients affected by an extreme form of psychosis.

Beginning in the 1960s, the research and surgical practices with transgendered patients carried out at the John Hopkins University helped to legitimize the category of *transsexual* both in the United States and Europe (Meyerowitz). However, in the case of Spain, the social and cultural diffusion of the *transsexual* category would not happen until two decades later. In this regard it is necessary to emphasize an important legal obstacle: genital surgery was not decriminalized until 1981. In short, in Spain, the category of the *transvestite* forms part of industrialism, while the medicalized category of the *transsexual* becomes completely hegemonic in the framework of post-industrial society.

The concept of *transsexuality* is a very useful example for illustrating that "categories are especially flexible and changing in relation to context." (Coll-Planes 261). Still today, the category *transsexuality* encompasses different subjectivities, bodily projects, and social practices. However, it is anachronistic to label gender practices as *transsexual* prior to the creation of this medical concept. In addition, from an anthropological viewpoint, to describe as *transsexual* the transgender realities of other cultures is an ethnocentric judgment that reduces the cultural and gender logics of other societies to Western biomedical parameters. Anachronism and ethnocentrism characterize the thinking of Western societies on transgenderism (Spain included). The homophobia and transphobia, typical of undemocratic societies also favors simplistic ways of thinking about transgender realities. Popular culture of late Francoist Spain is a clear example of how homophobic and transphobic societies deny, ignore, and simplify the enormous internal diversity of sexual and gender dissidence.

In the social imaginary of late Francoism and the Transition, the category of *homosexual* was used indistinctly to refer to and to label sexual and gender realities as diverse as *transsexual*, *gay*, and *transvestite.* Guasch (*La sociedad*), in his ethnography on the gay world of Spain in the 1980s, analyzes the system of social classification of homosexuality at that time.

Spanish society of the 1980s thought that depending on the intensity of effeminate homosexuals' desires to be women, they could be classified *transvestites* or *transsexuals* (in that order). Semi-erotic magazines from the popular culture of the period (such as *Party, Lib,* or *Interviu)*, that flaunted their supposed sexual openness, provide documentary evidence of this perspective. Despite the fact that the first academic studies in Spain on homosexuality published in the 1980s included transsexuals and transvestites under the heading of "homosexuality." That is the case of the anthropologist Alberto Cardín, who wrote a book with a revealing title: *Guerreros, chamanes y travestis: indicios de homosexualidad entre los exóticos* (*Warriors, Shamans and Transvestites: Indicators of Homosexuality among the Exotics*, 1984). Or the forensic doctor Alberto García Valdés, whose photographs of imprisoned homosexuals illustrate the existing difficulties at that time when it came to distinguishing among homosexuals, transsexuals, and transvestites.

Cinema and "underground graphic novels" also contributed to the shaping of a confused social imaginary regarding *transsexuals* and *transvestites.* In this regard, the importance of the *transvestite* detective Anarcoma (created by the cartoonist Nazario in 1980) should be mentioned. Anarcoma was a character outside standard gender classifications, drawn with both large breasts and a large penis. Regarding cinema, there were many films that portrayed confusing images of homosexuals, transsexuals, and transvestites. In this regard, *El transexual* (*The Transsexual*, José Jara, 1977), *Cambio de sexo* (*Forbidden Love*, Vicente Aranda, 1977), *Ocaña, retrat intermitent* (*Ocana, an Intermittent Portrait*, Ventura Pons, 1978), *Un hombre llamado Flor de Otoño* (*A Man Called Autumn Flower*, Pedro Olea, 1978), and *Vestida de azul* (*Dressed in Blue*, Antonio Giménez Rico, 1983), should be mentioned. The influence of film on popular representations of transvestism was notable, although "the lack of critical attention [...] to the cinema of the transition [...] does not correspond with the popular impact that it had on the Spanish" (Melero 12). Subsequently, with the powerful pedagogical contribution of the first Pedro Almodóvar films, Spanish society would refine its understanding of the distinction among these categories.

In Spain, during the 1970s and 1980s, *transvestites* and *transsexuals* were most visible in shows and cabaret: "in the seventies, the success of *transvestites* performing was so spectacular that no hall would lose the opportunity of having 'the most outrageous challenge to the imagination in their line-up'" (Pierrot 155). This visibility was constructed around ambiguity and playing with doubts regarding the "real" femininity of the artist. As Gómez and Pierrot explain, doubt would usually be resolved through the full nudity that marked the climax of the performance. Alberto Mira clarifies that "with the arrival of the transition [...] a new repertoire was imposed that included nudity [...] and the central acts of each show were constructed as a *strip-tease,* the climax of which would be full nudity, revealing the 'real' artist" (Mira 441). This is the case of the performance (much commented on at the time) of the actress Bibí Andersen (who later would become one Pedro Almodovar's "muses"). It consisted therefore in a liminality (or indeterminacy) that ultimately needed to be confessed and resolved in the eyes of the public. However, these types of acts where the performer showed his/her genitals were severely criticized by certain sectors of the performing world: "I will never show my genitals [...] I am not paid to show my penis [...] Bibí lives through her face and her penis; she has nothing else" (Pierrot 67).

Between cabaret acts and "nudie magazines," popular culture during the transition established that having or not having a penis was the central element in distinguishing between *transvestites* and *transsexuals*: the *transvestites* were thought of as "men with female hormones" that had not changed their sex through surgery, while *transsexuals* were those who had been operated on. In this period, the term transsexual was not yet well established in Spain, consequently, the term transvestite was commonly used to refer to all expressions of transgenderism. This can be seen in the popular reference to *transsexuals* as *operated transvestites.* Today, the hegemony of classifications from the biomedical paradigm regarding so-called *sexual and gender identity disorders* means that, both in scientific and popular culture, the word *transsexual* is used to refer to persons that modify their secondary sexual characteristics with hormones or through surgery, regardless of whether or not they also wish to operate on their genitals. At the same time, the term *transvestite* is used specifically for those persons that limit themselves to adopting dress associated with the opposite gender without wanting to carry out any other bodily transformation. Nowadays, many *transsexual* women get angry if they are labeled *transvestites* because they see this as questioning their essential femininity.

But in the Spain of the 1970s and 1980s, the figure of the *transvestite* was thought of as polymorphous and it included very diverse practices and identities. The popular imaginary defined the *transvestite* as a radical form of homosexuality in which effeminate males tried to approximate the stereotyped forms of being a woman: "in that period, transsexuality was something completely unknown and women transsexuals were seen as men that liked to dress like women, like *transvestites*, and adopt the most exaggerated stereotypes of femininity" (Garaizabal 51). The idea that there are varying degrees of homosexuality based on the intensity of effeminacy and the inclusion of the phenomena of transvestism and transsexuality as a *homosexual* phenomenon, was present in the popular imaginary and also formed part of the scientific narrative of some of the founders of modern sexology. That is the case of Richard von Krafft-Ebing, who at the end of the nineteenth century distinguished among three degrees of *sexual inversion* or *homosexuality.* According to him, it is in the most accentuated degree of homosexuality (the *metamorphosis sexualis* paranoica) where the origin of what would later be referred to as *transsexuality* is found, given that this form of homosexuality is characterized by men who, in addition to desiring sexual relations with other men, dress, feel, and act like women. Until the publication of what is now considered the foundational book of transsexuality, *The Transsexual Phenomenon* (1966) by Harry Benjamin, the scientific community had serious difficulties in distinguishing among homosexuality, transvestism, and transsexuality. However, the same Harry Benjamin contributed to that confusion by stating in 1953 that transsexuality constituted such a radical form of transvestism that its practitioners wished to change their sex (King 141). As it can be seen, it is possible to find in the medical narrative, hypothesis, and arguments that contributed to reinforce society's viewpoint, which saw in *transvestites* and *transsexuals* accentuated forms of homosexuality.

The recent history of homosexuality in Spain can be organized into three periods with very different characteristics: a *pre-gay* period, a *gay* period, and a *hyper-gay* period (Guasch *La construcción*). Applying this historical classification to the figures of the *transvestite* and the *transsexual*, the *transvestite* is the predominant character during the pre-gay period, when social categories defining sexual and gender dissidence were still being constructed. The transsexual category reaches its social and conceptual "plenitude" in the *hyper-gay* period: a time of clear democratic advances as the rights of sexual and gender minorities were recognized through the gay marriage, act passed in 2005. The *hyper-gay* period is also the time when some regions in Spain established specific hospital units for the treatment of transsexual persons; or when in 2007 the government led by the Socialist Party presented a law regulating "the rectification of register entries relating to a person's gender," which permits transsexual persons to apply for name change and gender change in official documents without "gender reassignment surgery." The side-effect of these initiatives has been established the medical narrative as the hegemonic conceptual framework to theorize transgenderism without considering the opinions of the transgendered. As a transgendered activist and researcher explains: "when *trans* activists want to be the active subjects in the debate over how to regulate transsexuality–medically, but also socially and legally–we have no space to do so" (Missé 41). In this process, *transvestites* become *transsexual* patients and lose part of the sovereignty they had to construct their own identities and corporeality.

The *pre-gay* period extended through late Francoism and the transition (1970s and 1980s). During that time, transvestites enjoyed a certain recognition and respect in the entertainment world and within certain intellectual circles on the Spanish left. The cartoonist Nazario's counter cultural characters, the debate around the transsexuality of Salvador Dalí's supposed lover (Amanda Lear), Ocaña's critical anti-capitalist "discourse," and the anti-militarism of the transvestite (which created serious problems regarding obligatory military service) wrapped this figure in a *progressive* veneer which contrasts with the denigrating and stigmatized treatment transvestites received in the subsequent *gay* period. This *gay* period spanned the 1990s and inaugurated the search for the social acceptance of homosexuality, led by a sector of the gay movement with strong ties to Spanish social democracy. This is also the period of success for the gay magazine *Zero* and its role in the campaign to present a respectable image of homosexuality. In this context, the excessive social visibility of *transvestites* distorted the socially *correct* image that this sector of Spanish gays wanted to communicate. In addition, during this time, Spanish *reality* television found in transvestites (gradually becoming *transsexuals*) a way to increase their audience. It is the time of television characters perceived as extravagant and excessive: such as "Veneno" (in the program *Esta noche cruzamos el Mississippi, Crossing Mississippi Tonight,* conducted by Pepe Navarro) or Carmen de Mairena (in *Crónicas marcianas, Chronicles from Mars,* conducted by Javier Sardà). It is precisely through these television programs that a new transphobic term to refer the transvestite reality appears: it is the word *travelo* or *travolo*, which is a mix of the Spanish term *travesti* and the name *Manolo* (a colloquial derivative of the name Manuel, very common among Spanish men). If Don Juan refers to the seductive and sophisticated

Spanish male, Manolo refers to the rural or provincial one employed in low-skilled jobs. Converting the *travesti* into the *travelo* Manolo illustrates the historical moment in which the *transvestite* is no longer a transgressive figure and, instead, it comes to be perceived by society as a grotesque figure.

Although they were the most visible champions of the social transformations related to gender and sexuality affecting Spanish society in the 1970s and 1980s, the transgendered were stigmatized in the gay media during the *gay* period. This happened because, in a context of the "masculinization" and social normalization of homosexuality in terms of a gay subculture, transvestites and transsexuals were expelled from gay centrality, their attitudes were considered contaminating the project of social integration led by "respectable" gay organizations: "the tense and ambivalent relationship that gay activists of the 1970s had with transsexualism, contrasted with the transphobic cruelty [...] practiced by a new gay model which was narcissistic, egocentric, "hard-bodied," and with no political commitment" (Vélez-Pelligrini 417). Thus, the gay subculture lost the sense of humor and self-parody that so many *transvestites* and *transsexuals* provided, and became clearly transphobic. The problems and needs of transgender persons had to wait until the twenty first century to once again become part of the progressive political agenda. In Gayle Rubin's sexual hierarchy, transsexuals occupy a lower place than gay men and lesbians. Perhaps for this reason progressive sectors of Spanish society first fought for the rights of gay men and lesbians and only much later for those of *transsexuals*.

The process described in this text, in which the *transvestite* of the late Franco period turns into the post-industrial *transsexual,* chronicles the change from the liminal (and sometimes even the grotesque) toward the regulated and stable. It is paradoxical that the complete social normalization of transsexuality (at least in terms of "political correctness" and the recognition of social rights) takes place in the *hyper-gay* period, precisely at the moment in which movements and *queer* theory in Spain start to claim the public *performances* of transvestism as if they represented the *epitome* of gender transgression. The gender subversion of uneducated transvestites in the *pre-gay* period (which was spontaneous, little theorized, and personal) is now imitated (without the same showmanship) by those devoted to queer theory that think that cross-dressing (or self-administering hormones) is the "cutting edge" of gender subversion. These forms of theatrical performance that imitate the *transvestites* of the past tend to forget the historical meaning of the period in which these performances were originally carried out. In this sense, the supposed subversive intensity of *queer performances* is not very original, and therefore anachronistic.

We also have to read the transition from the *transvestite* body to the *transsexual* one in terms of technological possibilities in the context of the market. These technological possibilities are used to encourage the standardization of bodies. Post-industrial society manipulates bodies in search of homogeneity, desiring bodies that do not smell, sweat, or disturb. Hence, the social process by which the *transvestite* body turns into the *transsexual* one is analogous to the process transited by other bodies. Esther Nuñez (77) formulated the idea that in post-industrial society discriminations based on the body are organized around a market structure. Nowadays we are told that all bodies are potentially desirable, as if hegemony and subalternity around definitions of beauty did not exist.

Liberalism defends the idea that all bodies compete in equal conditions in the market of desire because there are body modification *techniques* that allow the adjustment of personal demands of the erotic-sexual market. But these *techniques* are only available for those that can pay for them, even though this variable in the equation is often hidden. Where economic neoliberalism proclaims the free competition of the unregulated labor market, the ideology of *sexual neoliberalism* proclaims that all bodies participate equally in the market of erotic desire. The only thing required is to prepare oneself for it. In any case, there are all types of body modification technologies that can be used to turn the *transvestite* body into the *transsexual* one. As a result, the *transsexual* body can be adjusted (or not) to the social expectations of normality, depending on the frequency and the intensity with which these technologies are used. In other words, "those who are not normal do not want to be," and the discourses, identities and subjectivities ascribed to the bodies of "transgendered" persons can be analyzed as forms of resistance or adaptation to the process of late-modern rationalization that constructs the *transsexual* in a market context.

The current Spanish medical model of transsexuality is an imported product: "during the 1970s and 1980s, many European countries imported the North American model […] and developed and perfected units specialized in the diagnosis of transsexuality in hospital psychiatric departments" (Missé 30). In Spain, until 1981, carrying out gender reassignment surgery was a crime punishable with prison, although in that period some doctors started to independently offer consultation to transsexual persons regarding hormone treatment. It is in the first decade of this century that the public healthcare system began to provide assistance to transsexual persons. The first of many hospital units to treat transsexuals in Spain (referred to as UTIG, *Gender Identity Disorder Units*) was established in 1999, in the hospital Carlos Haya in Malaga. The decision to create new services for specific medical attention to transsexuals and to include gender reassignment surgeries in the public healthcare system it depends on each autonomous regional government. In other words, in Spain, the medical and legal existence of transsexuality is some twenty years behind the majority of developed countries.

This does not mean that there were no transsexual women during late Francoism and the Transition, but their existence was outside of the realm of possibility afforded by Spanish medical technology. Transsexual women that wished to be operated on had to travel abroad. In particular, they traveled to Casablanca in Morocco, which was an important center for gender reassignment surgery during the 1960s and 1970s. However, some Spanish doctors defied the prohibition on such surgery and operated clandestinely on. The death in the 1970s of the famous transsexual Lorena Capelli because of a peritonitis, after having a vaginoplasty in Barcelona, provoked a great uproar in the trans world. But the majority of transsexual women of the period, constructed their bodies and identities in a self-taught and autonomous manner, outside of the medical gaze. The administration of hormones was usually carried out with little or no medical control and, given the lack of surgical options and economic resources to travel abroad, there were transsexual women that resorted to clandestine injections of liquid silicone in their breasts, buttocks, hips or in their faces to feminize their bodies. This practice, carried out clandestinely due to its illegality, was very widespread in Spain, especially during the 1980s (Mejía 177–187). It is currently still practiced in large cities such as Madrid or Barcelona, although being now very uncommon. Generally, it was carried out by experienced transsexual women, who, in a private home, injected themselves with liquid substances (silicone, but also paraffin or even engine oil) with the objective of shaping their bodies. There are many serious health problems resulting from this practice, and it has caused the death of many transsexual women.

The establishment of special units for the treatment of transsexuals (UTIG) in certain public hospitals has resulted in an undeniable improvement in the well-being of transsexual persons. However, it has also consolidated the hegemony of the medical model regarding the creating the conditions for the possibility of transgenderism, no longer now being defined in terms of the transvestite, but only as the *transsexual.* The multiple sexual possibilities of the transvestite, which are summarized in the ironic phrase: "I am a lover from behind and from the front," is reduced to a homogeneous universe in which any form of bodily and gender transgression will be considered a nuisance, inappropriate, and sensitive of being institutionally regulated. In this way, the bodily subversion of the *transvestite* becomes a problem that must it be solved: from now on, it is necessary to remove body hair, put on make-up, dress, follow hormone treatments and, ultimately, operate on bodies so that these can be easily encapsulated in one of the two gender categories socially available (Mas). The *transsexual* body reconstructs, in this sense, the borders of gender that the *transvestite* had brought into question, and contributes to undermine any indeterminate form of gender. At present, trans persons *must* adjust their bodies to social expectations. For example, it is worth pointing out that in the ninth edition of the Spanish reality television show *Big Brother*, some of the residents of the town where the house was located gathered to yell at the contestants that one of them was not the woman she claimed to be because she had a penis.

The fight to depathologize transsexuality is helping to recover critical and "combative" discourses that were so present among transvestites during late Francoism and the transition. To be fair to the reality, the history of sexual and gender liberation must recognize the role played by transvestites in making sex/gender diversity visible in Spain. The contributions that they made from stages and cabarets had a pedagogical impact that prepared society so that, later on, it could adopt changes regarding gender and sexuality. Long before the first homosexuals came out of the closet, *transvestites* and *transsexuals* made previously unimaginable realities visible. Books and memoirs, such as those of Antonio Gracia (Pierrot) and Dardo Gómez give proof to this. As Mérida Jiménez (118) states: "the transvestite was a catalyst before becoming fashionable." It is time to thank them for their leadership and recognize these merits which we have denied them until now.

## Notes

1 A cultural critique of the Transition can be found in Vilarós (1998). For a more political analysis see Maravall (1982).

2 This chapter has been written as part of the research project entitled "Representations and practice in the process of the feminization of transsexual women" (Exp. 2011-0004-INV-

00124), funded by the Spanish *Instituto de la Mujer*, as well as it was conducted as part of the research project entitled "Representaciones culturales de las sexualidades marginadas en España (1970–1995)" ["Cultural representations of marginalized sexualities in Spain (1970–1995)"], FEM2011—24064, funded by the Spanish Ministerio de Economía y Competitividad.

## Bibliography

Benjamin, Harry. *The Transsexual Phenomenon*. New York: Warner Books, 1966. Print.

Billings, Dwight and Thomas Urban. "La construcción socio-médica de la transexualidad: interpretación y crítica." *Transexualidad, transgenerismo y cultura.* Ed. José Antonio Nieto. Madrid: Talasa, 1998. 91–116. Print.

Cardín, Alberto. *Guerreros, chamanes y travestís. Indicios de homosexualidad entre los exóticos*. Barcelona: Tusquets, 1984. Print.

Coll-Planes, Gerard. "El circo de los horrores: una mirada interseccional a las realidades de lesbianas, gays, intersex y trans." *Intersecciones: cuerpos y sexualidades en la encrucijada*. Ed. Raquel/Lucas Platero. Barcelona: Bellaterra, 2012. 255–276. Print.

Díaz Morfa, José. "Disforia de género." *Sexología Integral* 14 (2007): 83–88. Print.

Garaizábal, Cristina. "La trasgresión del género. Transexualidades, un reto apasionante." *Transexualidad, transgenerismo y cultura.* Ed. José Antonio Nieto. Madrid: Talasa, 1998. 39–62. Print.

García Valdés, Alberto. *Historia y presente de la homosexualidad.* Madrid: Akal, 1981. Print.

Gómez, Dardo. *Travestis*. Barcelona: Bruguera, 1978. Print.

Guasch, Óscar. *La sociedad rosa*. Barcelona: Anagrama, 1991. Print.

———. *Héroes, científicos, heterosexuales y gays. Los varones en perspectiva de género.* Barcelona: Bellaterra, 2006. Print.

———. "La construcción cultural de la homosexualidad masculina en España (1970–1995)." *Minorías sexuales en España (1970–1995). Textos y representaciones*. Ed. Rafael M. Mérida Jiménez. Barcelona: Icaria, 2013. 11–25. Print.

King, Dave. "Confusiones de género: concepciones psicológicas y psiquiátricas sobre el travestismo y la transexualidad." *Transexualidad, transgenerismo y cultura.* Ed. José Antonio Nieto. Madrid: Talasa, 1998. 123–158. Print.

Krafft-Ebing, Richard von. *Psychopathia Sexualis : avec recherches spéciales sur l'inversion sexuelle*. Georges Carré. 1895. Web. Sep 2013. <http://goo.gl/PN4Z5E>.

Maravall, José María. *The Transition to Democracy in Spain.* London: Croom Helm, 1982. Print.

Mas, Jordi. *Identidades gestionadas. Un estudio sobre la patologización y la medicalización de la transexualidad.* Universitat de Barcelona, MA in Anthropology and Etnography. Sep 2010. Web. Sep 2013. <http://goo.gl/9lvAVA>.

Mejía, Norma. *Transgenerismos. Una experiencia transexual desde la perspectiva antropológica*. Barcelona: Bellaterra, 2006. Print.

Melero Salvador, Alejandro. *Placeres ocultos. Gays y lesbianas en el cine español de la Transición*. Madrid: Notorious, 2010. Print.

Mérida Jiménez, Rafael M. "Memoria marginada, memoria recuperada: escrituras trans." *Escrituras de la sexualidad.* Ed. Joana Massó. Barcelona: Icaria, 2008. 105–125. Print.

Meyerowitz, Joanne. *How Sex Changed. A History of Transsexuality in the United States.* Cambridge: Harvard University, 2002. Print.

Mira, Alberto. *De Sodoma a Chueca. Una historia cultural de la homosexualidad en España en el siglo XX.* Barcelona: Egales, 2004. Print.

Missé, Miquel. *Transsexualitats: altres mirades possibles*. Barcelona: UOC, 2012. Print.

Nuñez Vidal, Esther. *Del tercer sexo a la disforia de género. Transexualidad, medicina y comunidades generodisidentes*. Barcelona: Universitat de Barcelona, DEA Sociología, 2001. Print.

Paredes, Francisca. "La nación se hace carne: la construcción del travestí como metáfora de la transición en *Una mala noche la tiene cualquiera*, de Eduardo Medicutti." *Hispanofilia* 149 (2007): 55–68. Print.

Picornell, Merçé. "¿De una España *viril* a una España *travestí*? Transgresión transgénero y subversión del poder franquista en la transición española hacia la democracia." *Feminismo/s* 16 (2010): 281–304. Print.

Pierrot. *Memorias trans. Transexuales, travestis, transformistas*. Barcelona: Morales i Torres, 2006. Print.

Ponce, Jose María. *El destape nacional. Crónica del desnudo en la Transición.* Barcelona: Glenat, 2004. Print.

Robins, Jill. "Andalucía, el travestismo y la mujer fálica: *Plumas de España*, de Ana Rossetti." *Lectora* 15 (2009): 135–158. Print.

Rubin, Gayle S. "Thinking Sex. Notes for a Radical Theory of the Politics of Sexuality." *Pleasure and Danger: Exploring Female Sexuality*. Ed. C. S. Vance. Boston: Routledge, 1984. 267–319. Print.

Turner, Victor. "Entre lo uno y lo otro: el periodo liminar en los 'rites de passage'." *La selva de los símbolos*. Victor Turner. Madrid: Siglo XXI, 2008.103–123. Print.

Vélez-Pelligrini, Laurentino. *Minorías sexuales y sociología de la diferencia. Gays, lesbianas y transexuales ante el debate identitario*. Barcelona: Montesinos, 2008. Print.

Vilarós, Teresa. *El mono del desencanto. Una crítica cultural de la Transición española (1973–1993)*. Madrid: Siglo XXI, 1998. Print.

# CHAPTER 4

# Embodiments of Class and Nation in Eloy de la Iglesia's Gay Films

Alfredo Martínez-Expósito
*University of Melbourne*

While most accounts of the twenty-three films directed by Eloy de la Iglesia (1944–2006) have focused on either their portrayal of social inequalities or their grasp of gay issues, questions related to how the body is portrayed and utilized have been largely taken for granted.[1] Yet, a close reading of his last gay film, *Los novios búlgaros* (*Bulgarian Lovers*, 2003), reveals a careful treatment of the body's visual rhetoric along the lines of a discourse based on class, nation, and sexuality. The different types of male characters defined by oppositions generated by these paradigms (privileged/subaltern, local/foreign, and gay/straight) receive a unique cinematographic treatment. For instance, well-off gay Spaniards are played by relatively unfit actors, while subaltern gay foreigners are played by young, fit, good-looking actors. Thus, *Los novios búlgaros* seems to respond to preconceived ideas about the physicality of certain human types and it does so in ways that are both complex and non-reductionist: focusing on individual differences amongst the several characters within each group; stressing individual evolutions; and suggesting that a given character can be reassigned to a different group. From this perspective, bodies are more than just mere physical supports for characters; bodies do embody values and ideological discourses. Taking *Los novios búlgaros* as a model, this chapter sets out to analyse de la Iglesia´s earlier gay films, *Los placeres ocultos* (*Hidden Pleasures*, 1977) and *El diputado* (*Confessions of a Congressman*, 1978), as instances of an embodied discourse not only on homosexuality but also on class and nation.

The significance of director Eloy de la Iglesia in the history of Spanish cinema has been often described in relation to his ability to interpellate audiences by means of an anti-academicist cinematography, an openly ideological approach to the two genres he cultivated (the thriller and the melodrama), and, above all, a combination of violence and politics that seemed to echo the country's general atmosphere during the troubled

Transition years. Unambiguously Marxist in his approach to cinema as a means to denounce and critique power structures, his genre films were the result, in most cases, of a conspicuous *auteur* awareness that organised and articulated his filmic practice as a call to action. De la Iglesia famously denounced academia and bourgeois notions of art and cinema as instruments of domination and social conformity; his own utilisation of the medium aimed precisely at exposing, from within, the exploitation and symbolic violence inherent to a social system based on deeply-ingrained inequalities. In his case, auteurism was a form of resistance to both the violence of society and the conforming agendas of commercial cinema—which, in the 1970s, was still subject to state censorship. It should not come as a surprise, therefore, that most accounts of his twenty-three films have focused on representational regimes of social inequalities and state violence, with thematic examples such as sexual exploitation, class differences, marginal lifestyles, illegal drugs trafficking and consumption, homosexuality, and political violence, among others.

> As an affiliated member of the illegal Spanish Communist Party (PCE) and a homosexual director, de la Iglesia's political and sexual orientations were clearly outside of official Francoist discourse. In the highly politicised context of the periods of Transition and early democracy, de la Iglesia was able to produce an explicitly 'homophile cinema' […] but in the late Francoist period he could only intimate and articulate it through the vehicle of the horror and the thriller genres.[2]

What, with a few eminent exceptions[3] has not been so often pointed out in relation to his films, is the central importance of the human body as a visual metaphor in most of these themes, in particular the male body. It would appear that, for de la Iglesia, the human body is not only the locus of all physical interactions (sex, violence) but also the visual canvas in which identities are played out (class, nation, gender). Interestingly, de la Iglesia's most productive years from a production viewpoint were the same years in which the Spanish media became the privileged vehicle of *destape* ("The Revealing"), with its assortment of exploitative (and largely distasteful) genres centred around the naked female body. More queer than feminist in his approach to the body, de la Iglesia did not avoid the exploitative gaze but focused his attention on the male body and on fairly alternative approaches to notions of masculinity. For instance, his choice of actors for male roles, gay or straight, is consistently marked by a preference for non-effeminate, unambiguously "masculine" types. As Juan Carlos Alfeo points out, in gay films of the 1970s there was a clear differentiation between effeminate and masculine gay characters:

> [O]tro grupo de personajes acentúan su masculinidad y hacen bandera de su buen porte, de su masculinidad, de todo aquello que, en fin, los igualaba a sus homólogos heterosexuales. Sin duda no es precisamente casual que algunos de los protagonistas homosexuales sean encarnados por actores que, en su momento, constituían auténticos iconos de [las masculinidades] para el público de la época, como pueden ser Simón Andreu, Javier Elorriaga, José Sacristán o Imanol Arias.[4]

For a Marxist filmmaker working under and against Francoist censorship, nothing could have been more appealing than collapsing ideological discourses into the semiotic container of the human body as a visual repository of exploitation and alienation. Far from resulting in an oblique, indirect, allegoric, and ultimately opaque technique, de la Iglesia's embodiment of ideology is, from today's perspective, one of the most transparent and lucid denunciations of state and social violence during the Transition. In her study of represented masculinities all along the Transition, Isabel Estrada rightly warns that "the transformation of the political system did not always influence the transformation of the social or sexual mores that had been disapproved of in the past;"[5] even when the right conditions for a radical change were created by the "intersection of the democratic political transition and the rise of the feminist movement in a socio-political moment that demanded a new model of masculinity,"[6] the gradual distancing from received patriarchal models of masculinity was motivated by the political rejection of the dictatorship than by the influence of feminist thought.

De la Iglesia's atypical career structure provides us with a unique vantage point from which to re-assess his Transition films: *Los novios búlgaros*, his last film, was shot after a very long silence that kept de la Iglesia away from the profession since 1987 while he fighted his addiction to heroine that started while shooting *El pico* (*The Shot*, 1983). *Los novios búlgaros* is set in contemporary Spain, a country that, in 2003, has sealed a pact of silence with regards to its own traumatic past; an affluent, reconstituted country for which many of the issues of the Transition, such as political violence, are no longer meaningful but that has made of the so-called *Cultura de la Transición* (self-imposed cultural consensus tightly controlled by the main political parties) its most venerable cultural axiom.[7] It is precisely this film that allows for a reconsideration of the importance of the human body in de la Iglesia's earlier films. The film is an adaptation, co-scripted by de la Iglesia, Fernando Guillén Cuervo, and Antonio Hens, as well as Mendicutti himself, of Eduardo Mendicutti's 1993 novel *Los novios búlgaros*. Published by Tusquets shortly after Mendicutti being shortlisted for the 1992 Premio Nacional de Narrativa, the novel was broadly interpreted as an important addition to the author's contribution to the growing body of gay-themed fiction that in the early 1990s was gradually gaining recognition as a popular genre. Ten years later, with the "homosexual" genre already well established in the market, de la Iglesia's adaptation emphasized the gay melodrama choosing to play down the LGBT political issues of the time—namely the campaign in favour of equal rights for same-sex couples that would eventually lead to a programmatic declaration by newly-elected PM Zapatero in 2004 and the reform of the marriage law in 2005. De la Iglesia's only overt political intent in *Los novios búlgaros* is to highlight the unfair conditions of migrants in a country that has forgotten too quickly its own migrant past. With a quality cast that included first-rate names such as Fernando Guillén Cuervo and Pepón Nieto, as well as newcomer Albanian-born Dritan Biba, the film enjoyed international distribution and was awarded the Jury Prize at the 2003 Philadelphia International Gay and Lesbian Film Festival.

The chronological distance between *Los novios búlgaros* and the rest of his production reveals the deep historical hiatus between the Transition years and the affluent Spain of the millennium. The country's extraordinary transformation, so obvious and visible in *Los novios búgaros* when compared to his films of the 1970s and 1980s, goes well beyond and above the economy: the transformation of Spain's culture and values can be traced, amongst other things, through regimes of representation and visualisation of the body. It would be hard to overestimate the influence of the economy over the symbolic: imagination, and therefore representation of bodies on the screen, becomes a commodity that consumers in post-materialist societies expect to be readily accessible. The proliferation of screens in a screen-dominated culture such as that of Spain means that screened bodies are as omnipresent as one could possible desire, in as many genres and varieties as one could possibly imagine. De la Iglesia's return to the cinema in 2003 is also a felicitous occasion for a comparison of largely similar topics and themes seen from different historical perspectives. *Los novios búlgaros* features basically the same representational concerns de la Iglesia had two decades earlier, as if they had been preserved unaltered in a time capsule.

Yet, despite the enormous and perhaps unexpected improvement of the country's economy, Spain in the early 2000s did not seem to have overcome the social and economic inequalities of earlier times. That is, at least, one of the most obvious continuities in de la Iglesia's oeuvre. Despite de la Iglesia's carefully crafted discourse of marginality and dispossession, his socially-aware films go to the core of one of the most important national discourses of Spain in the democratic period: the image the nation projects of itself and the reputation it enjoys in the rest of the world. While Spain is, by all accounts, one of the countries that most successfully repositioned its international image in the last quarter of the twentieth century, de la Iglesia's multiple marginalities work as an efficient reminder of the fundamental inequalities that persist in Spain's social fabric.

The point about Spain's international reputation is not a minor one. A rereading of de la Iglesia's films from a post-GFC (the global financial crisis of 2007) perspective reveals that his thematic continuities from the Transition to the Aznar years (1996–2004) map out some of the most salient criteria used to measure Spain's reputation. The social and legal status of same-sex couples, together with the decriminalisation of homosexual acts and the subsequent introduction of legislation against homophobia and discrimination based on sexuality, features prominently as a major instance of the country's reassessment of sexual minorities—often, namely by PSOE during the Zapatero years, presented as an example of progressive policies.[8] Social inequalities and the replacement of class struggle with an inter-class dialogue of sorts is also revealing of the country's social achievements: the local underclasses portrayed in de la Iglesia's Transition films are replaced, in *Los novios búlgaros*, with migrants from other countries, as if Spain had ceased to generate migrants and expatriates. Violence, one of the director's signature features, does not totally disappear in *Los novios búlgaros*, but it receives a rather sanitised visual treatment. Importantly, the powerful and explicit link between politics and violence that articulates landmark films such as *El diputado* and *El pico* all but disappears in *Los novios búlgaros*. Conversely, central elements of the reconstituted image of Spain that are absent in earlier films do appear in *Los novios búlgaros*: Spain as a desired destination for international travellers and migrants, together with the construction of the Spanish metropolis as a gay mecca; the portrayal of a society that glorifies individual freedom; the welfare state; and, underlying it all, a prosperous economy that, in 2003, does not show any signs of slowing down.

*Los novios búlgaros* is also revealing of a number of interesting achievements related to the representation of homosexuality. If, during the

Transition de la Iglesia was a lonely voice whose pioneering gay films were no less than ground breaking, in 2003 *Los novios búlgaros* clearly belongs to an established gay tradition. Facts are clear in this regard: while the homosexual content of his 1970s films was hardly supported by any literary or film tradition, *Los novios búlgaros* is an adaptation of a well-received novel by Eduardo Mendicutti, one of the leading voices of the gay genre in Spain; parts of the film are shot on location in the lively Chueca gay district, which before the 1990s was a derelict area where drug trafficking and criminality were rampant; the film features cameos by prominent gay personalities such as Eduardo Mendicutti and Luis Antonio de Villena. The time of educative gay narratives that proliferated in the 1970s and 1980s is clearly over: while both *Los placeres ocultos* and *El diputado* treat homosexuality "didactically,"[9] the narrative of *Los novios búlgaros* does not bother to justify, explain, contextualise, proselytise or moralise about homosexuality: its target audience is no longer an unarticulated society dominated by a default heteronormativity, as it was the case of earlier films, but a gay and gay-friendly market segment which is familiar with a well-established genre of gay films—a genre that was pioneered by de la Iglesia's own earlier titles. The apparent social normalisation of homosexuality in 2003 and its corresponding on-screen treatment by de la Iglesia contrasts with some comments inspired by his much earlier films, such as Haro Ibars' impatient remark about Eloy de la Iglesia's, Pedro Olea's, and Jaime Chávarri's inability to "tell the true life of the real homosexual who frequents gay bars and is not a rich man, a politician, a transvestite or a terrorist."[10] Quoting extensively scholarship on the wide-encompassing phenomenon of the visibilisation and normalisation of gay men, Santiago Fouz-Hernández points out that the increased visibility of homosexuality in the 1990s was due to a number of social factors:

> [G]ay visibility in Spain was ironically helped by the AIDS crisis during the 1980s and publicized sex scandals in the mid-1990s, notably the Arny club trials (a boy prostitution club in Seville frequented by celebrities) and the homophobic declarations of the mayor of Sitges, a well-known holiday resort internationally popular with gay men, that made headlines in 1996.[11]

In addition to all its continuities with previous modes of representation, *Los novios búlgaros* also contains a number of discontinuities regarding the representation of the male body if compared to de la Iglesia's gay films of the 1970s. Fouz-Hernández and Martínez-Expósito[12] identify three discontinuities: the conspicuous use of subjective camera angles (POV shots) from the perspective of the main gay character (which they relate to the use of a first-person narrative in Eduardo Mendicutti's novel), in contrast with the much more restrained use of subjectifying techniques in *El diputado* and *Los placeres ocultos*; the deeper and more meaningful level of socialisation of the gay character in the gay Chueca district, which is presented as much more rewarding than the characteristic double life of his predecessors; and, closely related to the latter, the fact that the main gay character's homosexuality is open and visible, thus rendering meaningless thematic devices that were widely used in gay films of the 1970s such as blackmailing and traumatic outings:

> Subjectivity, sociability, visibility and a lack of political engagement put *Los novios búlgaros* at a distance from de la Iglesia's earlier films and serve as indicators of the remarkable evolution of the modes of representation of the homosexual body in recent Spanish cinema. This evolution is symptomatic of the transformation of the legal framework, visibility (and, arguably, social acceptance) for Spanish lesbians and gay men in the thirty-year gap between *El diputado* and *Los novios búlgaros*.[13]

Perhaps *Los novios búlgaros*' most striking continuity with de la Iglesia's earlier gay films is the Marxist-inspired contrast between the two main male characters, which engage in a relationship strongly defined by economic, class, and nation differences, more so than by the homosexual narrative that sustains it. In fact, the contrast between the well-off Spaniard Daniel and the Bulgarian hustler Kyril is presented in oppositional terms using age, class, nationality, and sexuality as binary axes that set the characters apart from each other. Other narrative-induced discriminators contribute to this opposition, such as their respective emotional engagement with each other, Kyril's legal situation as a migrant in Spain, and, importantly for the visual rhetoric of the body, the different physiques of both characters, with Kyril representing the idealised muscular male body so prevalent in contemporary gay culture.

The importance placed upon the body's visual rhetoric becomes clear very early on in the film, with the image of Daniel's upper torso surrounded by the darkness of a dark room. This image, repeated at the film's end, frames the visual construction of the character: the isolation of his body, dimly lit in the centre of a dark frame, is an excellent metaphor of the paradoxical loneliness of a gay man physically surrounded by invisible bodies but emotionally aloof and romantically dissatisfied. Daniel and his gay friends are seen throughout the film in different gay venues that are easily associated with contemporary consumerist gay culture, such as gay clubs, saunas, and parties. Male nudity, an undeclared visual taboo in the 1970s, is part of the new on-screen codes, which means that the naked bodies of this group of characters are seen without any major fuss. This is also true of the group of Bulgarian hustlers, who are frequently seen in varying degrees of nudity. Sexual activity is shot using soft-porn techniques such as non-genital close-ups and medium shots.

In the film, there are two instances of the deliberate use of visual rhetorical devices to enhance the importance of the male body image. One of them is the intradiegetic use of a camcorder utilised by Daniel to shot Kyril and others in sexually explicit poses. This narrative device is of course connected to the pre-eminence given to Daniel's perspective throughout the film, and to the emphasis on a gay subjectivity that governs and articulates the whole narrative. Furthermore, images captured with Daniel's camera contribute to the audience's identification with his (gay) viewpoint, thus creating an interesting effect of multiple gazes that put (gay) desire and voyeurism in the centre of the film's poetics. Voyeurism is further emphasised by the fact that Daniel's body, in a position of power, is out of sight and not unveiled in any way when he uses his camera. An element of sadism has been suggested as underlying this visual device:

> [T]he sadism inherent in this voyeuristic setting, later confirmed by the client-costumer economic relationship he and Kyril engage in, does not translate into Daniel's active/penetrative role; sex scenes between him and Kyril reveal Daniel at the passive/receiving end, although he adopts an active role when having sex with another Bulgarian boy.[14]

The other rhetorical device is the use of vision and dream-like scenes associated to Daniel's perspective. As we shall see later, this is a narrative technique that Eloy de la Iglesia used in other films; it can also be seen in many Spanish auteur films, most notably by Surrealism master Luis Buñuel.[15] Daniel's visions and dreams contribute to the visual composition of his body as ambivalent and versatile—in opposition, again, to Kyril's fit and hard physique. In the first of the three visions he fantasises with the possibility of adopting a commanding role over Kyril, something that never occurs in his real life. In the second vision, he remembers himself as pubescent boy mesmerised with the image of a young man and a horse, the homoerotic undertones of which are by no means disguised or played down. The third vision introduces a metaphoric link between the horse, a uranium capsule, and a nuclear explosion. The film's sub-plot involving the illegal traffic of uranium does not appear in Eduardo Mendicutti's original novel;

apparently, it was de la Iglesia himself who insisted in introducing it in the film despite Mendicutti's misgivings. The nuclear blast story brings with it apocalyptic images of death and bodily meltdown that complement and echo instances of real-life physical damage and decay such as Kyril's hand scars, some characters' comments about sexually transmitted diseases, and, finally, the shocking image of a dead boy when Daniel and Kyril visit Bulgaria. Daniel's ghastly visions are effective reminders about the impermanence of the pleasures and hedonism otherwise privileged by the narrative.

If the distance between the Transition films and *Los novios búlgaros* is indeed demonstrative of social and political changes in Spain during the 1980s and 1990s, a retrospective analysis of his earlier films from the vantage point of his last film reveals a number of interesting continuities: some have to do with power relations (e.g. the equation between *quinquis* or petty thieves of the seventies and migrants of the new century; the national adscriptions of Basques and foreign migrants), others with the representation of the male body (regimes of showing and hiding; the body as proxy for discourses on sexuality and class), and others with cinematography and visual grammar (use of visions and dreams within the narrative; use of close ups and other framing devices to signify relations between characters; melodrama as a governing narrative principle). Most of these continuities can be traced back to de la Iglesia's beginnings as a director of horror films and thrillers[16] in the late 1960s. By the time he was ready to include homosexuality as a leading theme in his films without having to deal with censorship (*Los placeres ocultos* was released in 1977), he had already been using many of the aforementioned devices. For example, the use of nationalism to illustrate power relations was already present in *Juegos de amor prohibido* (*Forbidden Love Games*, 1975), a highly allegorical drama in which a high school teacher kidnaps two of his students for no apparent reason other than the pleasure of dominating them. The on-screen composition of the teacher's character starts with a mention to the 1934 essay *In Defense of Spanishness (Defensa de la Hispanidad)*, by Basque-born Ramiro de Maeztu, before unfolding a range of Nazi-like germanophile icons including the persistent use of Wagner's music in his huge but decadent mansion. Also in the same film the body becomes unambiguously a metaphor for a number of ideas: scars and other signs of bodily violence punctuate a narrative of domination and humiliation that ultimately points to a discourse on limitless power and the vulnerability of all individuals to its alienating effects. Thus, the bodies of the young couple of students who for most of the film represent a rather chaotic and juvenile libertarian society (as opposed to the teacher's rigid and stale imperial world) in the last scene suddenly became as tidy and orderly as the teacher used to be. The film's critique of rigid social hierarchies and the inevitability of class domination is fully embodied in the characters' physicality, dressing, hair styles, body integrity, and kinetic relations. The fact that the film was heavily censored, making parts of the narrative hard to follow or simply meaningless (interview) does not affect this regime of visual embodiment and its heavily symbolic poetics: according to the director, "the film aspired at being hermetic."[17]

De la Iglesia's national and cultural self-identification as a Spanish rather than Basque director is far from surprising in the context of late Francoism and Transition. Yet, the fact that he sought to gradually reposition his own allegiances from the Spanish Communist Party to the Basque Left in the 1980s should not be mistaken for an opportunist tactic. While de la Iglesia was hardly ever a militant Basque director, Joseba Gabilondo has made the very illuminating point that a number of Spanish directors that identified with minority or minoritised groups (he mentions queer, women, Basque) choose to erase or disguise their identities as a strategic move:

> I suggest that these filmmakers negate their own identities in order to effect a violence that, if effected by the state, would rob them of their identity and desire: that is, of their capacity for *jouissance*. For there is an element of enjoyment in negating one's own identity in order to break the state's monopoly on negation. It is important to recognize that Basque cinema adopts a similar strategy.[18]

In 1978, the same year de la Iglesia's iconic *El diputado* was released, another truly iconic film hit the Spanish screens, which contained some of the most enduring and lasting images of the whole Spanish cinema of the period. *El sacerdote* (*The Priest*, 1978), featuring Simón Andreu as the troubled father Miguel, is an extraordinarily complex analysis of the human body as a site of tensions, contradictions, paradoxes, and struggles. By focusing on the figure of a priest subject to chastity and obedience vows, de la Iglesia was able to combine two of his life-long obsessions, sex and power, making the body the ultimate ideological arena. The film contains a number of explicit scenes of body punishment that include the use of flagellum and cilice in the lead up to the notorious scene in which father Miguel, tortured by his inability to control his sexual desires, decides to castrate himself with pruning shears. Of the many visually significant scenes in the film, there are two that are particularly relevant for their relation to de la Iglesia's bodily poetics. The first is one of the many reverie moments that feature in all his films. When visiting his mother in the village, father Miguel remembers in flash-back a scene of his puberty: the village boys swim and play naked by the river, then they turn their attention to their penises, the largest of which is Miguel's own who is pressured by the group to have sex with a goose. The scene, a daring combination of homoeroticism and zoophilia, would have never passed censorship only a year before (censorship was formally disestablished in late 1977); framed as a child memory of a practicing Catholic priest, it was simply scandalous from a moral perspective. Politically, its combination of Rousseauianism and utopian egalitarianism embodied in innocent pubescent boys was a powerful reminder to the pre-referendum Spain of 1978 of the huge gap between utopia and totalitarianism. The setting of *El sacerdote*'s narrative in 1966 coinciding with the one-party referendum that Franco won with 98.1% of the vote is of course intentional, as are the several scenes featuring in the background a large street billboard in which the dictator supports the "yes" vote.

The second scene is father Miguel's prayer in front of an image of Christ in the cross. Reminiscent of the Spanish Baroque, the figure of Christ emphasizes the physical suffering: wounds, facial expression, the chromatic contrast of blood and flesh, the foreshortened position of his body, the crown of thorns. The suffering, squalid body is minimally covered by a loincloth. Father Miguel's starts his prayer by begging fortitude to overcome his sexual urges, but it soon becomes an agitated grievance about the power of flesh over spirit. Alternate point of view shots of the cross from father Miguel's perspective and vice versa create the impression of a dialogue. In the end, father Miguel reproaches Jesus Christ for allowing the body to dominate human nature—and the Catholic Church for hiding Christ's genitalia (hence sex and sexuality) under a modesty cloth. It is Christ's body in the cross, perhaps the body that most frequently has been portrayed and represented in the entire history of Western art, that encapsulates all the tensions between flesh and spirit as well as the paradox of obedience (both compliance and submission at once). Conversely, father Miguel embodies the tensions and contradictions of the Catholic Church in a post-Vatican Council II world, as well as the growing concern regarding political relations between the Curia and the Spanish State in the months leading to the December 1978 constitutional referendum and the January 1979 Concordat. Eloy de la Iglesia repeatedly denied any intention to deal with specifically religious themes in

*El sacerdote*;[19] yet, the historical coincidence with such important milestones cannot be ignored.

Both *Juegos de amor prohibido* and *El sacerdote* are closely related to the gay films de la Iglesia shot in 1977 and 1978—*Los placeres ocultos* and *El diputado*. The thematic and stylistic continuities earlier mentioned are all present in these films. The body—the male body in particular—is the visual platform that allows de la Iglesia to articulate discourses on class and nation focusing on inequalities, power structures, and domination. Using an orthodox Marxist perspective, the body is a commodity that can be exchanged, bought, and sold. Also, looking at these films from the vantage point of *Los novios búlgaros*, the body can be interrogated about its potential for subjectivity, sociability, visibility, and de-politization. In fact, de la Iglesia's pioneering attempts to create an on-screen visual regime for gay bodies was also the first attempt to open representational modes up to new paradigms. If Marxism provided de la Iglesia with a workable paradigm to represent gay men in the 1970s as unequal actors subject to capitalist exchanges of sex, desire, goods, and cash, both *Los placeres ocultos* and *El diputado* contain the seeds of non-Marxist approaches in peripheral but important ways—such as the Feminist-inspired concept of embodiment that queer art and theory would later turn into a central representational tool.[20]

Hence, while *El diputado* was arguably an excellent piece of ammunition in the ideological struggle between the emerging Left represented by filmmakers who militated in the Spanish Communist Party like Juan Antonio Bardem and Eloy de la Iglesia himself on the one hand and the largely *alienated* Spanish society on the other, it was also an early queer film in which the gay character is saturated with multiple identities. All de la Iglesia's gay films feature a struggling, unequal relationship between an older man and a younger guy—the former unambiguously gay despite some bisexual innuendos and the latter either heterosexual or bisexual. Scholarship on de la Iglesia's gay films unanimously emphasise the unequal relations that articulate these films.[21] Such asymmetry has lead Fouz-Hernández and Martínez-Expósito to postulate the existence of a version of *paideia* in these films:

> Whilst the younger boy has no financial stability, no job and is frequently seen wearing informal clothes or semi-naked, the mature homosexual men are invariably well-situated professionals (a bank office director, an MP, a well-off consultant) who wear relatively expensive clothes and are rarely seen undressed. The Greek-love model is made clear not only by these differences, but also by the fact that the youngster relies on the older man for financial improvement and a sense of

direction; this is particularly clear in *Los placeres ocultos* (Tropiano 1997: 162–164). The Greek paradigm is further emphasized by the fact that the youngster's sexuality is kept deliberately ambiguous.[22]

Asymmetrical roles in same-sex relations could indeed be taken to evoke idealised versions of homosexuality in ancient cultures; and there is little doubt that the Greek paradigm has been used historically as a cultural, even moral, legitimation of love and sex between men. In the context of politically-driven Spanish *Transición*, though, it would appear that de la Iglesia's Marxist-inspired oppositional dialectics is closely related to the asymmetrical relations and the power struggle they generate. Violence in these stories is both physical and symbolic: de la Iglesia's homosexuals are frequently the victims of homophobic violence and the camera does not spare audiences the view of marred and scarred bodies. The gay character in *Los placeres ocultos* happens to be writing a novel aptly titled *Los heridos* (*The Wounded*).

Asymmetry does seem to play yet another role. In the context of the growing contestation to patriarchal models of masculinity that was starting to gain attention in the mid-1970s (with 1975 as a key milestone as United Nations named it the International Women's Year), the proliferation of models of masculinity represented a clear stance against the uniformity of patriarchal masculinity as a single, universal model. Far from offering same-sex relations made up of mirror-like individuals, de la Iglesia takes the principle of difference to an extreme and creates couples that embody oppositional relations over age, class, nation, sexuality, and virtually any other identity marker. With regards to the representation of the homosexual, de la Iglesia represents a landmark in the history of Spanish cinema for his emphasis on the masculine and his rebuttal of the effeminate model, which had been prevalent in previous popular representations. Alberto Mira points out that in both *El diputado* and *Los placeres ocultos* effeminacy is associated with reactionary bourgeois attitudes that militate against gay liberation:

> Homosexuales afeminados cotillas, egoístas e insolidarios. Este tipo aparece de manera recurrente en el cine de Eloy de la Iglesia como representantes de la mezquindad, y los veremos también en *El diputado*. No se trata de una elección casual. La actitud del director está en sintonía con la del activista, que consideraba este modelo reaccionario, y su protagonismo nocivo para la liberación homosexual. Desde otras posiciones homófilas, el tratamiento que se hace del homosexual afeminado [...] ha sido criticado: hay evidentemente una diferencia entre dar

> protagonismo a un homosexual de aspecto 'respetable' y hacer sistemáticamente de los homosexuales afeminados personajes poco atractivos.[23]

Interestingly, de la Iglesia's disinterest for effeminacy extends to *Los novios búlgaros* despite the fact that the original novel by Eduardo Mendicutti, as many other novels and short stories by the same author, features a much more sympathetic use of effeminate expressions. While Mendicutti's main contribution to a gay political agenda consists arguably of his broad use of humour as a factor of homosexual normalisation,[24] de la Iglesia's earlier approach in the 1970s was to raise political awareness of gay people; for instance, in *El diputado*, the arrival point of the narrative is the coming out of a closeted congressman, a political intervention that takes homosexuality out into the public arena.[25]

The out-of-the-closet homosexual bodies of de la Iglesia's early films remain as unassuming and out-of-sight as they were in the closet. These bodies are not sexualised, they do not belong to the *destape* genre; on the contrary, they are put forward as embodiments of political discourses that link the repression of ideology with the repression of identity (including sexual identity). The political content of *Los placeres ocultos* may not be as unmediated as that of *El diputado*, but the coming-out scene possesses a strong ethical component in that the courageous public homosexual is elevated to a category of personal dignity that the film denies to other kinds of homosexuals—not only the effeminate.

## Notes

1 This chapter was conducted as part of the research project entitled "Representaciones culturales de las sexualidades marginadas en España (1970–1995)" ["Cultural representations of marginalized sexualities in Spain (1970–1995)"], FEM2011—24064, funded by the Spanish Ministerio de Economía y Competitividad.

2 Lázaro-Reboll 129–130.

3 See, for instance, Fouz-Hernández and Martínez-Expósito 114–118, Perriam 135, and Melero 219–262.

4 "A subset of [gay] characters existed whose masculinity and good looks were over-emphasised as was anything that made them similar to heterosexuals. It is no coincidence that some homosexual characters were embodied by actors that, at the time, were considered by the audience icons of masculinity, such as Simón Andreu, Javier Elorriaga, José Sacristán or Imanol Arias" (Alfeo 149, my translation).

5 Estrada 269.

6 *Ibid.* 66.

7 Martínez *passim.*

8 Martínez-Expósito "Branding (and) Authenticity" n. pag.

9 De Stefano 58.

10 "Hasta aquí y hasta ahora nadie nos ha contado la vida del homosexual de verdad: del que va a bares gays, frecuentador de guetos; del marica ni rico, ni político, ni travestí, ni terrorista. En fin del hombre de la calle, con sus problemas, con sus vivencias a veces trágicas y a veces divertidas" (Haro Ibars 91, my translation).

11 Fouz-Hernández 191.

12 Fouz-Hernández and Martínez-Expósito 118.

13 *Ibid.*

14 *Ibid.* 117.

15 Babington and Evans n. pag.

16 For an alternative formulation of the horror-thriller dyad, see Lázaro-Reboll 127 ff.

17 "Quiere ser una película hermética, cargada de simbolismo" (Aguilar 123, my translation).

18 Gabilondo 277.

19 Aguilar 137.

20 See, for example, Butler.

21 Hopewell 164–178, Smith n. pag., Fouz-Hernández and Martínez-Expósito 114–118.

22 Fouz-Hernández and Martínez-Expósito 115.

23 "Homosexuals that are effeminate, blab, selfish, uncommitted: this type emerges in a recurrent way in the films of Eloy de la Iglesia, including *El diputado*, as representing meanness. It is not an accident. The director's and the political activist's stances coincide: politically, de la Iglesia considered this type reactionary and damaging for gay liberation. This harsh treatment of the effeminate has been criticised by other gay critics" (Mira 504, my translation).

24 Martínez-Expósito, "Humor y narración gay," n. pag.

25 Mira 509.

## Films by Eloy de la Iglesia Mentioned

*Bulgarian Lovers* [*Los novios búlgaros*]. Screenplay by Fernando Guillén Cuervo, Antonio Hens, and Eloy de la Iglesia with Eduardo Mendicutti. Dir. Eloy de la Iglesia. Altube Filmeak, Conexión Sur, Creativos Asociados de Radio y Televisión, Televisión Española, 2003. Film.

*Confessions of a Congressman* [*El diputado*]. Screenplay by Eloy de la Iglesia and Gonzalo Goicoechea. Dir. Eloy de la Iglesia. Figaro Films, Ufesa, Prozesa, 1978. Film.

*Forbidden Love Games* [*Juegos de amor prohibido*]. Screenplay by Eloy de la Iglesia, Juan Antonio Porto, and Antonio Corencia. Dir. Eloy de la Iglesia. Arturo González Producciones Cinematográficas, 1975. Film.

*Hidden Pleasures* [*Los placeres ocultos*]. Screenplay by Rafael Sánchez Campoy and Eloy de la Iglesia with Gonzalo Goicoechea. Dir. Eloy de la Iglesia. Alborada P.C., 1977. Film.

*The Priest* [*El sacerdote*]. Screenplay by Enrique Barreiro. Dir. Eloy de la Iglesia. Alborada P.C, 1978. Film.

*The Shot* [*El pico*]. Screenplay by Gonzalo Goicoechea and Eloy de la Iglesia. Dir. Eloy de la Iglesia. Ópalo Films, 1983. Film.

## Bibliography

Aguilar, Carlos. *Conocer a Eloy de la Iglesia.* San Sebastián: Filmoteca Vasca, 1996. Print.

Alfeo, Juan Carlos. "Evolución de la temática en torno a la homosexualidad en los largometrajes españoles." *Dossiers Feministes* 6 (2002): 143–159. Print.

Babington, Bruce and Peter William Evans. "The Life of the Interior: Dreams in the Films of Luis Buñuel." *Critical Quarterly* 27, no. 4, (2007): 5–20. Print.

Butler, Judith. *Gender Trouble: Feminism and the Subversion of Identity*. New York: Routledge, 1990. Print.

De Stefano, George. "Post-Franco Frankness." *Film Comment* 22 (1986): 58–60. Print.

Estrada, Isabel. "Transitional Masculinities in a Labyrinth of Solitude: Replacing Patriarchy in Spanish Film (1977–1987)." *Bulletin of Spanish Studies* 83, no. 2 (2006): 265–280. Print.

Fouz-Hernández, Santiago and Alfredo Martínez-Expósito. *Live Flesh: the Male Body in Contemporary Spanish Cinema*. London: IB Tauris, 2007. Print.

Fouz-Hernández, Santiago. "Queer in Spain: Identity without Limits." *Queer in Europe: Contemporary Case Studies*. Ed. Lisa Downing and Robert Gillett. Burlington: Ashgate, 2011. 189–202. Print.

Gabilondo, Joseba. "Uncanny Identity: Violence, Gaze, and Desire in Contemporary Basque Cinema." *Constructing Identity in Contemporary Spain: Theoretical Debates and Cultural Practice*. Ed. Jo Labanyi. New York: Oxford UP, 2002. 262–279. Print.

Haro Ibars, Eduardo. "La homosexualidad como problema sociopolítico en el cine español del postfranquismo (o cómo aprendí a dejar atrás toda esperanza al penetrar en un cine." *Tiempo de Historia* 52 (1979): 88–91. Print.

Hopewell, John. *El cine español después de Franco, 1973–1988*. Madrid: El Arquero, 1989. Print.

Lázaro-Reboll, Antonio. *Spanish Horror Film*. Edinburgh: Edinburgh UP, 2012. Print.

Martínez, Guillem *et al. CT o la Cultura de la Transición*. Barcelona: Debolsillo, 2012. Print.

Martínez Expósito, Alfredo. "Humor y narración gay en *Los novios búlgaros* y *Fuego de Marzo*, de Eduardo Mendicutti." *Una ética de la libertad: la narrativa de Eduardo Mendicutti*. Ed. José Jurado Morales. Madrid: Visor, 2012. 171–190. Print.

Martínez Expósito, Alfredo. "Branding (and) Authenticity in Pedro Almodóvar's Films." *La Nueva Literatura Hispánica* 16 (2013): 91–112. Print.

Melero, Alejandro. *Placeres ocultos: gays y lesbianas en el cine español de la transición*. Madrid: Notorius; Cáceres: Fundación Rebross, 2010. Print.

Mira, Alberto. *De Sodoma a Chueca: una historia cultural de la homosexualidad en España en el siglo XX*. Barcelona: Egales, 2004. Print.

Perriam, Chris. *Spanish Queer Cinema*. Edinburgh: Edinburgh UP, 2013. Print.

Smith, Paul J. "Homosexuality, Regionalism, and Mass Culture: Eloy de la Iglesia's Cinema of Transition." *Modes of Representation in Spanish Cinema*. Ed. Jenaro Talens, Santos Zunzunegui, and Tom Conley. Minneapolis: U of Minnesota P, 1998. 216–251. Print.

Tropiano, Stephen. "Out of the Cinematic Closet: Homosexuality in the Films of Eloy de la Iglesia." *Refiguring Spain: Cinema/Media/Representation*. Ed. Marsha Kinder. Durham: Duke UP, 1997. 157–177. Print.

# CHAPTER 5

# Queer Pastoral: Rural Homoeroticism on Film during the Early Years of the Spanish Transition

Alberto Mira
*Oxford Brookes University*

### The Spanish Transition and Representation

The political transition brought a number of changes with impact on politics, society, cultural attitudes, and representation in the arts in general and film in particular.[1] Central to these is the end of censorship legislation in April 1977: suddenly, novelists, filmmakers were able to depict "more" things, to explore aspects of reality that had not been allowed by the regime. Topics could be broached, historical facts could be brought to light and bodies could be exposed. But beyond the events and subjects of representation, more subtle changes in perspective broadened the range in terms of re-signification: certain signifiers with fixed meanings during Francoism, could now be presented in different ways, sometimes to say exactly the opposite. This process of re-signification was one of the ways in which Francoist ideologies could be challenged and "new," more libertarian ones were put in place. "Religion" or "youth" are obvious examples of this process. In this chapter I will focus on one such process of re-signification, that of the idea of the *aldea* ("village") or rural enclave, particularly as it was represented in connection to changing notions of sexuality.

Films of the late seventies show the Spanish rural life literally expanding, being re-drawn in its meanings and implications. Always subject to the logic of metaphor (as in the Generación del 98 musing on the Castilian landscape) representation of rural life had been for decades subject to strict ideological discourses. In a country that until the 1950s was demographically more rural than urban, the "aldea" was used to represent some kind of Spanish essence dominated by the Church, a bulwark against the tide of historical change, a repository of moral values. In this sense, one needs to point out that such official view was not "natural." Nineteenth and early twentieth century writers critical with Spanish identity and political choices had consistently used country settings to denounce social evils in their novels. The focus of criticism (as for instance in novels by Benito Pérez

Galdós and Emilia Pardo Bazán) was *caciquismo* ("despotism"). Both views of the countryside, a progressive one that presented it as primitive and unfair and a reactionary one, clashed in the early decades of the twentieth century and the clash is still evident in narrative during the Francoist period (for instance in the novels of Camilo José Cela or the short stories by Ignacio Aldecoa). Film, however, was a different matter. The reactionary representational agenda took over officially in 1939 (the first version of Francoist censorship legislation was put in place in 1938), asserting total control on plots and images, but the view of the mythical, de-historicized "aldea" can be seen already in pre-Francoist classics like *La aldea maldita* (*The Cursed Village*, Florián Rey, 1930), *Nobleza baturra* (*Aragonese Virtue*, Florián Rey, 1935), *Morena Clara* (*Dark and Bright*, Florián Rey, 1936), *El cura de aldea* (*The Village's Priest*, Francisco Camacho, 1936) or *La malquerida* (*The Unloved*, José López Rubio, 1939). All of these had Francoist updates. According to this view, devout and meek villagers were always happily subjected to the law of God which at the time of *Nacional-Catolicismo* ("National-Catolicism") coincided with the law of the Francoist regime. There could be abuses of authority. Landowners could seduce or slander the daughters of honest God-fearing workers, and girls did get pregnant out of wedlock (as in, respectively, *Nobleza baturra* and *La aldea maldita*), but the imposed ideological narratives that provided closure for plot events were eminently stable: transgression had to be paid for, the Church dictated morality in everyday life. In terms of gender ideologies, patriarchal masculinity (which demanded femenine submission) was the absolute rule. In the end there was always a priest to sanction the right behavior and to reinforce a vision of life. Narration was structured so that the balance achieved in the end reinforced the reactionary agenda at the heart of the Francoist counter-revolution.

Increasing migration from the village to the cities from the 1950s created more anxiety about urban life which is slowly articulated into the old narratives. Whenever a contrast between the urban and the rural was represented, the latter stood for traditional virtues that the former corrupted. One key example is *Surcos* (*Furrows*, José Antonio Nieves Conde, 1951), where urban corruption threatens the lifestyles and family values of labourers who feel forced to migrate to Madrid. This trend for insisting on a clash between rural and urban life in terms of values reaches a high point in the 1960s through a series of films reminding audiences of values that were, in the softer version of Francoism, "better" and "more humane." A typical plot that demonstrates this point is *La ciudad no es para mí* (*City Life Is Not for Me*, Pedro Lazaga, 1966), starring Paco Martínez Soria, in which rural values are used lightheartedly as an indictment on urban modernity. For many years this was the biggest box office hit in Spanish cinema, due to the popularity of its star but also to a simple message that seemed to connect with contemporary cultural anxieties. Martínez Soria became indeed a durable stereotype, an icon of reactionarism, imposed in a time of crisis, when urbanization had *de facto* overtaken rural lifestyles. He portrayed the traditional *paleto* ("hick"): more than simply non-intellectual he was anti-intellectual (the film is very aware of the threat posed by new "ideas" which challenge old doctrines), happy with the limitations of patriarchal ideology and all the wiser because of those limitations. In *La ciudad no es para mí*, Martínez Soria moves to the city to live with his family. Shocked by the excesses of urban life, he will have a beneficial impact on his family helping them deal with love and sex in a more fulfilling way and strengthening family ties. Martínez Soria comes across as a rural Mary Poppins, who has a down-to-earth recipe for the evils or modernity: go back to traditional values.

This anxiety about modernity addressed through a reactionary political agenda is one of the sites for struggle in the cinema of the post-Franco period. The early years of the Spanish Transition (before the Socialist electoral victory in 1982) offer a wealth of manifestations and a flood of unorthodox images that seem to refute the idea of rural virtue. Most films of the 1977–1982 period are uncouth cinematically, dramatically uneven to say the least and artistically negligible, but there is a rawness and urgency in dealing with current events and with what had been repressed that is still amazing (sometimes shocking) in its variety. Classical narrative depends heavily on time and budget, on following certain storytelling traditions through the use of a *mise en scene* that requires certain polish to work. Filmmakers had neither during the early transition (before the Socialist government put into practice a system to support certain idea of Spanish cinema). Films had to succeed merely through audiences' attendance[2], and audiences were hungry for discourse that could articulate the changes. Their stories are hardly self-sufficient and rely heavily on the knowledge of what was going on in the country, which makes them particularly apt for cultural readings.

Throughout the period, reactionary ideological agendas coexisted with radical experiments, particularly in the case of sexuality, one of the key areas of expression for filmmakers in this period. The limits between underground themes and aesthetics are blurred in the years around the writing of the 1978 Constitution. Bigas Luna's early features *Bilbao* (*Bilbao*, 1978) and *Caniche* (*Poodle*, 1979) are good examples of loose, non-classical, narratives as more apt to represent non-orthodox views of sexuality than straightforward ones. Storytelling conventions can act as a kind of superego to limit the power of desire and experimentation. In this sense the looser narration of Bigas Luna's films (or Francesc Bellmunt, or Ventura Pons, or Gonzalo Suárez, or pre-transition Eloy de la Iglesia or Iván Zulueta, Jaime Chávarri or the earliest Almódovar films, to give just a few examples) can be seen as refusing to close a gap between desire and language.

New filmmakers soon made use of the new permissiveness to show a radically different view of rural life. Although most of these representations were firmly within the boundaries of patriarchal heterosexism, a small number of films provide images of the countryside which are carnivalesque, orgiastic, and queer. The countryside has ceased to be the site for the triumph of the law and has become a sexually fluid version of the classical Arcadia, an idealized *locus amoenus* filled with non-orthodox sexualities. It is interesting that so many of these films show tensions, specifically, in the representation of homosexuality and homoeroticism as a contested area. Although outside of the official gay movement, some of the figures discussed here (Ventura Pons, Emili Teixidor, Eduardo Blanco-Amor, Bigas Luna, Ocaña) had personal investment in the sexual freedom allowed by the Transition period. The old view of the sanctity of rural life overseen by the Church was treated cynically. Following the anti-clerical tradition in pre-Franco Spanish literature, the countryside became now the place for lustful priests, sexual behaviour, and class chaos. In the late seventies it looks increasingly like the countryside is the site for disorder and an emerging modernity. Narrative disconnections and carnivalesque aesthetics are just two aspects of early transition cinema that convey desire as resistant to labels or even more as challenging the very possibility of being labelled.

*El extraño viaje* (*Strange Voyage*, Fernando Fernán-Gómez 1964) was one of the most suppressed Spanish films of the sixties, and at the core of its satire is the questioning of moral standards in a small village and a precedent to this re-signification of country life. From the first image in the film (Maria Teresa Ponte holds up a brassiere) it is clear that the film's view will be an ironic comment on the prudish sexless representations of rural life during Francoism. When the lascivious matriarch played by Tota Alba forces Carlos Larrañaga to dress as a woman, rural life acquires a queer edge that was unknown of in Spanish cinema of the time (with the exception of Buñuel's *Viridiana*, which was actually made only three years before Fernán-Gómez film in 1961). The film is one of the earliest projections in Spanish cinema of the fear of matriarchalism that will later be developed in *Furtivos* (*Poachers*, José Luis Borau, 1975) or *La muerte de Mikel* (*Mikel's Death*, Imanol Uribe, 1984). Non patriarchal sexualities become more and more central as a sign of critical non Francoist cinema, and in a way, it is one of the key ideas cinema of the transition keeps on revisiting.

Following the lead of Fernán-Gómez's obscure (at the time) feature, films of the 1970s, the countryside stops being "safe" and sexually orthodox. One early example is *La portentosa vida del padre Vicent* (*The Prodigious Life of Father Vincent*, Carles Mira, 1977), which represented traditional motives in the life of Saint Vincent in such extreme fashion as to make them ridiculous. Narrated as a series of loose episodes and starring Albert Boadella (the leader of Catalan theatre company Els Joglars), the film resists a coherent, logical reading and appears as a cinematic version of a Valencian "falla," with a general meaning which is clear but not articulated in terms of story. Such carnivalesque aesthetics, common to Els Joglars and other films by Mira like *Jalea Real* (*Royal Jelly*) or *Con el culo al aire* (*Caution to te Wind*, both released in 1980), is one privileged way to convey the unstability of gender and to criticize traditional morality.

At this point, it's worth remembering that the distinction between queer and gay, between polymorphous sexuality and sexual *identity* is at the same time critical and epistemological. On the one hand one can produce queer readings based on one of the central starting points of queer theory (adapted from Freud's "polymorphous perverse" concept) about the instability of identity in general and gender identities in particular. Gender identities are not essential aspects of people's psychological makeup, but are adopted through cultural pressures and repetition. On the other hand, however, one can postulate that "gay men" or "lesbians" are distinctive groups and therefore reinforce their identity and use such identity to organize struggle against repressive forces. During the 1970s in Spain, the latter version of sexuality was represented by the official gay movement[3]. The former view, closer to what is known today as "queer theory" was less distinct (being less easy to articulate) and had less public or political support. Both views, however, are well represented in films of the period.

Whereas the city can encourage modern identities, in the country the boundaries seem to be more porous, to the point that "identity" as a concept is less central. The political films of Eloy de la Iglesia (*Los placeres ocultos*, *Hidden Pleasures*, 1977 and *El diputado*, *The Deputy*, 1978) or Pedro Olea´s *Un hombre llamado Flor de Otoño* (*A Man Called Autumn Flower*, 1978), made during this period, used the trope of "coming out" in line with the general impulse of the gay movement.[4] There is a strong impulse in both films towards closure, "becoming" seems to be an important part of the political project. In the countryside, however, "coming out" or "becoming gay" seems to be beyond politics. *La muerte de Mikel* is a good example of this odd stasis. Odd because it is a film that explicitly deals with politics, but seems to be full of gaps and silences in telling the story of self awareness (Mikel's sexuality seems to be queer, but it's certainly not represented following the political project of the gay liberation movement). Uribe wanted to tell a story of the conflict between a homosexual and nationalist Basque politics, but in the representation of the former, he finds it hard to follow the agenda of the gay movement, as if "identity" and "coming out" were not central aspects in the evolution of the homosexual. The ambivalent relationship Mikel has with transsexual Fama can be read along the same lines: the film deals with a desire that resists definition in terms of set categories.

Along similar lines, *Ocaña. Retrato intermitente* (*Ocana, an Intermittent Portrait*, 1978) is the film that most consistently represents the countryside as a sexual arcadia. Historian Vicente J. Benet[5] is the latest articulating a certain agreement about the film being a sign of growing acceptance of the gay movement in Spain. However, when one listens closely, there is nothing "gay" about the view of sexuality articulated in Ocaña. This is implied in many of his "intermittent" self-dramatizing scenes, but it is particularly clear in the way the protagonist narrates his own experience of sexuality. Some sections of his monologue refer to life in Cantillana before moving to Barcelona in 1971. The way the Sevillian village appears in these reflections is interesting. Rural life does appear as taking place outside history and class struggle, and although coming to Barcelona is presented as some kind of liberation, one cannot help thinking that the experience of sex and sexuality in that context was very fulfilling. In fact, it is Ocaña himself who insists on the bliss of those years in which everybody seemed to be available privately no matter how harsh explicit homophobic discourse was. It is the site of violent homophobia, but the protagonist's descriptions go beyond this to show up a version of sexuality which is clearly polymorphous and pre-gay.

## Queering the "sainete"[6]: *El vicari d'Olot*

As we have seen, representation of the "aldea" in Francoist cinema was ideologically predetermined. But, beyond the ideological implications, signifiers were also fixed in terms of local stereotypes. Andalusian, Aragonese or Castilian rural cultures were treated as typical, as disposable clichés used by central Francoist culture. The "regionalism" of Francoism was distinctly different from the different "nationalist" agendas in Catalonia, the Basque country and Galicia all developed (to different degrees) in the nineteenth century. National Catholic Spain saw itself as a unity with superficial differences that were a proof of variety but not of essential national identity. These differences were exploited (often for comic effect) in the "sainete." The rural variety of this dramatic genre is a blueprint for many representations of rural life during Francoism. In such representations, the reality of the countryside was replaced by humour and simplicity with little satirical content: audiences were invited to laugh at these characters rather than establishing a complicity with the author. One of the key cultural impulses of the Transition was a shift in the way Spain's cultural diversity was represented. And the cases of regions with a strong nationalist history were particularly interesting.

Catalonia's natural landscape had been one of the *loci* of Catalan nationalism in song and literature. The Catalan landscape, people with wise old men who knew about repression and the value of roots, dispensing advice (like the grandfather Sisset in Lluís Llach's canonical song "L'estaca" written in 1968) automatically brought to mind the yearning of national self-expression. Rural Catalonia was presented as the soul of the country, the perfect complement to the practical, hardworking, bourgeois urban Catalonia. Scarcely represented on film during the Franco period[7], the rural landscape had been at the heart of Catalan nationalist writing during the 1960s and early 1970s as the expression of some deep truth about Catalan identity. At the same time, in common with the rural representations of Francoism, the nationalist Catalan rural enclaves were represented as patriarchal and sexless. Although brimming with history and nationalist ideals, sexuality was conventional in these representations and in the work of iconic Catalan writers on the countryside like Josep Pla.

In this sense, Ventura Pons decision to work on a rural "sainete" has important implications. He was in fact sexualising the sexless, both in terms of genre and in terms of nationalist traditions. Josep-Anton Fernàndez has written extensively on how official Catalan culture under the auspices of Convergència i Unió (CiU, the coalition made up of two conservative parties that ruled Catalonia until 2003) had an impact on the representations of non-orthodox sexuality from 1980.[8] *El vicari d'Olot* (*Olot's Vicar*) constitutes a rare glimpse of the possibility of an approach to Catalan culture which was sensual, Mediterranean and libertarian. Freedom was indeed one of the drivers in Pons' filmmaking. In Pons' films, freedom is associated to self-expression rather than identification with pre-defined political alternatives. The same can be said about his view of sexuality. Later in his career he would provide clear articulations of this idea of sexuality as individual freedom in *Carícies* (*Caresses*, 1998), *Amic/Amat* (*Beloved/Friend*, 1999) and in looser, more frivolous Mediterranean "sainetes," close in their perspective to *El vicari*, such as *Que t'hi jugues Mari Pili?* (*What's Your Bet, Mari Pili?*, 1991) or *Aquesta nit o mai* (*Tonight or Never*, 1992) all of them set in a progressive Barcelona full of sexual opportunity.

The film was one of the most popular Catalan films of its time and had one of the starriest casts of the period, made up mostly of Catalan actors, including Enric Majó, Rosa Maria Sardà, Maria Aurèlia Capmany, Fernando Guillén, Mary Santpere, Anna Lizaran, Joan Monleón, Núria Feliu, Marina Rossell, Amparo Moreno, and Montserrat Carulla. The initial success of screening in Barcelona surprised everyone, although once dubbed into Castilian the film didn't do well.[9] Pons suggests that it was the dubbing itself that robbed this film of its "authenticity," and sense of location.[10] Clearly, standardization imposed by dubbing (robbing the film from its authenticity) hurt the film's effect by uprooting it. It remains an obscure film, almost forgotten by its director, who didn't seem to have a lot to say about it in his memoirs. Made at the same time as Convergència i Unió (CiU) won the Catalan government elections in 1980, it signals the beginning of end of a short-lived age in which official national culture did not attempt to shape behaviour by providing earnest and slightly prudish Catalan nationalism.[11] With CiU came a new notion of cultural identity based on the promotion of national history based on sentiment, pushing aside the more modern, culturally diverse and sexually provocative worlds of Ocaña, Bigas Luna or Els Joglars. Although cheeky, carnivalesque films continued to be made (for example by Francesc Bellmunt, or Ventura Pons himself), it is unusual to see again the view on reality proposed in films like *Caniche*, *Bilbao*, *Salut i força al canut* (*Catalan Cuckold*, 1979), *L'orgia* (*The Orgy*, 1978) or *Ocaña*.

Co-scripted by Emili Teixidor[12], *vicari* is one of the fullest expressions of a libertarian attitude towards sex and the Church that became widespread in cultural manifestations during the early transition. On the one hand the plot is related to the "sainete" tradition as reinterpreted by Luis García Berlanga, in which a group of popular types interact around a central situation, clashing among them and creating a moderate amount of chaos, as in *Plácido* (*Placido*, 1961), *Calabuch* (*The Rocket from Calabuch*, 1956) or *La escopeta nacional* (*The National Shotgun*, 1977). There is a strong satiric element in that those types are clearly representative of power figures of the period (the corrupt right wing politician, the high ranking prelate, the nuns in the school). So, rather than just laughing "at" the characters, as in the traditional brothers Quintero rural "sainetes"[13], we share the authorial point of view in gently mocking real types and situations. Along with Berlanga and popular satire, the *comedia sexy* ("sex comedy") so popular in the period[14] constitutes an important frame of reference for this film.

The unnamed village where the film's events take place is very different from the well-behaved villages of Francoist cinema: although there are clueless nuns and priests, and they are still prominent citizens and have power in running the place, almost every other character had a secret life that the events of the plot will bring into the open. There may be two factions clashing in the film, and two different perspectives are represented, but in the end they share a down-to-earth outlook. If the countryside in *El vicari d'Olot* is a metonym of Catalonia, then the idea conveyed is far more libertarian than what audiences had been used to, particularly when articulating discourse on the nation. The title refers to a traditional verse, and, in the fashion of popular entertainment, the film is presented as an example or demonstration of the veracity of the verse, presented as common wisdom: "El vicari d'Olot té pels al ninot, se'ls vol treure i no pot"[15] ("The Vicar in Olot has hairs in the puppet, he wants to pluck them out but can't"). In the film this is used to illustrate the central idea of the impossibility of denying one's own nature. In that way, "human nature" is placed at the center of the plot. But rather than the version espoused by bourgeois ideology, what we have here is a "nature" which doesn't fit into the matrix of relationships predetermined by heterosexism.

The Vicar (Enric Majó) is introduced in the film in an act of repression: he wakes up, supposedly in the midst of an erotic dream, to whip himself up seeking self-punishment for a transgression he can't control. The Vicar is a respected figure in town, generally tolerant of prostitution and slight sexual misdemeanours. He does pay lip service to catholic morality and resists the advances of the village "beatas" (fervent churchgoers played, among others, by singers Marina Rossell and Núria Feliu). Although shocked by homosexual behaviour (he spots from a window his neighbour the pharmacist frolicking with the local omnisexual stud), he doesn't do anything too serious to condemn it or hinder it. Both life in this village and its representation in mainstream film would have been just unthinkable only five years earlier. The turning point in the film is the visit of a high ranking priest with Vatican connections (played by Valencian comedian Joan Monleón) who, aware of the misbehaviour spreading among the population (known in the media as "la oleada de inmoralidad," "a wave of immorality") and in an effort to galvanize conservative forces, decides to organize a conference of catholic morality. That will make the village the focus of attention and probably bring in the authorities in order to repress untoward behaviour. Interestingly, the attempt is countered by all characters in the film that want to be left in peace and keep the Church and its morality away from their lives. Ramoneta, the local whore (Rosa Maria Sardà in her film debut) calls her prostitute friends from Barcelona, who are joined by gay activists, drag queens, transsexuals, and assorted sexual outcasts. They all congregate and demonstrate at the door of the council; the clash between traditional Catholic mentality and the new forms of sexuality becomes blatantly obvious. The scenes in which the demonstration is represented are shot as a street party, reminiscent of the different feminist and gay demonstrations of the period.

This image is put into practice in Pons' multi-layered network narrative. Characters do lead a double life. The mayor has a virginal wife and a mistress, the Vicar has sexual dreams, the beatas hide their desire for the Vicar, and the whore is a devout Christian and the monsignor in the past sired a baby. One of the characters is a representative of polymorphous desire. Bernat (Enric Cusí), the son of a local landowner, has a wife, and at the same time has relationships with both the Vicar's maid and the (male) pharmacist. In the context of Spanish masculinities, characterized by a clear distinction between machos and *maricas* ("faggots"), Bernat is of particular interest, as it challenges deeply held notions and, most importantly, does so without too much emphasis, as if such polysexuality was "normal."

The plot also develops a second, even more interesting strand focusing on the Vicar himself. The outcasts work out a plan according to which he will be entrapped to have sex with a popular transsexual prostitute and then threaten to make this public. In the turn of events, the Vicar's main struggle is not with his fear of being exposed but with his own desire. His character arc is in the end about accepting his own desire and allowing himself to have a relationship with the prostitute: the chaste priest discovers a masculinity which is not quite heterosexual. Meanwhile, Ramoneta has unearthed some evidence that the high ranking monsignor had an illegitimate daughter in the past. Without much resistance, he will cynically stop battling against the prostitutes and proposes a more ambivalent, less hostile version of his catholic conference. Although the catholic conference still takes place, the Vicar's opening statements are about tolerance and respect for sexual difference and individual choices.

In *El vicari d'Olot*, Ocaña's rural world is expanded and illustrated. Desire is first acknowledged as something that is inextricable linked to human experience (as the rhyme says, "i no pot," "he just can't"). The film presents a clash between two struggling viewpoints at the time, and gives an articulate voice to those who refused the repressive programme of Francoism. The *comedia sexy* ("sex comedy") had been encouraging a sexualized view of life, but it was always patriarchal, it suggested women had to accept being passive objects of desire and that desire was always male and straight. Pons is proposing instead an approach to desire which is plural and ambivalent as it challenges established gender stereotypes particularly traditional masculinity. All kinds of characters are allowed to express some desire, including the lesbian nun played by Lizaran or the reactionary Mayor. Bernat is unrepentant about his affairs with both sexes, adultery is not renounced, the prostitutes defend their view of sex as commercial enterprise and the pharmacist does not back up one step in expressing gay sexuality. It is actually the pharmacist (Fernando Guillén) who articulates for the Vicar the key message of the film: people are the way they are and they have to be accepted. In terms of closure, the film most resembling *El vicari d'Olot* was the contemporary *Gay Club* (Ramón Fernández, 1981), in which a group of homosexuals working in a gay bar in a village need to join forces to unmask the hypocrisy of a reactionary politician who wants to close them down.

*El vicari d'Olot* ends with the celebration of the morality conference. But the threat of repression has disappeared. The Vicar closes the plot by making a speech about the need for tolerance and acceptance of difference. Following the loose approach that characterized the film, plot strands remain essentially open. We never know whatever happened to Bernat, the pharmacist, the beatas or the pregnant girl, although the film seems to suggest they will be free following their desires and even the Vicar will be able to indulge in his fantasy with the transsexual prostitute. Most importantly, we don't have any final answers about his "sexual identity." After human nature and sexual chaos has been vindicated, what one "is" doesn′t seem to matter much. The Arcadia has become a place that replaces sexual repression for sexual expression.

### Gonzalo Suárez's *Parranda* and the Representation of Queer Sexuality

Gonzalo Suárez's *Parranda* presents a very different approach to the fluidity of sexuality in a rural background. The film is based on the 1959 novel by Eduardo Blanco-Amor written in Galician (the original title is *A esmorga*) during the writer's exile in Buenos Aires. Like *El vicari*, *Parranda* is geographically precise, and it attempts to reveal some "deep truth" about Galicia through the events happening in the countryside (this is clear both in the novel and in the script adaptation, but less prominent in the film version); and as in *El vicari* what the film suggests about patriarchalism in the heartlands challenges official national discourses. The relationship between plot and national identity is metonymical. The novella is set in the Galician countryside, near Orense ("Auria"), under unremitting rain and the main action covers twenty four hours. Whereas *El vicari*, the "sainete" and the comedia sexy broke up the sexual boundaries through carnivalesque *jouissance*, the main impulse of this film is tragedy and fluid sexuality is just an aspect of life rather than the main driver in the narrative.

The novella is largely developed as a monologue which constitutes the declaration of Cibrián "El Castizo," a labourer who suffers from epilepsy (which he calls "el pensamiento," "the thought") in front of a judge whose words are silently represented in the text through dots. El Castizo is both narrator and commentator of the events, although his perspective is severely limited. He is accused of being involved in a series of crimes (a fire, a murder, a housebreaking) although his precise implication is unclear. He states that he spent the previous day with the actual perpetrators, his friends El Bocas ("Big-mouthed") and Milhomes ("Milhombres" in Castilian or "Thousand Men"). Cibrián met the friends on a Monday morning, when they were still drunk from the weekend's *parranda* ("spree") and tagged along. In a long day of drunken stupor, a complicated chain of events led to Milhombres stabbing El Bocas and then being killed by the police. Although not the main narrative focus, Cibrián's commentary keeps circling around the "truth" of the relationship between Bocas and Milhombres: Milhombres is represented as basically homosexual (but sometimes expresses fascination with female sexuality, which may or may not be genuine). Whereas Bocas appears to be a traditional heterosexual, several elements in character construction complicate the definition. Given the narrative voice (Cibrián) can't pin Bocas' feelings down in exact terms, readers only have ambivalent words in which feelings and desire are confounded. If Bocas is not "a homosexual," he is certainly not "a heterosexual" either. Unless, of course "heterosexuality" has *always* been made up of a mix between the patriarchal and the homoerotic as Eve Kosofsky Sedgwick suggested in *Epistemology of the Closet.*[16]

The novella was adapted into an excellent script by Blanco-Amor himself after his return to Spain in 1967 and he kept on revising this until 1971.[17] Given the very restrictive and very precise censorship laws in force during the period, Blanco-Amor knew his script could not make it to the screen, but this may have helped him to make his decision without any kind of compromises in terms of content. His work is detailed and more specific than the narrative fiction in conveying Blanco-Amor's intentions regarding the representation of homosexuality. Critics have suggested that homosexuality was ambiguous in the original (the focus of conventional readings even today is "rural Galicia" rather than gender dynamics), and Blanco-Amor used the film script to make it more explicit.[18] Clearly, however, although traditional "homosexuality" is difficult to accommodate in Blanco-Amor's work, queer desire is articulated in the original as the motivation for the character dynamics in the story between Milhombres and Bocas. To what extent this affects Cibrián is even more ambiguous: he claims disgust, but there is also evidence of fascination; he stays with his friends out of loyalty towards Bocas but is unclear how his own desire is involved in the whole situation.

Bocas's role remains complex, but now we have an authorial voice (Blanco-Amor's) to expand on such complexity. In the case of El Bocas, Blanco-Amor writes:

> *Es el macho elemental, fuerte y magro, si puede ser, guapote, cuenta siempre consigo, con su fuerza, su coraje y su estampa pero ignorándose "estéticamente." Su presunta relación homosexual con el Milhombres es muy compleja y, según parece, poco o nada espontánea por su parte y en cuanto a iniciativa. Quizá obedezca a un fondo de narcisismo inconsciente, de dandismo potencial, de contradicción profunda, todo ello nada infrecuente en la laberíntica psicología galaica, aun en la popular. De todos modos, tal como se desprende del texto de la*

> *novela, el Bocas necesita o busca la borrachera para "consentir" la compañía de Milhombres y tolerar (o provocar) "sus atrevimientos."*[19]

Several aspects in this description move away from a traditional homo/heterosexual distinction into a queer view of masculinity. Firstly, one needs to note that homosexuality is presented by the author as "alleged," i.e., it is not homosexuality as described by others, but something more "complex." Although Bocas' public identity is heterosexual, narcissism leads him to be receptive to Milhombres's attentions. "Ambivalence" is a recurring word in characterizing El Bocas' behaviour.[20] The fact that he links such muddy attitude to Galician "popular" or "folk" identity adds to the universalizing element in Blanco-Amor's intentions. At the same time, he is presented as "the quintessence of masculinity" (macho elemental), which suggests the paradigm used by Blanco-Amor is infused with a queer view of sexuality. Indeed this portrait of El Bocas suggests that this mix between male violence, repression and homoeroticism may be typical (rather than exceptional) of male identity in general.

Blanco-Amor's description of Milhombres sticks slightly closer to sexual stereotypes, but in between brackets he adds some advice which is still nuanced enough to articulate a complex view of masculinity. Blanco-Amor was reluctant to use a very narrow label to describe Milhombres. He is perceived as a homosexual by other characters, but this clashes with received descriptions on rural homophobia. The novel seems to be saying that he is indeed a homosexual and at the same time not exactly what people think homosexuals are like.

> *(ojo con hacer el personaje "en marica," especie siempre desagradable en todo el espectáculo. Su afeminamiento en muy poco depende de los gestos, pasitos cortos y habituales ratimangos del tipo convencional; es algo más hondo, matizado e interno que exige un gran talento en el actor).*[21]

As we can see, in his description Blanco-Amor is at pains to balance the stereotype and the variation. He dismisses a version of homosexuality based on straightforward imitation of "faggoty" gestures and replaces it by a less definable desire.

These authorial interventions are good starting points when framing the film itself and discussing the way it has dealt with the basic approach proposed by Blanco-Amor. In 1977, Gonzalo Suárez, a director well known for his literary, cinematically experimental leanings, worked from Blanco-Amor's script on a version of *Parranda*. He retained many of Blanco-

Amor's ideas and the events are by and large (with an important exception, as we'll see later) the same as described by the novelist. In particular, the film retains (and to some extent strengthens) the idea of a "queer Arcadia" in which sexualities are resistant to patriarchalism. As in the novel and the Blanco Amor's script, prostitution is central to life in Auria. Cibrián (played in the film by José Sacristán) has decided to marry La Rajada, who earns a living as a prostitute; the small town has several brothels and its inhabitants all seem to have complex libidos that don't fit into the fixed categories of heterosexual identities. The script develops further a "queer" character that only appears very late in the original narrative and was somewhat more developed in Blanco-Amor's script: Socorrito, a young woman who was raped in the past; ever since she is obsessed with dolls and with "making babies" with someone who "smells" properly. Rather than obsessed with sex and rape, she seems to have an obsession with maternity and keeps on stealing dolls even from children playing. In Suárez's film she's the one opening the story as a sphinx that introduces the audiences to a world of twisted, displaced desires.

Another manifestation of queer masculinity that presents interesting differences in regard to the original novel can be found in the character of Andrada. His beautiful wife (which he keeps largely hidden in his mansion) becomes an obsession with the characters, especially El Bocas (played by José Luis Gómez). El Bocas declares repeatedly that he wants to have sex with her. The novel and Blanco Amor's script clearly state that she was only a mannequin. In the film, the scenes concerning this woman are more ambiguous and what seems to be straightforward in the original sources is here presented through ambivalent *mise en scene* (the doll is played by an actress and at one time the image doubles in a mirror reflection). Even if she is represented as a doll, she is ambiguously reimagined as a human being from the perspective of El Bocas (who has been exposed to opiates) and such double perspective is conveyed to audiences complicating the reading of the character and our perspective on El Bocas: Is he deceiving himself? How does this acute lust correspond with his narcissism?

A different display of non-orthodox sexuality is specific to Suárez's version of the script and is only hinted in Blanco-Amor's work. He added another example of sexual heterodoxy in the character of the "Escribiente" played by Fernando Fernán-Gómez. The character appears, first as someone who is trying to dispose of a corpse. It becomes clear that he might have murdered the man, who was his wife's lover, although the story he tells the three friends (visualized in subjective flashback by Suárez) states that he was called upon disposing of the body by a student of his who was a married lady. Later, when the protagonists spend some time in a brothel, we learn that the character is a customer and he demands to have sex in coffins. It is up to audiences to develop this character in terms of necrophilia and murder, and this ambiguity is very much at the heart of *Parranda*'s rhetoric. More tellingly, this character whose behaviour has been seen as erratic and ambivalent, spinning stories that are revealed as false and therefore the character who has probably most to hide in the film, is seen at the narrative closure stating in writing that Cibrián killed himself in guilt desperation after his testimony. Both the novel and Blaco-Amor's script make it clear that Cibrián dies by his own hand, but the film suggest he is killed by the Guardia Civil, the statement being just another lie by the Escribiente.

The focus of queer sexuality in the novel and Blanco Amor's version of the script was the relationship between El Bocas and Milhombres (the latter played by Antonio Ferrandis in the film). Although Suárez underlines the queerness of sexualities in Auria, the fact is that this particular aspect is not fully developed through imaginative *mise en scene* in the actual film. To begin with, homoerotic feelings are harder to identify in the film; the very ambivalence expressed in Blanco-Amor's notes means it required inventive approaches avoiding both the idea of general friendship and "faggoty" characterizations. Maybe confused by the way sexuality challenges received notions, Suárez preferred to keep the objective elements, but kept from suggesting anything else. Letting emotions become expressed only in terms of their consequences in the events makes those feelings go unnoticed. In the end, only previous knowledge of the novel can suggest homoerotic desire in a first viewing, and a rich, complex approach to homoerotics of masculinity is avoided.

## Conclusions

Indeed at this point one can only underline the difficulties that the queer paradigm poses for representation (not to speak of politically effective representation). It is relatively easy to build a "gay" ("identitarian") plot based on motives like coming out or coming to terms with one's own sexuality, and it is easy con characterize "a homosexual" as there are repertories of imagery one can use. In moving away from identities, we are risking obscurity and the kind of ambivalence that won't work well in terms of mainstream cinema. It was more effective to work on the kind of canvas proposed by Pons in *El vicari d'Olot*, in which the creation of libidinal arcadias come out of the addition of individual choices and articulated through camp and satire rather than the depth model of complexity proposed by Blanco-Amor and only partially realised by Gonzalo Suárez. It is also interesting that "queerness" in the films is better conveyed as a canvas of different characters than in the precise relationship between Bocas and Milhombres.

Rather than exploring these challenges (also posed by films like Jaime Chávarri's *A un dios desconocido* [*To an Unknown God*], made in 1977 or Iván Zulueta's *Arrebato* [*Rapture*] in 1980) Spanish cinema moved in the direction of exploring and defending identities as fixed and stable. This runs parallel to the fact that the countryside becomes less and less a preferred space for the exploration of sexuality. From 1982, with the rise of power of the Socialist Party, the Spanish Transition enters a different stage. One of the aims of the Socialists will be the regulation of cultural practices. In terms of the film industry, the key innovation was a pack of measures known as the Ley Miró (1983). The government set clear criteria for "quality" in film, and only films following those criteria were likely to achieve full funding under the law. Central criteria were thematic and referred to films based on literary works or representing Spanish history. Because films on earnest historical topics tended to receive more support, producers preferred to embark on projects with such historical topics, which led to a wave of Civil War and post-War films. The Ley Miró had consequences for the representation of the countryside. The arcadia model of fluid sexualities that we have described was replaced by another in which the countryside is the site of historical or political struggle. The best examples of this shift in the representation of rural life are Montxo Armendáriz's *Tasio* (*Tasio*, 1984), and, especially, Mario Camus' *Los santos inocentes* (*The Holy Innocents*, 1984) one of the key Spanish films of the post Franco era. In both films issues of sex and gender identity are treated conventionally, following patriarchal logic, and the focus is political or social oppression. Queer sexualities will remain a central area for plot construction and representation in Spanish cinema, but its context will be the urban romantic comedy: the specific link between rural life and fluid sexual desire that turned certain films into statements on the nature of human relationships had been overcome by the *comedia de costumbres* ("popular comedy").

## Notes

1 This chapter was conducted as part of the research project entitled "Representaciones culturales de las sexualidades marginadas en España (1970–1995)" ["Cultural representations of marginalized sexualities in Spain (1970–1995)"], FEM2011—24064, funded by the Spanish Ministerio de Economía y Competitividad.

2 According to Ventura Pons film like *El vicari d'Olot*, returned his investment (30% of the total capital) in just a month, which illustrates a very different financial model from today's. See Campo Vidal 53.

3 Although much of the writing underpinning homosexuality at the time reads today as queer theory *avant la lettre*. See Mira 465–473.

4 See Martínez-Expósito and Mérida's chapters in this volume.

5 Benet 384.

6 A *sainete* is a short comic play with popular characters.

7 A telling example is the lack of Spanish film versions of Àngel Guimerà's *Terra Baixa* (1896) one of the key representations of rural Catalonia and one of the most popular dramatic texts written in the Spanish territory (the exception is a very primitive 1907 film by Fructuós Gelabert) in spite of the fact that it was a well known text internationally (for instance it was made into an opera in 1903 by Eugen D'Albert).

8 Fernàndez *Another Country* 190.

9 Pons 190.

10 For the strong sense of Catalan location in the film see Pons in Campo Vidal 54: "Yo hablaba desde mi cultura, mi entorno, mi sensibilidad, mi sentido del humor…," "I spoke from my cultural roots, my surroundings, my sensitivity, my sense of humour."

11 Fernàndez *Another Country* 190.

12 Teixidor would go on to write in 2003 the source novel for the Agustí Villaronga film *Pa negre* (2010) another queer rural fantasy, although this time dark and earnest contrasting with his work for Pons.

13 For instance *Malvaloca* (1912) or *Mariquilla Terremoto* (1930).

14 For instance, *El virgo de Visanteta* (Vicente Escrivá, 1979) beat box office records at the time.

15 This was actually the starting point for the whole film, proposed by Teixidor to Pons, the rest of the script was improvised around this idea. See Pons 159.

16 Sedgwick n. pag.

17 Intro by Luis Pérez Rodríguez in Blanco-Amor n. pag.

18 The interpretation of sexuality in the novel *La Parranda* is problematic: the very ambivalence in the text allows critics to project on the characters homophobic language. See Allegue 11.

19 Blanco-Amor 36. "He is the essential male, strong and muscle-bound, if possible he should be handsome, he always rely on himself, on his strength, on his courage and his looks, but at the same time he pretends to care little for his looks. His alleged homosexual relationship with Milhombres is very complex and, as it seems, almost or completely lacking in spontaneity and initiative on his side. This may be due to a deep seated unconscious narcissism, potential dandyism, deep contradiction, all of this not too infrequent in the labyrinth of Galician psychology, even in popular instances. In any way, as the novel suggests, El Bocas needs or seeks drunkenness in order to 'accept' Milhombres' company and tolerate (or provoke) his cheeky 'excesses'."

20 See for instance Blanco-Amor 48.

21 Blanco-Amor 37. "be careful not top lay the character 'as a faggot,' a species always distasteful in every artistic manifestation. His effeminacy does not come across so much in gestures, short steps and the usual peculiarities of the conventional type; it is

something deeper, nuanced, part of an inner self that will require a great talent from an actor."

## Films Mentioned

*A Man Called Autumn Flower* [*Un hombre llamado Flor de Otoño*]. Dir. Pedro Olea. José Frade Producciones Cinematográficas S.A. and Panorámica. 1978. Film.

*Aragonese Virtue* [*Nobleza baturra*]. Dir. Florián Rey. Compañía Industrial Film Español S.A. (CIFESA). 1935. Film.

*Beloved/Friend* [*Amic/Amat*]. Dir. Ventura Pons. Els Films de la Rambla S.A., Televisión Española, Canal+ España, Televisió de Catalunya, and Departament de Cultura de la Generalitat de Catalunya. 1999. Film.

*Bilbao*. Dir. Bigas Luna. Figaro-Ona Films. 1978. Film.

*Caresses* [*Carícies*]. Dir. Ventura Pons. Departament de Cultura de la Generalitat de Catalunya, Els Films de la Rambla S.A., Televisió de Catalunya, and Televisión Española. 1998. Film.

*Catalan Cuckold* [*Salut i força al canut*]. Dir. Francesc Bellmunt. Prozesa. 1979. Film.

*Caution to te Wind* [*Con el culo al aire*]. Dir. Carles Mira. Andro, Ascle Films, and Globomedia. 1980. Film.

*City Life Is Not for Me* [*La ciudad no es para mí*]. Dir. Pedro Lazaga. Pedro Masó Producciones Cinematográficas. 1966. Film.

*Dark and Bright* [*Morena Clara*]. Dir. Florián Rey. Compañía Industrial Film Español S.A. (CIFESA). 1936. Film.

*Furrows* [*Surcos*]. Dir. José Antonio Nieves Conde. Atenea Films. 1951. Film.

*Hidden Pleasures* [*Los placeres ocultos*]. Dir. Eloy de la Iglesia. Alborada P.C. 1977. Film.

*Mikel's Death* [*La muerte de Mikel*]. Dir. Imanol Uribe. Ariete Films, Cobra Films, and José Esteban Alenda. 1984. Film.

*Ocana, an Intermittent Portrait* [*Ocaña. Retrato intermitente*]. Dir. Ventura Pons. Prozesa and Teide P.C.1978. Film.

*Olot's Vicar* [*El vicari d'Olot*]. Dir. Ventura Pons. Cop-Nou, Germinal Films, Profilmar P.C., and Teide P.C. 1980. Film.

*Placido* [*Plácido*]. Dir. Luis García Berlanga. Jet Films. 1961. Film.

*Poachers* [*Furtivos*]. Dir. José Luis Borau. El Imán Cine y Televisión. 1975. Film.

*Poodle* [*Caniche*]. Dir. Bigas Luna. Figaro Films. 1979. Film.

*Rapture* [*Arrebato*]. Dir. Iván Zulueta. Nicolás Astiarraga P.C. 1980. Film.

*Royal Jelly* [*Jalea Real*]. Dir. Carles Mira. 1980. Film.

*Strange Voyage* [*El extraño viaje*]. Dir. Fernando Fernán-Góme. Ízaro Films and Pro Artis Ibérica. 1964. Film.

*Tasio* [*Tasio*]. Dir. Montxo Armendáriz. Elías Querejeta Producciones Cinematográficas S.L. 1984. Film.

*The Cursed Village* [*La aldea maldita*]. Dir. Florián Rey. Florián Rey-Pedro Larrañaga. 1930. Film.

*The Deputy* [*El diputado*]. Dir. Eloy de la Iglesia. Figaro Films, Ufesa, and Prozesa. 1978. Film.

*The Holy Innocents* [*Los santos* inocentes]. Dir. Mario Camus. Ganesh Producciones Cinematográficas and Televisión Española. 1984. Film.

*The National Shotgun* [*La escopeta nacional*]. Dir. Luis García Berlanga. Impala and In-Cine Compañía Industrial Cinematográfica. 1977. Film.

*The Orgy* [*L'orgia*]. Dir. Francesc Bellmunt. Producciones Zeta. 1978. Film.

*The Prodigious Life of Father Vincent* [*La portentosa vida del padre Vicent*]. Dir. Carles Mira. Ascle Film. 1977. Film.
*The Rocket from Calabuch* [*Calabuch*]. Dir. Luis García Berlanga. Águila Films and Films Costellazione. 1956. Film.
*The Unloved* [*La malquerida*]. Dir. José López Rubio. Ufilms S.A. 1939. Film.
*The Village's Priest* [*El cura de aldea*]. Dir. Francisco Camacho. Compañía Industrial Film Español S.A. (CIFESA). 1936. Film.
*To an Unknown God* [*A un dios desconocido*]. Dir. Jaime Chávarri. 1977. Film.
*Tonight or Never* [*Aquesta nit o mai*]. Dir. Ventura Pons. Antena 3 Televisión, Els Films de la Rambla S.A., and Idea. 1992. Film.
*What's Your Bet, Mari Pili?* [*Que t'hi jugues Mari Pili?*]. Dir. Ventura Pons. Els Films de la Rambla S.A. 1991. Film.

## Bibliography

Allegue, Gonzalo. "Presentación." *Parranda.* Eduardo Blanco-Amor. Gijón: Trea, 2001. 5–13. Print.
Benet, Vicent J. *Cine español. Una historia cultural.* Barcelona: Paidós, 2013. Print.
Blanco-Amor, Eduardo. *La parranda e outros guions ineditos.* A Coruña: Centro galego de artes da imaxe, 1994. Print.
Campo Vidal, Anabel. *Ventura Pons. La mirada libre.* Madrid: Fundación Autor, 2004. Print.
Fernàndez, Josep-Anton. *Another Country: Sexuality and National Identity in Catalan Gay Fiction.* London: Manley, 2000. Print.
———. "The Authentic Queen and the Invisible Man: Catalan Camp and Its Conditions of Possibility." *Journal of Spanish Cultural Studies* 1 (2004): 69–82. Print.
Mira, Alberto. *De Sodoma a Chueca. Una historia cultural de la homosexualidad en España en el siglo XX.* Barcelona: Egales, 2004. Print.
Pons, Ventura. *Els meus (i els altres).* Barcelona: Proa, 2011. Print.
Sedgwick, Eve Kosofsky. *Epistemology of the Closet.* Berkeley: U of California P, 1990. Print.

# CHAPTER 6

## From Stage to Screen: *Flor de Otoño*'s Transitional Impersonations

Rafael M. Mérida-Jiménez
*Universitat de Lleida*

Throughout the Spanish decade of the 1970s, many different tensions met between the supporters of the dictatorship and those who fought to establish a fully recognized democratic regime.[1] After General Francisco Franco died in 1975, on November the 20th, a fortunate political transition process began that led to a system of civic freedoms guaranteed by the Constitution passed on referendum in 1978. However, I have always considered pertinent to point out that, despite the collective success, the lights and the shadows that bring this political transition should not be forgotten (Mérida Jiménez 67–68). Establishing a comparison, which I believe revealing, the *Partido Comunista de España* ("Spanish Communist Party") was legalized on April 1977 but the FAGC (*Front d'Alliberament Gai de Catalunya,* "Gay Liberation Front of Catalonia")—which organized the first demonstration to fight for the rights of the sexual minorities in the *Ramblas* of Barcelona—had to wait until July 1980 in order to see its legal status recognized. In other words, during the Spanish Transition, the political elites felt less panic towards the Communists than towards the queers. First of all because faggots subverted the masculinity patterns and the heteronormativity imposed during decades by law.

I will focus, throughout this chapter, in the recreation of masculinity and femininity, "homosexual" and "trans," during the decade of 1970s, through an analysis of the theatre play *Flor de Otoño: una historia del Barrio Chino* (*Autumn Flower*, 1972), by José María Rodríguez Méndez and its film adaptation (*Un hombre llamado Flor de Otoño*/*A Man Called Autumn Flower*, 1978), brought to the cinema by Rafael Azcona (scriptwriter) and Pedro Olea (scriptwriter and director). The two goals of this article are to confirm the transformations of some of the discourses about the sexual otherness—here related with the theatre-related sphere—which had a deep impact in Spain during one of the main social tension ages of its recent history and to evaluate the prominent differences that split both creations and its significances. I am clearly echoing one of the first proposals of the essay "Thinking Sex," published in 1984 by Gayle Rubin: "Disputes over sexual behaviour often become the vehicles for displacing social anxieties, and discharging their attendant emotional intensity. Consequently, sexuality should be treated with special respect in time of great social stress" (Rubin 138).

**Trans Contexts**

Before evaluating the two works mentioned above, it is necessary to place them in a double context: historic-political and cultural. Regarding the first one, it has to be recalled that the main characteristic of the extreme catholic social model imposed by Franco's dictatorship (1939–1975) was the control over and the repression of sexuality, especially women and those pretending to escape from the heteronormative orthodox patterns: the conservative law from the Second Republic known as *Ley de Vagos y Maleantes* ("Vagrancy Act"), modified in 1954, and the *Ley de Peligrosidad y Rehabilitación Social* ("Law of Social Dangerousness and Social Rehabilitation") passed in 1970 and not repealed until 1978. The misdemeanor known as "disorderly conduct" allowed the persecution of gays, lesbians and transgender people and brought most of them to prison and/or to medical treatments which used devastating therapies, as the activist Armand de Fluvià (2003) pointed out, as well as Arnalte (2003), Mira (2004), Olmeda (2004), and Soriano Gil (2005) have, among others, evaluated.

Nevertheless, from the end of the 1960s, this repressive legislation coexisted with a timid tolerance—always under control—in the bars opened in big cities, especially in Barcelona, where new LGT networks of sociability began to show up. As a result of this paradoxical situation, small night clubs or cabarets opened and showed spectacles where female impersonators and transsexuals performed as the autobiographical testimonies of Pierrot (2006) and Dolly Van Doll (Matos, 2007) confirm. After the dictator's death and with the abolition of censorship, an "erotic boom" unleashed in Spanish society. Its first expressions were heterosexual—which contributed to make audiences wide and varied—and staged in less gloomy and quite affordable new clubs whose shows began to include trans performers. Raids became more irregular, so the theatrical trans "growth" began a golden age where very different typologies of performers cohabitated and which was brought to the big screen.

An analysis of the dramaturgical and cinematographic production during the decade of the 1970s would confirm the coexistence of at least four typologies of trans masculinity/femininity associated to the stage sphere. First of all, a "trans feminine" universe related with the people who underwent irreversible male to female sex reassignment surgeries—including vaginoplasty—could be analysed. That is the case of Dolly Van Doll or Lorena Capelli, whose biography and her unfortunate death inspired the film *El transexual* (*The Transsexual*, 1977) directed by José Lara. Dolly Van Doll stated in her such significant autobiography *De niño a mujer*:

> Mi naturaleza ha sido un error absoluto. Yo he nacido con piel de mujer, con formas de mujer, con espíritu de mujer y con ademanes de mujer. No he sido nunca un hombre absoluto: es decir, con los atributos de un hombre en cuanto a genitales, o pelo, o músculos. Un hombre homosexual, no. Yo creo que he nacido mujer con ese pequeño error de complemento: con unos atributos masculinos pequeños y equivocados que resultaban un contrasentido en mi forma de ser y de amar.[2] (Matos 69).

*De niño a mujer*—a title that refers to the Julio Iglesias song "De niña a mujer"—constitutes an original example of vital review in which the transsexual person denies and obeys Nature in order to finally adjust. This process happens without arguing, with an intimate satisfaction by the heteronormative discourse, in the company of a Christian model of personal overcoming, capitalist and masculine despite its presumed natural contradictions and shared with many trans during that decade.

Closely related with this first sphere within the Spanish context of the Transition, there would be a second one. The connected with the "trans ambiguous" people whose genitalia kept being masculine—and which is more important they could be shown of it generating a greater expectation among masculine and feminine audiences—although they look biological women thanks to different body treatments. The most known example was the film *Cambio de sexo* (*Sex Change*, 1977), by Vicente Aranda, featured by Victoria Abril and Bibí Andersen. The actress Victoria Abril portrayed a young guy wanting to be a woman and who finally got an operation after a long but happy physical and psychological process. Andersen was, in real life, the young club star who appears in Aranda's film and who performed herself on the stage at her early twenties, long before she became one of the "Almodóvar girls." Bibí Andersen, without undergoing sex reassignment surgeries (the opposite happened in the film, though), stated in 1978: "I am not homosexual, neither transvestite nor cross-dresser. I am transsexual." The actress also affirmed that "como yo quería darme a conocer en el espectáculo, jugué con este recurso"[3] (Pierrot 142). Manuel Vázquez Montalbán described her in his novel *El pianista* (1985), as it follows:

> El chorro de luz abandonó al presentador y al pianista y se fue hacia la derecha hasta tropezar con una escultura de mujer, melena oleante, facciones de niña sensual, un poderoso cuerpo sinuoso enfundado en un traje de lentejuelas y de un corte de la falda salía una pierna torneada unida a la tierra por un zapato rojo. Sólo la anchura del cuello era un ruido visual en aquel conjunto armónico que había sobrecogido a la sala, las mujeres vencidas en su contemplación crítica y los hombres a disgusto por la sospechosa atracción que tenían que confesarse. La estatua se puso en movimiento. El alto cuerpo se movía con ligereza y los brazos, tal vez excesivos como el cuello, servían para mover el micrófono manual y para subrayar la majestad de las evoluciones estudiadas.[4] (Vázquez Montalbán 88–89).

A third field, the one that better connects with the two works I am going to analyze in this chapter, it would be the female impersonators' world which would be related with those who only cross-dressed on the stage, updating the model of the *imitadores de estrellas* ("stars' imitators") previous to the Spanish Civil War (1936–1939). One of the best imitators was Modesto Mangas, better known as Madame Arthur, who showed a more traditional identity. Starting with the fact that he equally referred to himself as masculine or feminine and continuing with his rejection to medical and surgical procedures which had been spread among his trans colleagues: "Yo recomiendo que nadie se ponga hormonas, porque yo llevo cuarenta años de transformación, he sido la primerísima figura en España y parte del mundo sin tenerme que poner tetas"[5] (Pierrot 57). Jean Baudrillard probably recalled Madame Arthur when he took an anecdote in the first pages of *Seduction* (21; originally published in 1979 as *De la séduction*) where transvestites from Barcelona keept their mustaches and showed their hairy chests.

In front of the feminine essentialist transsexuality shown in the film *Cambio de sexo* (which at the very end of the movie a surgeon graphically explains what the sex-change operation is about), Ventura Pons managed to present a fourth kind of transvestism in the documentary *Ocaña, retrat intermitent/Ocana, an Intermittent Portrait*, 1978). The director showed a more transgressive type through José Pérez Ocaña's personality, who developed an art of provocation in the streets of Barcelona by wearing old-fashioned women clothes. The Sevillian painter, who accidentally died in 1983, impersonated the spirit of the counter-culture in Catalonia together with his friend Nazario, the most important gay comic book author in Spain. This film contains some shootings of theatrical scenes, together with confessional sections or dramatic monologues as well as unusual performances.

Bibí Andersen defined herself as transsexual and Ocaña rejected labels: he did not consider himself as "transvestite," although he transvestited himself. He probably did not consider transvestite because the term was mainly used in that moment to those who work in shows as the films *El transexual* and *Cambio de sexo* presented. Ocaña did not consider himself as "homosexual" although he was part of the first demonstration organized by the FAGC, as we can see in the pictures of the documentary—where we can read the demand to repeal the Law of Social Dangerousness and Social Rehabilitation. Ocaña stated, in a television interview broadcasted in the celebrated television series *La Edad de Oro* (*The Golden Age*) by Paloma Chamorro (October 1983), that his transvestism would be a "visual art" although it looks obvious that is about an art which, furthermore, is committed. A transvestism, remarked Ocaña, born "para provocar, para divertirme y para reírme con la gente."[6] Masculine and feminine at the same time.

## A Story from the *Barrio Chino* ("Red-Light District")

During this golden trans age, it came the premiere of the film *Un hombre llamado Flor de Otoño* (1978) by Pedro Olea, with a script written by the director himself and Rafael Azcona, that adapted the José María Rodríguez Méndez theatrical play (written in 1972 and published in 1974 but not brought to the stage until 1978). There are several different reasons that could explain this late staging of the play; however, the economic and technical ones should not be undervalued. *Flor de Otoño: Una historia del Barrio Chino* is a play that requires an unusual amount of performers (the total quantity of characters exceeds the number of forty), and that shows considerable scenography and wardrobe changes. Secondly, I believe the nature of its subject matter did not make the premiere attractive to producers either: a production of these characteristics can only be set up if it is expected to be an undeniable success for the audience. It is surprising anyone got interested in a play where the leading role was a lawyer from the bourgeoisie in Barcelona that transvestited himself and performed in the red-light district cabarets around 1930 and who, moreover, joined in the anarchists' protests against the dictatorship of the General Miguel Primo de Rivera (1921–1930). Too jumbled or complex for the taste and the pockets of those years, especially if, thirdly, the text is nearly bilingual, a weird mix between Spanish and Catalan, and not easy to understand if the original text is respected. In addition, this theatrical play is deeply political. As it happens with other works by Rodríguez Méndez, he attacks the present through the recreation of a tumultuous period of the Spanish History (a technique that he used in many of his plays. For example: *Bodas que fueron famosas del Pingajo y la Fandanga* (*The Great Day Pingajo and Fandanga Got Wed*) in 1965, related to the Spanish colonial empire crisis in 1898). What is also very interesting now for my goals is that *Flor de Otoño: Una historia del Barrio Chino* shows a scarce empathy and a perplexing distancing towards its characters and, especially, towards its leading role.

Lluís de Serracant is a thirty-year-old lawyer from Barcelona, who is single and homosexual and cohabitates with his mother—who indulges and overprotects him—who lives an unconfessable double life and who during the play debuts as a singer in a fashion night club in the red-light district with the nickname of "Flor de Otoño." Rodríguez Méndez seems to criticize him from all different fronts: as a product of a monarchic and decadent bourgeoisie, as a hypocrite and inconsistent man, as someone whose interest in anarchism is pretty artificial, as a not very masculine type and almost permanently effeminate and trivial… In sum: the author avoids to concede a minimum heroic status to him, so it becomes very difficult to identify with someone who barely can redeem himself despite the final shooting. The light that Rodríguez Méndez projects it is guided through a homophobic discourse. Even though it is admirable that the message the author wanted to transmit is liberal and against the injustices described in the play, his speech around Lluís/Flor de Otoño turns out to be deeply conservative, as it was an essay written by the author in those same years: *Ensayo sobre el machismo español* (1974).[7] A man of his time, the author shapes him from a pre-gay archetype, hyperbolically feminized, subordinate and mining: such option can be validated in some of the comments made by the rest of the characters as well as in the stage directions made by Rodríguez Méndez. From his initial introduction as "un individuo flacucho, pálido, con gafas, embutido en un abrigo oscuro que parece totalmente indefentso"[8] (Rodríguez Méndez, *Bodas,* 133),[9] who is introduced by his mother as "premio extraordinario en la Facultad, una lumbrera"[10] (134), Lluís de Serracant speaks with "voz mariquela"[11] (134).

A later stage direction, while the reader attends his first night transformation, does not leave any room for doubt:

> Mientras tanto, se ha iluminado un rincón de la escena y vemos al LLUISET, o sea, la criaturita que ha producido tamaño terremoto moral. Está en una especie de "garçonnière" tapizada de rojo. Sobre una mesita reposan las gafas. El LLUISET se nos aparece ahora muy distinto del que vimos en la entrevista con el secretario del Gobierno Civil. Vestido con pantalón, faja y camisa de "smoking," sin gafas, parece un gigoló maricuela. Se está contemplando al espejo. Alisándose los cabellos y poniéndose fijador. Se advierte que lleva bastante tiempo acicalándose. Utiliza pulverizadores, pomos de perfume y mil menudencias. Mientras se acicala silba alegre. Entretanto, seguimos viendo al fondo el grupo de la familia mimando una larga y dolorosa despedida. El LLUISET se aleja del espejo para contemplar su figura. Marca unos cuantos pasos de "claque," luego se coloca las manos en las caderas y avanza hacia el espejo con andares de "vamp" cinematográfica estilo Mae West. (…) Vuelve al espejo. Luego descuelga la capa y se la coloca muy terciada, a lo flamenco, y marcha por el escenario como una cupletista flamenca. Coge una flor de un "bouquet" y se la coloca en la oreja. Se mira. No le gusta y se quita la flor.[12] (Rodríguez Méndez, *Bodas*, 140–141).

Rodríguez Méndez, a great connoisseur of the twentieth-century theatrical tradition in Barcelona, used the genealogy of those female impersonators who enjoyed a glory age during the 1920s and the 1930s. Actually, it must be said Flor de Otoño was a historical performer but with a different genealogy.[13] It is also clear by the fact that the author places him in a real performance night club, the "Bataclán" (132), and that he mentions another of the most known concert halls in the red-light district before the Civil War, "La Criolla" (131).

Lluís, as well as some of the *imitadores de estrellas* ("stars' imitators") glossed by Álvaro Retana in *Historia del arte frívolo* (1964), comes from the local bourgeoisie and feels pleased by his transformations, on and off the stage. His creator minimizes his masculinity when he addresses him by the diminutive "Lluiset," he draws him as "happy" (meaning "gay"), and he feminizes him among the "thousand triffles" of his "garçonnière" through a portrait between the "cinematographic vamp" and the "flamenca singer of cuplés."

Nevertheless, from my perspective, the construction of this character did not seek laughter from the spectator but for rejection or, at least, a great distancing. However, the transformation does not remain fulfilled until another stage direction describes Flor de Otoño in the "Bataclán" right before his show: "casaca de lentejuelas,"[14] "una pluma de varios colores"[15] in top hat, "labios pintados en forma de corazoncito"[16] (147)… The author underlines that his trans lead reminds us that "una Marlene Dietrich misteriosa y arrogante. Canta con aquella voz cascada parecida a la de la 'Bella Dorita' y se mueve con avezado aire de 'vamp' estrepitosa"[17] (148). The female impersonator that Flor de Otoño is appears ridiculed—directly and indirectly—through the paratexts the author writes as the creator does not admire his performing qualities nor his glamour.

Something similar can be said about the audience attending the club where Flor de Otoño debuts, although the people gave her "una salva de aplausos ensordecedora"[18] and a "total" success (151–152) after her first musical act. Why is that disliked? Because probably it was consistent with the description of "Bataclán," which is used as a urban microcosm but becomes, in fact, as a bull's-eye that Rodríguez Méndez points to in a merciless way: "bohemios, chulos profesionales, burgueses camuflados, extranjeros que van de paso para visitar la Exposición, anarquistas, jugadores"[19] (143)… The same idea could be said about Lluís' friends: Ricard dresses in "a dandy way," although "no puede evitar su cara de macarra, con sus bigotazos y patillas"[20] (168); Surroca is introduced as a "un ex boxeador, con veleidades ácratas"[21] (145). According to the author:

> Lluiset era la Barcelona que yo tengo vivida y que tiene un misterio casi indescifrable, una poesía sórdida curiosa, una rebeldía soterrada, procedente de la delincuencia portuaria, aplastada por el peso de una burguesía puritana, insufrible... Yo quería expresar ese conflicto compuesto por varias clases sociales en la lucha sorda, que sólo se dan en Barcelona y no creo que en ninguna otra parte del mundo: una clase burguesa repugnante, una clase proletaria aburguesad, una clase inmigratoria balbuceante en la diáspora, una clase encanallada y delincuente, como hay en Nápoles, que convive con las otras y se transforma camaleónicamente según épocas.[22] (Thompson 154–155).

The father's lack of respect for his creatures it is openly noticed in the episode that relates in the second part of the work, which is set in the "Cooperativa Obrera del 'Poble Nou'"[23] (173). Between factories and blue-collar workers, this proletarian settlement it is no less described as the "el siniestro rostro del suburbio ácrata e industrial"[24] (173). Before the bomb explosion that was supposed to blow up in the Serracant family business and also before the confrontation between the police and the workers that favor the final imprisonment of Lluís/Flor de Otoño together with his two friends, we confirm again Rodríguez Méndez hostility against all of them:

> Allá, junto a uno de los ventanales, se sienta FLOR DE OTOÑO-LLUISET, vestido con un atuendo híbrido entre macarra y pistolero: gorrilla elegante, una bufanda anudada coquetamente al cuello y jersey de cuadros azules y blancos bien entallado que describe sus formas pectorales y cintura. Pantalón gris, zapatos blancos. Si no

estuviera en tal sitio podía ser un deportista de Montecarlo. El SURROCA se halla entretenido con una radio de galena que extiende sus alambres sobre su gran cabezota y tapa sus orejas con enormes auriculares. El RICARD con su abrigo de gran vuelo echado sobre los hombros, el sombrero de ala flexible y bohemia echado hacia atrás, a lo gánster, le está dando el parte del día.[25] (Rodríguez Méndez, *Bodas*, 173–174).

It seems like Rodríguez Méndez used the leading figure of the transvestite as the quintessence of the masculine inauthenticity at the same time as it looks like that he hates Ricard's prostituted masculinity and Surroca's foolishness. This attitude goes side by side with a use of a really plain range of characters that follows with a minor intensity the stele of the best independent political theatre in the Europe of the 1950s and the 1960s than the obscure Spanish one, between Goya's Black Paintings and Valle-Inclán's grotesque. The author misses the individual and collective transgressive potential of Flor de Otoño by denying individuality and erodes his revolutionary capability. He does so to the extreme that the whole play could be considered a bitter and embittered piece, where the prevailing mood is that of contempt for the bourgeoisie and for the military, for the students and for the working class, or for the red-light district as a metaphor of Barcelona. It's a nihilistic piece that destroys itself as well as all masculinities.

## Transformations

It may surprise, after this brief analysis, the statement saying that the script written by Rafael Azcona and Pedro Olea almost constitutes its antithesis. But it is like that in most of the shots and details. That dull and skinny character coincides with the appearance of the popular Spanish actor José Sacristan who had the leading role in the film although the script transforms him into a hero/heroine which is indefinitely more complex: his belonging to the bourgeoisie is used to reinforce anarchist ideals, his masculine femininity is active, his intelligence and cleverness are stunning. The scriptwriters believe that we can identify with their Flor de Otoño because the new character firmly beliefs and fights for individual and collective ideals of transformation. In this sense, the film subplot, in which the preparation of the attack against the train that has to bring General Primo de Rivera incognito to Barcelona unfolds, is specially relevant. wherein that scene, besides some hilarious scenes "in drag", we can hear from Lluís' mouth a speech of notorious ideological solvency about the union disputes, in the context of the fights of the time: neither Lluís himself nor his coworkers are despised by the scriptwriters and their fears and bravery are described with authenticity.

One of the newer aspects of the adaptation it would be, in this sense, the consideration of the leading role's sexuality. The "Lluiset" character from the play by Rodríguez Méndez was a homophobic narrative from the pre-gay "effeminate" model; without stopping from being, when intimacy favors it, the "Lluís" character from the script by Azcona and Olea seems to configure himself from a progressively gay model, according to the analyzed patterns by Óscar Guasch. It becomes very interesting to confirm that, although in the very first movie scenes his presence is ambiguous, just as the plot draws on, the kind of discourse that leads around his sexuality, very close to the public "pride," the director slips and projects the character towards the historic reality of Barcelona in 1977 and 1978, where the movie was shot (the one in whose Ramblas there were gays, lesbians, and trans demonstrations). In fact, towards a reality that obviously still was a Utopia because the legislation that imprisoned those who dare to commit "disorderly conduct."

From this perspective, the intimate relationship that Lluís and Ricard show becomes a visible milestone, although apparently is anodyne, as Alberto Mira has pointed out:

> Ricard, el amante de Lluís, muestra una masculinidad convencional, a pesar de lo cual su afecto resulta ejemplar. Cierto es que el romance homosexual se ha despojado de toda pasión, pero también de melodrama. Si bien el relato cuestiona muchas cosas (la unidad familiar, la ideología burguesa, la represión policial, la violencia machista), no existen dudas o inestabilidades en la relación entre Lluís y su amante, que se presenta como estable y tan convencional que no merece comentario. Se trata de un raro intento de normalización de la pareja homosexual que no encontramos en ninguna otra de las películas homófilas de la Transición. [...] Lluís de Serracant se presenta así como uno de los escasos ejemplos de "héroe homosexual" en el cine español.[26] (Mira 501).

Both the theatrical Lluís de Serracant as well as the cinematographic one will end up being executed on the same military wall at the Montjuïc castle, but while one of them will get there because of his "fag" inconsistencies, the other will do it because of his political commitment without forgetting his final identification as a trans person when, before getting out of the cell and going with his two friends in front of the firing line, he made-up his lips with carmine. I believe this scene is an excellent metaphor of his self-perception considering that he decides to get rid of his stigma at the very last moment of his life, not by hiding but by showing himself through a very queer practice of visibility, a pride of vital and sexual self-affirmation.[27]

Is it true that the character played by Sacristán appears a little bit blurred in that scene but, in my opinion, the film would reflect more a "trans coming out" in front of his mother than a "gay" one—a different issue it would be that gays could appropriate the transvestite confession or identify themselves with that scene. Lluís' interpretation could be evaluated, nowadays at least, more a "transgender" than a "homosexual" or "gay" performance. For example, if we analyze the language that he uses in order to refer to himself/herself: it would not be a man who had lost his masculinity but a trans person who combines and controls gender performances, masculinizing femininities and feminizing masculinities up to his convenience, inside and outside the stage. The "outside" turns out to be extremely interesting. On the screen, Lluís/Flor de Otoño join together some of the "role models" that Esther Newton (97–111) claimed, in the fifth chapter of *Mother Camp,* to the female impersonators in the U.S. in the 1960s: talent consciousness, extreme care in the clothes and the make-up, concern about their presence on the stage, sense of humor… However, Lluís takes a step forward, influenced by an anarchist ideal that American colleagues did not have, that distinguishes when he decides to go out with female clothing and to show up in front of the military wall with his lips made-up. If, according to Newton (111), "only by fully embracing the stigma itself can one neutralize the sting and make it laughable," Flor de Otoño dramatizes and transforms it into a much more radical neutralization.

I would like to begin the conclusions with an anecdote that appears in the volume *La Barcelona de los años 70 vista por Nazario y sus amigos* (Nazario 109). It explicitly refers to the night event where Sacristán enters into his family's home, dressed as a woman, to talk to his mother about his sexual identity:

> Durante el rodaje de la película *Flor de otoño* usaban el portalón del edificio como casa del protagonista José Sacristán, que entraba y salía por la noche disfrazado de mujer tambaleándose sobre unos tacones no muy bien ensayados. La "trupe" de Nazario y Ocaña se burlaba desde los balcones de la "representación ficticia" de lo que ellos mismos repetían a diario en su ir y venir a fiestas, "rambleos" y festivales.[28]

Despite this mirror game between the Ocaña's "trans imagery" and the "transvestite" one of Flor de Otoño that I mentioned at the beginning, it may not be misleading. In front of the conservative imagery of Rodríguez

Méndez's work, in Olea's film we confirm a much more libertarian approach; the *closet* from the first one stays wrecked at the end due to the second, as if he was spreading the news of the first groups that reclaim sexual freedom of lesbians, gays, and trans (as the Front d'Alliberament Gai de Catalunya) during the Spanish Transition. That is what happens in barely six years, the ones between the play and the film. Between the last years of the Francoist Dictatorship and the first democratic elections, Flor de Otoño had won the authenticity battle, which was the freedom one. In this sense, it gains special importance that some of the most known drag queens during that decade, as Paco España (together with no less than a really young Pedro Almodóvar interpreting a female impersonator), performing together with José Sacristán in the theatrical show and backstage which is recreated in the movie.

In the comparative analysis of the Rodríguez Méndez drama and the Azcona and Olea cinematograph adaptation—as it also could be considered after the analysis of Vicente Aranda and Ventura Pons films—it seems to me that it would confirm one of Judith Butler's most attractive proposals regarding *drag*. In her text *Bodies That Matter* (125), the American philosopher suggested that there could not exist an intimate relation between the *drag* and the subversion since the *drag* could show both the denaturalization as the re-idealization of the heterosexual gender hyperbolic rules. That is the case of the leading roles of *Cambio de sexo* and the theatrical *Flor de otoño.* On the other hand, if we think in Ocaña's *retrat intermitent* and in the cinematograph version led by José Sacristán, we can accept Butler's proposal whereby the *drag* is subversive when it shows the imitative structure through which the hegemonic gender produces itself and when it questions the heterosexuality as a natural aspiration. In my opinion, moreover, the comparison between both pieces would confirm the terrific gender roles variation as well as the masculinity and femininity conceptions which reflects, as a mirror, the social, historic, and political tensions and transformations that took place in Spain during the 1970s, between the last years of the Francoist Dictatorship and the first years of the hopeful democracy.

## Notes

1 This chapter was conducted as part of the research project entitled "Representaciones culturales de las sexualidades marginadas en España (1970–1995)" ["Cultural

representations of marginalized sexualities in Spain (1970–1995)"], FEM2011—24064, funded by the Spanish Ministerio de Economía y Competitividad.

2 "My nature has been a complete mistake. I was born with a woman skin, with women shapes, with a woman soul, and with women gestures. I have not ever been a man at all: therefore, with men attributes regarding genitalia, or hair, or muscles. Neither a homosexual man. I believe I was born a woman with that little accessory mistaken: with small and wrong male characteristics which resulted to be nonsense with my way of being and loving."

3 "As I wanted to be known in the show business I played with that resource."

4 "The stream of light abandoned the presenter and the pianist and it went to the right until it came across with a woman sculpture, wavy mane of hair, features of a sensual girl, a powerful sinuous body squeezed into a sequin dress and from a skirt cut came out a toned leg connected to the ground by a red shoe. Just the width of the neck was a visual noise in that harmonic combination that had shaken up the club, the defeated women in their critical contemplation and the annoyed men by the suspicious attraction they had to confess. The statue took on. The tall body moved with lightness and her arms, maybe excessive as the neck, served to move the manual microphone and to emphasise the majesty of the learned evolutions."

5 "I recommend everyone to not use hormones because I spent forty years in transformation, I have been the very first leading figure in Spain and in part of the world without having to put boobs on."

6 "To provoke, to have fun, and to laugh together with the people."

7 Thompson developed a very interesting reading of the relationship between plays and essays. In his opinion, "Flor de Otoño, in a paradoxical way, can be seen as another representative of *machismo*, in the tradition of the casual, comical criminality of Manolo and the arrogant, irresponsible sensuality of Pichi, drawing on and transforming popular culture and the language of the streets. Of course, Flor de Otoño is far from *macho* in the conventional sense of the term […]. Nevertheless Flor proudly claims to be 'flamencona', and expresses a local loyalty akin to the pride of the other *machos* in their *patria chica*" (Thompson 158).

8 "*A thin, pale individual wearing glasses. HE is wrapped in a dark overcoat and seems utterly helpless*" (Rodríguez Méndez, *Autumn,* 8).

9 All quotations refer to the José Martín Recuerda edition (Rodríguez Méndez, *Bodas*) and all their translations to the Marion Peter Holt translation (Rodríguez Méndez, *Autumn*).

10 "Graduate with honors, a luminary of the courts" (Rodríguez Méndez, *Autumn*, 8).

11 "*In an affected* […] *voice*" (*Ibid.* 9).

12 "*Meanwhile, the lights have come up on a corner of the stage and we see LLUISET–that is, the dear child who has produced such a moral earthquake. HE is in a kind of bachelor's apartment carpeted in red. His glasses lie on a small table. LLUISET appears to us now very different from the way we saw him at the interview with the secretary of the municipal office. Dressed in pants, cummerbund, and tuxedo jacket, with his glasses off, he looks like a gay gigolo. HE is looking at himself at the mirror, smoothing back his hair and applying pomade. We notice that he is taking time grooming himself. HE uses atomizers, colognes, and a thousand other trifles. While he is fixing up, HE whistles happily. Meanwhile, we continue to see upstage the family group miming their drawn out goodbyes. LLUISET steps back from the mirror to admire himself. HE clicks his heels rhythmically, places his hands on his hips, and walks toward the mirror vamp-like in the manner of Mae West. (...) and returns to the mirror. Then HE takes down a cape and holds it crosswise, flamenco style, and marches across the stage like a flamenco cabaret singer. HE takes a flower from a bouquet and places it over his ear. HE looks at himself, doesn't like the look, and removes the flower*" (*Ibid.* 13–14).

13 Flor de Otoño was a real historical figure. Michael Thompson transcribes the following remarks from Rodríguez Méndez: "[Flor de Otoño] era un personaje del barrio chino, que trabajaba como travestí en un cabaret, con otras estrellas también rutilantes, como 'La Cubanita', 'La Asturianita', y que tenía afinidades anarquistas hasta el punto de participar en el asalto al cuartel de Atarazanas. Pero todo lo demás es invención mía: que fuera abogado laboralista por las mañanas, que perteneciera a la alta burguesía de Barcelona, que tuviera un trágico final" (Thompson 164).

14 "*Sequined coat*" (Rodríguez Méndez, *Autumn,* 20).

15 "*A multicoloured feather*" (*Ibid.* 20).

16 "*His lips painted in the shape of a small heart.*" (*Ibid.* 20)

17 "A mysterious and a haughty Marlene Dietrich. HE sings with a raspy voice like that of 'Bella Dorita' and moves with the worldly air of a showy vamp" (*Ibid.* 20).

18 "*A burst of thundering applause*" (*Ibid.* 23).

19 "*Vagrants, Bohemians, hustlers, camouflaged individuals from good society, foreigners visiting the city for the International Exposition, anarchists, gamblers*" (*Ibid.* 15).

20 "*His large moustache and sideburns*" (*Ibid.* 38).

21 "*Ex-boxer, with anarchist sympathies*" (*Ibid.* 18).

22 "Lluiset represented the Barcelona that I have known. It has an almost unfathomable mystery about it, a strange and sordid poetry, a hidden rebelliousness, all coming out of the underworld of the docklands, stifled by the weight of a puritanical, insufferable bourgeoisie… I wanted to express this conflict between several warring social classes, which exists in Barcelona in a form that I don't think is found anywhere else in the world: a repugnant bourgeois class, a gentrified proletariat, an emerging class of immigrants from various parts of Spain, and a corrupt criminal class, like in Naples, coexisting with the others and adapting chameleon-like from one period to another" (Thompson 187).

23 "*The Poble Nou Workers' Cooperative*" (*Ibid.* 41).

24 "*The sinister ambience of an anarchist, industrial neighborhood*" (*Ibid.* 41).

25 "*Next to one of the windows FLOR DE OTOÑO-LLUISET is sitting, dressed in a hybrid get-up, part street smart and part gangster garb: an elegant cap, a scarf knotted coquettishly around his neck, and a checked, close-fitting sweater that outlines his pectorals and waist. Gray pants, white shoes. If he weren't in such a place, he could be a sportsman from Monte Carlo. SURROCA is amusing himself with a battery radio that extends its wires over his big head and covers his ears with enormous earphones. RICARD, with a flowing top coat over his shoulders, his soft-brimmed Bohemian hat pushed back gangster style, is giving the news of the day.*" (Rodríguez Méndez, *Autumn Flower*, 41–42).

26 "Lluís' lover, Ricard, shows a conventional masculinity despite the fact that his affection is exemplary. Is it true that the homosexual romance has stripped off all passion but also melodrama. Although the story questions many issues (the family unit, the bourgeois ideology, the police repression, the macho violence), there are no doubts or instabilities in the relation between Lluís and his lover, who is presented as stable and so conventional that does not deserve a comment. It is about a weird attempt of normalizations of the homosexual couple which cannot be found in none of the Transition homophile films. […] Lluís de Serracant is presented as one of the limited examples of the 'homosexual hero' in the Spanish cinema."

27 The movie critic José Luis Guarner pointed out keenly, in the review he wrote after the premiere of the film in 1978, what if follows: "No es un análisis, ni una descripción precisa lo que pretende *Flor de Otoño*. Lo que a Olea le interesa es indicar que Lluís es travestí como desafío a la sociedad a que pertenece [...] morir como una mujer puede ser finalmente la mejor manera de morir como un hombre." (Guarner 29). "What *Flor de*

*Otoño* expects is not an analysis nor a precise description. What Olea is interested in is that Lluís is a transvestite as a challenge to the society he belongs to [...] to die as a woman can finally be the best way to die as a man."

28 "During the shooting of *Flor de otoño,* the crew used a building's entrance hall as the leading role José Sacristán home, who got inside and, dressed as a woman and who was tottering on heels in a not very rehearsal way. Nazario and Ocaña's troupe made fun of their 'fictional representation' from the balconies, the same that they used to do in their daily lives: attending parties, 'rambleos', and festivals."

## Films

*A Man Called Autumn Flower* [*Un hombre llamado Flor de Otoño*]. Dir. Pedro Olea. José Frade Producciones Cinematográficas S.A. and Panorámica. 1978. Film.

*Ocana, an Intermittent Portrait* [*Ocaña. Retrato intermitente*]. Dir. Ventura Pons. Prozesa and Teide P.C.1978. Film.

*Sex Change* [*Cambio de sexo*]. Dir. Vicente Aranda. Impala and Morgana Films. 1977. Film.

*The Golden Age* [*La edad de oro*]. Dir. Paloma Chamorro. Televisión Española. 6 October 1983. Television broadcasting.

*The Transsexual* [*El transexual*]. Dir. José Jara. 1977. Film.

## Bibliography

Arnalte, Arturo. *Redada de violetas. La represión de los homosexuales durante el franquismo.* Madrid: La esfera de los libros, 2003. Print.

Baudrillard, Jean. *Seduction.* Trans. Brian Singer. New York: St. Martin's P, 1990. Print.

Butler, Judith. *Bodies That Matter: On the Discursive Limits of "Sex."* New York: Routledge, 1993. Print.

Fluvià, Armand de. *El moviment gai a la clandestinitat del franquisme (1970–1975).* Barcelona: Laertes, 2003. Print.

Guarner, José Luis. "Flor de Otoño." *Fotogramas.* 1978: 29. Print.

Guasch, Óscar. "La construcción cultural de la homosexualidad masculina en España (1970–1995)." *Minorías sexuales en España (1970–1995). Textos y representaciones.* Ed. Rafael M. Mérida Jiménez. Barcelona: Icaria, 2013. 11–25. Print.

Matos, Pilar. *De niño a mujer. Biografía de Dolly Van Doll.* Córdoba: Arco Press, 2007. Print.

Mérida Jiménez, Rafael M. *Cuerpos desordenados.* Barcelona: U.O.C., 2009. Print.

Mira, Alberto. *De Sodoma a Chueca. Una historia cultural de la homosexualidad en España en el siglo XX.* Barcelona: Egales, 2004. Print.

Nazario, ed. *La Barcelona de los años 70 vista por Nazario y sus amigos.* Vilaboa: Ellago, 2004. Print.

Newton, Esther. *Mother Camp: Female Impersonators in America.* 1972. Chicago: University of Chicago, 1979. Print.

Olmeda, Fernando. *El látigo y la pluma. Homosexuales en la España de Franco.* Madrid: Oberon, 2004. Print.

Pierrot. *Memorias trans. Transexuales, travestis, transformistas.* Barcelona: Morales i Torres, 2006. Print.

Retana, Álvaro. *Historia del arte frívolo.* Madrid: Tesoro, 1964. Print.

Rodríguez Méndez, José M. *Ensayo sobre el machismo español*, Barcelona: Península, 1974. Print.

———. *Bodas que fueron famosas del Pingajo y la Fandanga/Flor de Otoño: Una historia del Barrio Chino*. Ed. José Martín Recuerda, Madrid: Cátedra, 1979. Print.

———. *Autumn Flower.* Trans. Marion P. Holt. New Brunswick, New Jersey: Estreno Contemporary Spanish Plays, 2001. Print.

Rubin, Gayle. *Deviations: A Gayle Rubin Reader*, Durham: Duke University Press, 2011. Print.

Soriano Gil, Manuel Á. *La marginación homosexual en la España de la Transición*, Barcelona: Egales, 2005. Print.

Thompson, Michael. *Performing Spanishness. History, Cultural Identity and Censorship in the Theatre of José María Rodríguez Méndez.* Bristol: Intellect, 2007. Print.

Vázquez Montalbán, Manuel. *El pianista,* Barcelona: Seix Barral, 1985. Print.

# CHAPTER 7

## Undressing Masculinity: Male Dress and Accoutrements in Four Female Spanish Characters

Elena Madrigal-Rodríguez
*Universidad Autónoma Metropolitana-Azcapotzalco*

### The Man I Am

Gender and embodiment have produced extreme combinatorial typologies, like the one Lucía Etxebarria expresses in "Príncipe del silencio."[1] The first verses of her poem convey the longing for a primeval body that would solve the conflict of being a man trapped in a woman's body. To the reader's surprise, the ultimate resolution comes when the lyric voice accepts categorically her being a woman in a man's body:

> Y entonces te encontré: la mujer que yo soy
> en un cuerpo de hombre…[2]

The poem is central to this essay because it plays with the idea that the body can be isolated from one's own sense of being and looking, of unity and otherness. Following Lacan, it could be said that this is because biology belongs to the domain of the symbolic, to the same space where masculine and feminine images occupy the site of the "I" and the "Other,"[3] indistinctively, alternatively, or simultaneously, we might add. The poem also talks about the beginning and the end of a quest, leaving the reader free to imagine the particulars of such a journey, and more important, perhaps, what it means to be a man or a woman in a body that conceals its biology to the reader.

It is in this gap that we may imagine the poetic subject trying a constant shifting of codes until it finds the ones that suit it. We can picture it, naked and dressed, in a constant reenactment of imagery and behavior in front of a mirror. The mirror is a must, because even though the poetic subject expresses itself through the voice of an "I," it is the look of a collective Other that will ultimately sanction the appropriateness of private and public renderings. Iterability, rituals, and performativity allow the poetic subject to reproduce, recreate, and adjust to the grand systems of values of gender since, as Judith Halberstam has proposed, the "cardinal rule [of gender is that] one must be readable at a glance."[4] So, the body with its "correct" gestures and postures does not suffice to produce the mirage of being a man or a woman, for it needs complementary homogenized and visible markers, such as clothes, accessories, and cosmetics.[5] In short, "Prince of Silence" allows us to think of gender as a set of attributes people assimilate and embody. In those terms, gender is unstable, but it paradoxically relies on external stable markers.[6]

## A Deeper Look into the Literary

To explore these ideas further, I propose to ponder four other literary works where non-male characters adopt indicators of being male. The idea is not new in a field populated by female adventurers, fortune hunters, or warriors in their male clothing. By choosing pieces that are part of the lesbian literary corpus, the novelties would be the desire female characters express for other women and the ways masculinity functions in these self-contained worlds, where male characters are often erased, for the exclusion of the masculine does not equate to "writing the obituary of [hegemonic] masculinity."[7] Since masculinity is turned into a secondary or even silent presence in these fictional settings, it would be worth it to unveil the "negotiations between bodies, identities, and desire"[8] that affect both plot and characters.[9] By locating masculinities where they seem to be nonexistent, the subterfuges that sustain conventional masculinity become apparent. The exercise is framed by a "dismissal of any understanding that masculinity is a singular, biological, inevitable, core construct of males."[10] And, as Annalisa Mirizio has pointed out, regardless of embodiment, images of powerful women rely on traditional manly values still.[11] So, the challenge would be to reflect on the workings of a privileged visual order that matches external masculine markers and systems of values such as aggressiveness, power, or public validation.[12] The lines of analysis would be dressing, sex-desire, and alterity formation, three narratives that persist despite the publication places and dates and the literary time frames of these novels.

In relation to dressing, it has historically been a differentiator of the sexes. As such, following Mirizio, it is "el referente icónico de una presunta esencia."[13] The overreactions wearing the wrong clothes may still provoke[14] attest to the power of dressing, leading us to agree with David W. Foster in that "la ropa y adláteres [han sido convertidos en] un formalismo destinado a afirmar categóricamente lo que no existe ni funciona como tal."[15] The precariousness and ambiguity of sex differences anchor in niceties—such as haircut—[16] targeted to "men" and "women" and that exceed decoration or utility purposes. The minuscule details[17] add up so as to construct female or maleness or, as happens to the characters we will look into, place subjects under "various degrees of cross-dressing and various degrees of overt masculine representation"[18] in an overlapping of gender and power.

But for representation to take place, the imaginary presence of the Other who looks—of that Other who censors nakedness and dressing alike—is absolutely necessary. It is this Other who determines the binaries man/woman, masculine/feminine departing from dressing and accessories. The force of this look is such that Tod W. Reeser speculates why Margaret Thatcher or Janet Reno would be perceived as "masculine" and Hillary Clinton as "feminine." He also asks his reader to think of Wonder Woman and to imagine "another […] one with an androgynous outfit, small breasts, and short hair, but with exactly the same powers—"[19] to consider how these minor changes alter the reader's idea of fe/male power. Or take the first two female-to-male transsexuals tips and the anxiety they reveal about not being legible by the social glance: "[to] be seen by society as [one's] correct gender [:] Get guy clothes. […] Go for whatever haircut […], as long as it's a guy style."[20]

Charo Lacalle has developed a three-leveled axiology to explain the overlapping of attributes over dressing.[21] The first level is the epistemic and it is based on material traits and the words to describe them (like "silk"). The second is the ethic and it consists of attaching a concept to a material trait, such as "lush." The third level is the aesthetic and compels people to assign artistic tags, such as "elegant." Lacalle's proposal helps to understand that despite changes in fashion, a piece of fabric or garment may constantly be at the center of desire. Her ideas also incite to locate the masculine/feminine constructions in this less dynamic side of clothing. Indirectly, we could also understand how "stable gender and sexual signifiers [such as dressing] provide a much stronger base toward which others can direct and, more important, understand their attraction and desires."[22] Sex-desire, our second line of analysis, crosses easily the three axiological layers. It inserts outfit in a seduction circuit that involves the self and its yearnings—like being male—and the Other who sanctions the clothes. Claudio Guerri explains that appropriate dressing "nos puede llevar desde la superficie hasta los abismos del placer"[23] in this circuit.

In the novels, dressing not only triggers desire between lovers, but the formation of wider tribes or, as Halberstam would explain, "sexual subculture[s with their own] structures of social, sexual, and casual interaction."[24] Male dress, emblematic of virility as Christine Bard proposes,[25] plays a key role in establishing limits between larger lesbian/hetero collectives as well as among those grouped under the lesbian category. The limits pass almost unnoticed for the non-lesbian characters, whereas "insiders" are not disoriented by the male dress. On the contrary, wearing masculine outfits becomes a fine weapon for lesbians to bond and to exclude. The point is not to forget that masculinity is still there.

The novels to comment are *Las sombras del Safari* by Gilda Salinas (1998), *Beatriz y los cuerpos celestes* by Lucía Etxebarria (2001), *La insensata geometría del amor* by Susana Guzner (2001), and *La mansión de las tríbadas* by Lola Van Guardia (aka Isabel Franc, 2002). Briefly, the characters in each one of them provide various elements to ponder masculinity in female embodiment. For example, although *Las sombras...* takes place in 1950–60's Mexico City, the reason to include it here is the group of manly Basque *pelota* ("ball") women players (pelotaris) who had to cross the Atlantic to escape from regime in Spain. *Beatriz...* portrays the after Franco dictatorship breaking apart of family and school, institutions that had detained direct control of gender mores and practices. The novel also insists on depicting critical attitudes and the development of a new conscience on sex and love matters. *La insensata...* offers an interesting contrast between male secondary characters and masculine attributes in a lesbian romance, and *La mansión...* is based on a utopian erasure of virile bodies.

## The Novels

### *El puño de Orúe... la temida, violenta, monstruosa mano derecha de Orúe*[26]

The character of Orúe stands out from the twenty-four vignettes that make up the non-linear novel *Las sombras...* First her hand and fist, then her six-pack abs and trimmed hair, become a synecdoche for her physical power, strong personality, and womanizing skills. Some constant non-fiction details make Orúe more credible from her introduction to her dawn. Her story and sex life begin when barely a teenager she is taken to Mexico by iconic singer Lola Flores, "La Faraona":

> Tenías poco más de quince cuando te trajo Lola la Faraona, eras como su juguete, te prestaba a su tocaya, la gran Lola mexicana. Y a ti también te divirtió meterte entre las sábanas de las cantantes; una para que llenara de música las nostalgias de la madre patria, otra para que echara a remojar lo que habría de convertirse en tu nueva historia.[27]

Orúe then appears living in the then luxurious Bosque Hotel along with a Basque *pelota* team and playing at the fancy Frontón Metropolitano.[28] Like some other girls in her team, Orúe spends her nights at the Safari bar in a man's outfit: "Orúe con la camisa abierta casi hasta el ombligo, pantalón blanco, cero panza, ni una lonja, botas, pelo muy corto, copetito de rizos."[29] Another character in the story explains the reason for her to find in dressing a way to let her maleness be known: "Eso, lo de la ropa [era] importantísimo, porque en aquel tiempo nadie se vestía con pantalones para ir a trabajar, es más, las únicas de pantalón eran las pelotaris y uno que otro general."[30] Orúe perhaps did not dare to wear trousers as her outdoor clothes, but she did wear her sports uniform also as her party dress, so that everyone at the bar would know that she belonged to the "*canalla*" ("lousy"), or manly lesbians, and was opposed to the "*femmes*."[31] As such, Orúe shared with her fellow women *pelotaris* a power renowned by locals and that granted her privileges in their small world, such as being given a good table by the scenario:

> En la mesa de pista van a quedar los grandes generales del Frontón Metropolitano [...] todas de pantalón blanco, con las camisas abiertas y los senos libres de ataduras, firmes como bíceps inflamados y con un paliacate de cinturón; recién bañadas, el pelo embarrado de los lados, muy corto... y copete. Machas. Ya quisieran los pelotaris vascos ser tan machos como ellas.[32]

Her attire also differentiates her type from the tribe of dandy women. Brushstroke described, Chechelín is the character that stands for this second group: "Chechelín con traje de hombre, camisa *sport*, botines, sombrero y hasta un puro, deliberadamente a la moda de los cuarentas."[33] Despite both characters share an "absolutely meticulous [care] about their masculinity from the short haircut to the men's shoes,"[34] Orúe has her uniform as token of her middle class position and of her only chance of "wearing not feminine clothes."[35] As proof of their masculinity, Orúe and Chechelín measure their fighting abilities with each other. Their open physical violence is not shared by other manly women, however. Carolina, another pelotari, for example, flees every time there is a brawl, or Silvia Olga, a singer who left Cuba because of the Revolution, brandishes her guitar to protect herself.[36]

The years in which characters dressed freely ended abruptly for Carolina first and then for Orúe when they are deported during the times of persecution of foreigners in Mexico. Orúe has lost much of her physical strength and of her potent personality by then. Behind her is perhaps one of those real Catalan women who pioneered women sports in Mexico,[37] but most important, a character that condenses a will to be rude, virile, and commanding in a traditional, manly way.

*No me sienta bien el pelo tan corto. ¿Por qué me empeño en raparme de esa manera? Y, ¿es necesario que lleve siempre esas botas de pocero tan poco femeninas?*[38]

This is how Beatriz rephrases her mother's complaints about her rebelliousness. Beatriz has found that above drinking, drug dealing, and stabbing a guy, looking manly annoys her mother to the point of exasperation. Behind the war of clothes between Bea and her mom, there is a gender script that still functions "in remarkably consistent and restrictive ways," as Halberstam puts it.[39] Bea is pleased by the reactions her looks provoke. She assimilated her mannish style when she was studying in Edinburgh, but the process was not easy. Although she knew how unconventional her appearance had been since she was a child,[40] her gender assignment with its corresponding dress codes was confronted when she went to an only-girls bar in Edinburgh. There she despises:

> La mayoría [de las chicas que] llevaba pelo corto y vestía pantalones [...] uniformadas en sus supuestos disfraces de hombres, fumando cigarrillos con gesto de estibador y ceño de mal genio, las piernas cruzadas la una sobre la otra, tobillos sobre rodilla, en un gesto pretendidamente masculino.[41]

Lines ahead, she would recount her outfit in very similar terms like the ones she used to differentiate herself from a "congregación de petardas y marimachos [...] que llevaban el pelo rapado al uno y teñido con peróxido, que vestían camisetas de talla infantil y chaquetones de peluche y zapatillas de jugador de fútbol búlgaro."[42] Bea has gone far beyond her initial contesting of the blue color for boys[43] by admitting the power and freedom she profits from a man's look. Part of such liberty is the distance she can take from "El enemigo [que eran] el pasado, el franquismo, los matrimonios heterosexuales que se habían convertido en cárceles para los cónyuges y para sus hijas."[44] The gaps that would differentiate Bea's generation from their mothers are far from clear-cut, however. Fearless dealer, heavy drinker, and once stabber Bea is also capable to dress herself for an interview with Charo, the mother of Mónica, a great love of Bea's, for example. Bea explains that for the meeting "[se ha] vestido para la ocasión con un conjunto gris básico y sereno [...] e incluso [se] he maquillado los ojos para suavizar el efecto estridente de [su] pelo rapado al uno."[45]

Since Charo is a business woman, Bea guesses she would consider her crew cut fashionable. Her thought is another example of how Bea produces ethical comments based on dress aesthetics, this time in relation to somebody from an older generation. Despite being hypercritical, Bea is not able either to realize the paradox Mirizio notices about the powerful and famous woman whose clothing is ruled by male values.[46] In Charo's case, she is wearing her hair short and "un traje sastre color chocolate de corte muy masculino cuya austeridad endulza una corbata rosa pálido anudada, para mayor informalidad, sobre un cuello abierto."[47] Or when describing her mother's appearance, Bea says that "[su] melena corta rubia y su traje sastre de corte impecable le confieren [...] un aire a lo Marlene Dietrich."[48] The profuse and well-chosen adjectives that echo fashion jargon contrast with the coarse terms Bea applies to the outfit of both tomboys and femmes, adding to the complexity of her character thus.[49]

Bea also shares her will to break with stereotypical gender roles with other girls, such as Caitlin, her Scottish girlfriend. Once more, dressing is turned into an expression of rebelliousness and change, this time in its unisex variant which, following Bard, turns sexual dimorphism into a possibility.[50] In Caitlin's case, when she erases expected gender markers in her wardrobe, paraphernalia, and haircut she cancels all possible erotic signaling to the heterosexual male look. Bea explains:

> Caitlin no era, al menos aparentemente, una mujer sexual. No exhibía su cuerpo, no llevaba nunca ropas que permitieran adivinar cómo eran sus músculos o sus curvas, no se maquillaba, no se arreglaba el pelo, no estaba tatuada, ni siquiera llevaba pendientes, y mucho menos *piercing*. En suma: nunca intentaba destacar ninguna parte de su anatomía.[51]

As well as the tomboys at the bar, Bea and Caitlin alter masculine accoutrements to try new identity blends that would encompass eroticism. Bea provides a good example of how a masculinity marker on a female embodiment can trigger deep emotions of love and passion:

> En [...] la Body Shop [...] me detengo frente a un bote de Activist, la colonia que usaba Caitlin, una fragancia de hombre que imita al Antaneus de Chanel. [...] durante los próximos dos meses [...] sólo podré recordarla a través de un olor.[52]

Bea and Caitlin have paved the literary way for more subversive and contradictory manners of realizing masculinity with slight but significant changes in dress. The point is that masculinity in the novels they inhabit is still the grade zero to imply power, force, and even violence.

*El espejo me devolvió una imagen con una cierta "pluma" pero desenfadada, elegante y sexy.*[53]

The epigraph for this section comes from a passage in which María, the main character of *La insensata...*, expresses her mood, her lesbianism, and biases such as her class and "taste." Eva, her lover, is also extremely aware of fashion and how other people perceive her and her companions. In matters of clothes, Eva directs verbal aggressions mainly against two manly-looking lesbians: Amparo and Silvia. For instance, Amparo is classified as a "[l]esbiana y de las heavy, a juzgar por las trazas [:] [... un] severo atuendo de chaqueta y pantalón gris oscuro [al que] sólo le faltaba una corbata a rayas diagonales para completar la viva estampa de un obrero vestido de domingo."[54] Eva also ridicules Amparo's name[55] and her full breasts under a "camisa de clásico corte masculino;"[56] she also calls Amparo "marimacho [and] empleada de gasolinera,"[57] and she even threatens to assault her physically. Eva targets Amparo's gray hair as well in order to complete an exclusion based on Amparo's manly way of dressing and her age. Eva's attitude epitomizes a new age group of young fashionable lesbians who overlook the struggles for freedom of previous generations. Due to a complex narrative strategy, Amparo and Silvia symbolize the courage their generations needed to confront "[el] fanatismo y la exclusión cuyo ejercicio en lo privado no hubiese sido posible sin el aparato público, religioso, científico y médico que lo legitimara"[58] from the rise of Francoism to the enforcement of the Ley de Peligrosidad y Rehabilitación Social[59] (1970–1979).

Eva's attack on Silvia is also contemptuous. Silvia's body features—skin color, age, or height—and the clothes she wears are placed on the same degrading plane. She is also a "mamarracha"[60] who is "rapada al dos,"[61] and follows a look that reminds closely the one Bea made of some of the Edinburgh bar girls:

> muy en boga entre cierto ambiente lésbico: pantalón vaquero negro Calvin Klein a ser posible, camisa igualmente negra o a cuadros tipo leñador de Nebraska, zapatones abotinados, cinturón de cuero que obligadamente debe caer al desgaire

> unos quince centímetros una vez trabado en la hebilla, ni una pizca de maquillaje y un modo muy característico de fumar de costado cogiendo el pitillo con todos los dedos.[62]

Coincidentally, María also decides to try the outfit she has chastised to outrage not her mother, but Eva, who is used to shopping at the fancy boutiques on Ortega y Gasset, an emblem of her wealthy, idle position. María describes the trespassing of limits of her "feminoide"[63] look to adopt one that exposes her lesbianism as follows:

> Tenía ganas de ponerme [...] algo transgresor, y tras unos momentos de cavilación me decanté por unos vaqueros negros y una blusa de corte bastante masculino del mismo color. [...]
>
> —¡María! ¿Qué te has puesto? —[Eva] protestó airada al verme—. Se nota a la legua que eres lesbiana.
>
> —Soy lesbiana, Eva [...].
>
> [S]eguí batallando con el cinturón para lograr ese efecto de caída libre desde la hebilla que completaba el look Silvia. Me concedí, eso sí, una buena mano de maquillaje para contrapuntear el efecto lesbi [...] El espejo me devolvió una imagen con una cierta "pluma" pero desenfadada, elegante y sexy.[64]

At the end of the argument, Eva admits she finds María's look intensely exciting.[65] Perhaps what Eva really desired most was her lover's semi-manly outfit that came along with María's bragging of being out of the closet. The complexity of this arousal—with its infinite combinations of the women's bodies and male accoutrements—challenges the idea that traditional masculinity is the sole source of confrontation among lesbians, a fine reading that escapes Susana Guzner even.[66]

Another controversial scene in the novel is the physical confrontation between María and Eva, which Castrejón interprets as a chance for the characters to recompose themselves.[67] However, the lovers' reaction seems closer to the difficulties hegemonic masculinity faces when confronted with emotions or problematic situations. The two gorgeous and classy lesbians of *La insensata...* can also embody one of the meanest attributes of masculinity in its expression against women, exposing it as a detectable and descriptive construction.

### "*Allí [estaba] la inspectora García, ataviada con tejanos, pelo suelto y lentillas.*"[68]

Ana Corbalán has pointed out two interrelated features of Isabel Franc's novels: their contempt for male characters—if none at all—and their harmonious utopian female and lesbian community settings.[69] Prophylactic *masculinicide*, for example, is at the core of *No me llames cariño*. The inspector Emma García chases the pink ribbon serial murder, a criminal who intends to stop gender violence by killing male abusive partners, and whose hallmark is a pink ribbon she ties to the corpses' penises. The ribbon functions as a metonymy of a desire to castrate phallic power. As we have observed in the comments to *Beatriz...*, pink and ribbons have been associated with girlhood, sensitivity, and weakness, in consequence. So, the act of imposing a girl's marker on the male sex organ detaches symbolically the overriding power of manhood from the body so that the feminine can become the imposer of male attitudes and values, such as force, violence, and superiority.

Apart from the physical extinction of men, Franc renovates a women writers tradition Elaine Showalter describes as the depiction of communities of amazons or places located in desert zones or in the frontiers of idyllic locations.[70] The farm of *La mansión...* is one of those places. Franc excludes men from it in the novel by not having male characters at all and by using the feminine grammatical possibilities of Spanish—as Monique Wittig had done before with French—[71]instead of the supposedly neutral and academically accepted masculine forms. Franc gives continuity to the "a" strategy to evince lesbian independence from men. Corbalán and Castrejón praise Franc's gesture, but overlook the argument that the "a" strategy in *La mansión...* could be taken as an inversion of homophobia and misogyny to produce heterophobia and misandry. As Jean-Louis Jeannelle has pointed out, such textual practices and fictional strategies go against the vindication of other gender expressions,[72] and lead to a widening of the gaps gender theory and human rights seek to shorten.

However, in the literary field, Franc's mistreatment and exclusion of men open a critic possibility of masculinity. Her outstanding ability for irony and humor invites her readers to mock at orthodox masculinity with her portrayal of inspector García, for example. As a result, masculinity loses force but gains complexity. The masculine appearance of the character cannot certainly debase gender biases, but it does expose some of its most irksome archetypes, such as the male detective. García also wears glasses, her hair up, a "camisa blanca abrochada hasta el penúltimo botón,"[73] and a manly uniform—like Orúe once did. But to characterize it, Franc compares it to the suits conservative politician Loyola de Palacio[74] popularized. So, the image of García rests on that of the woman in politics who adds a manly marker to project her power. García also puts her hands into the pockets of her pleated trousers several times,[75] creating an original epithet for the character. Since the movement is mechanical, it adds a humorous touch to the man's piece of clothing García wears due to her profession.[76]

Being a detective, García never denies her intuition. This aptitude goes in combination with manly dressing but not necessarily to solve a crime. At the beginning of the novel, for instance, without knowing why, she decides to wear "jeans, camiseta cuello de barco y una cazadora tejana,"[77] an outfit that makes her feel confident. By the end of the story, a similar description reveals that the first combination was a *prolepsis* of a new love for García.[78] Besides her intuition, García acknowledges her body as the site of her pleasure. This time she falls in love with the alleged criminal, a doctor who during an exploration makes García's nipples react, and who is delineated at one point wearing "un vestido de lino con cuello de pico [,...] falda por encima de las rodillas [... y]; una rebequilla a juego,"[79] in a stereotypical contrast against García's masculine look. The misunderstandings and unfulfilled expectations that surround an apparent femme-butch coupling add to Franc's jokey portrayal of masculinity.

Despite the funny moments, García has left in *La mansión...* the category of the clumsy detective due to her constant introspection. She is hyper-conscious of her doubts, failures, weaknesses, as well as her strengths and capabilities. She is also aware of how consistent her masculine appearance must be since she holds a position of authority and wants others to recognize it, her collaborator Montse Murals in particular. Franc has explained that Murals functions as the close partner of García as Watson is for Sherlock Holmes, but includes a caring friendship between the two women and a deferential "usted" treatment.[80] Two excerpts exemplify Franc's parody of this literary device and how concerned García can be of transgressing the manly values associated to the uniform:

> 1
>
> —¿Qué se me ha puesto, Murals? —preguntó García arrugando la nariz.
>
> —«212» de Carolina Herrera. [...] Una colega me dijo que es una colonia muy buena y que da un toque de distinción a quien la lleva —exclamó orgullosa.
>
> [... García] lanzó una severa mirada a la agente y le espetó:
>
> —Pues no pega con el uniforme, la verdad.[81]
>
> 2
>
> [Murals] no llevaba uniforme, pero además, se había quitado las gafas de sol y mostraba una hermosa mirada de ojos claros.
>
> —Se ha puesto rímel, ¿no? —le estaba preguntando.
>
> —Sí —sonreía la agente.

—Muy bien, Murals, pero cuando esté de servicio no quiero verla con rímel, ni con sombra de ojos, ni colorete, ni nada por el estilo. ¿Estamos?

—Estamos, jefa.[82]

The fact that García respects Murals decisions about her appearance in private, but not when on duty, turns the inspector into a guardian of the police institution and of the public eye. The cultural association of perfume and make up with femininity speaks about the clear-cut limits of the male/female spheres, their fragile foundations, how easily they can be transgressed, and the courage it takes to do so. Age difference between García and Murals may also play a role in their views on the uniform since, as Bard explains, the police profession has dared to superimpose masculine and feminine markers in the recent history.[83]

**Closing Comments**

Orúe, Bea, María and Eva, and inspector García epitomize lesbian resort to traditional masculinity in manners and appearances that vary slightly in a context of extreme sociopolitical control and its aftermath. These characters do not cross-dress, nor do they feel men trapped in a woman's body. Besides seducing, these characters adopt almost the same masculine clothes and accessories to reassure themselves about their strength and freedom to defy conventions despite the risk of exceeding their empowerment and turn violence against themselves or their lovers. The manly attitudes that go with their dressing pave the way for Orúe to start a life as she wants it far from oppression at home. For Bea, they mean the courage to leave home as well as to protect herself from being raped. For María, they are seduction and out-of-the-closet strategies, whereas for Amparo and Silvia they represent rage turned into activism in favor of equality, and for inspector García they are the means to fight for justice. As Julia Kristeva has explained, "sin la afirmación fálica, les habría sido imposible [a estas mujeres], sin duda alguna, hacer realidad su singularidad."[84]

These characters need others to insert them in a collective imaginary in which masculinity is made evident by the same resources to signify power. The gender system functions beyond the characters' will; it is imposed on them for, as Sloop proposes, the idea of the "immutable" body is at the core of gender culture[85] with its heteronormative understandings.[86] Conversely, borrowing Halberstam's words,[87] female bodies may refuse some traits of their assigned feminine gender as well as reify others related to conventional male gender, resulting in a "reconsolidation of dominant masculinity"[88] and its related reconfiguration a certain definition of femininity.[89] The embodiment of masculinity can occur because masculinity is not tied to the phallus, but to its phallic—heterocratic—signifiers, such a haircut style, a type of belt or shoes. Tod Reeser observes a similar phenomenon in another context and advances an applicable commentary:

> Such a move or strategy can serve to reveal stable masculinity as fictional since the net result is not a man but a gender hybrid. This strategy is itself a kind of asymptotic masculinity [...] in which a woman purposely approaches masculinity through signs (such as dress) but never reaches masculinity or passes as a man. The goal [...] is not to reach masculinity, however, but to approach and then subvert it from within, to mimic it, in order to show that it is not unapproachable.[90]

To a large extent, masculinity is approachable because dress has disputed territories to bodies[91] and pieces of clothing for codified genders are available to almost everyone. The open or concealed morality, ethics, and aesthetics of dressing take part in such approachability. For instance, Orúe's uniform cannot be separated from her physical strength or Eva's judgments replicate gender, class, and age disparities. A close reading of literary works may reveal the processes behind the constructions of masculinity and even propose criticism and erasures.

The analysis above, for instance, has underlined two main types of erasures: of the male character and of the workings of the gender system that still patronizes man's supremacy. The accomplishments have been partially successful since they constitute a step towards equity and equiphony.[92] They have also laid the foundations for other types of representations, like the one in the novel *El primer caso de Cate Maynes* by Clara Asunción García, starred by a fe-male detective who tries hard to get rid of her own discriminating and exclusionary actions and thinking. In other words, detective Maynes tries to overcome the axiological heterosexual universe that surrounds her. Needless to say, she is learning to be good at undressing masculinity and male dress in the process.

## Notes

1 This chapter was conducted as part of the research project entitled "Representaciones culturales de las sexualidades marginadas en España (1970–1995)" ["Cultural representations of marginalized sexualities in Spain (1970–1995)"], FEM2011—24064, funded by the Spanish Ministerio de Economía y Competitividad.

2 Etxebarria, *Estación del infierno*, 113: "Prince of Silence." "For many years I longed for / my primeval body / the body I used to inhabit / in another life, because I was not a woman / and I felt like a man trapped in my body / And then I found you: the woman I am / in the body of a man…"

3 Zaoui 50.

4 Halberstam 23.

5 David William Foster considers that sexual binaries rest on three levels: genetic-biologic, sexual secondary characteristics (tone of voice, body hair), and correlated tertiary sexual characteristics: clothing and general appearance. See his insightful analysis in *Ensayos*, 193, 224, and 248, especially.

6 For related ideas, see Frohlich 138.

7 Whitehead 9.

8 Halberstam 38.

9 Feminist criticism is to be credited for the systematic reading of silences in order to disclose gender inequities and how they have erased women's history and achievements. Several authors in men studies acknowledge the crucial contribution of feminism to the formation of their field. See Millington as well as Minello's "Masculinidad/es: un concepto en construcción" and "Los estudios de masculinidad."

10 Whitehead and Barrett 27.

11 Mirizio 141.

12 These triads may synthesize the core masculine attributes, for "[a]ggressive masculinity is alive and well," express Whitehead and Barrett (7), an idea that Alsina y Borràs and Victoria Sau share in their contributions to the volume *Nuevas masculinidades*, edited by Àngels Carabí and Marta Segarra. Another attribute is the validation of manliness mostly within the public instead of the private sphere.

13 Mirizio 141: "the iconic referent of an alleged essence."

14 A recent case occurred when Sudanese Muslim Lubna Husein was brought to court for wearing trousers in 2009.

15 Foster 189–190: "clothing and trifles [have become] a formula aimed at the categorical affirmation of what does not exist and does not function in formulaic terms."

16 Haircut may also spring overreactions like the ones dressing transgression causes. Julio Medina, a survivor from Castro's detention camps, reminds the strict haircut Cuban Revolution leaders demanded from young males (see Almendros 123). The chapter "Modas, costumbres y extravagancias" ("Fashions, customs, and eccentricities"), under the "La Revolución y lo extranjero" ("The Revolution and the Foreign") section, regulated such matters well into the 1970s (*Ibid.* 179–180).

17 Sloop 64.

18 Halberstam 87. The author includes references about the sartorial and erotic style of some women cross-dressers in the 1920s and a thoughtful commentary on *The Well of Loneliness* that underlines the preponderance of appearance over a highly questioned essence (see pages 90–99, 153–55, and note 48 on page 288). Tracing the links between the epochs, languages, and cultures that separate Radclyffe Hall's novel from the ones we are studying is beyond the scope of this essay.

19 Reeser 134.

20 "How to Pass."

21 Lacalle 255–57.

22 Sloop 97.

23 Guerri 276: "may take us from the surface to the depths of pleasure."

24 Halberstam 77.

25 Bard 20. Her study focuses on the history of trousers, but most of her observations apply to other pieces of male clothing and accessories as well. Bard also includes an exhaustive archival research on trousers in France from a feminist point of view.

26 Salinas 108: "Orúe's fist… the frightful, violent, monstruous Orúe's right hand."

27 *Ibid.* 158: "You were a little over fifteen when the Spanish Lola la Faraona brought you, you were like her toy, La Faraona lent you to the great Mexican Lola. And it was funny for you too to get into both singers' sheets; so that one would quench your longing for your mother land, and the other would prefigure your new story."

28 *Ibid.* 159. The Frontón Metropolitano was opened in 1952. Some chronicles indicate the place was inaugurated by a group of women pelotaris who embarked on the Magallanes ship from Spain to Mexico during the years 1951–1952. Many of them looked for other places to play after the Metropolitano was closed in 1972 (Garritz 183–184).

29 *Ibid.* 109: "Orúe in a shirt wide open almost to the navel, white trousers, no belly fat, boots, crew cut, a quiff of curly hair."

30 *Ibid.* 39: "That thing, clothing, was very important, because back then nobody wore trousers for working, in fact, the only ones who wore trousers were the female pelotaris and one general or another."

31 *Ibid.* 115.

32 *Ibid.* 39: "The table by the dance floor is for the Frontón Metropolitano great generals […] all in white trousers, their shirts open and their breasts free from bonding, firm like swollen biceps and a cotton scarf to the waist; bathed, their hair licked on the sides, crew cut… and quiff. *Machas*. The male Basque pelotaris wished they were as macho as those girls." See also 109.

33 Loc. cit.: "Chechelín in a man's suit, sport shirt, boots, hand, and a cigar even, deliberately in a forties' look."

34 Halberstam 120. Although Halberstam's characterization corresponds to "studs" from the 1850s, it applies perfectly to the present case.

35 *Ibid.* 107.

36 Salinas 43 and 22.

37 There might be an Orúe who inspired the character. In a recent interview, María Elena Hernández Cazarín of Mexican origin explained that she fell in love with the sport after watching Catalan pelotari Blanca Orue play who, by the way, presented María Elena with her first racquet (Pardo). María Elena began playing in Madrid in 1972 after the Frontón Metropolitano in Mexico was closed and she lives in Spain still (Acosta).

38 Etxebarria, *Beatriz,* 33: "Crew cuts don't suit me. Why do I insist on cropping my hair that way? And, is it necessary for me to wear those so unfeminine well-digger boots?" For similar ideas in the novel, see also page 53.

39 Halberstam 118.

40 Bea remembers: "A los doce años […] [m]ientras [sus] compañeras se llenaban el pelo de horquillas rosas hasta que su cabeza adquiría el aspecto de un puesto de mercadillo de domingo, e invertían la paga de tres domingos en la adquisición de la imprescindible sudadera de algodón en tonos pastel, [ella] […] leía […] desde Balzac a Thomas Mann" (Etxebarria, *Beatriz*, 139: "when [she] was twelve […] while [her] classmates wore pink hairpins until their hair looked like a Sunday street stall and spent their allowances in a uniform cotton pastel shade sweatshirt, [she] would rather […] read […] from Balzac to Thomas Mann.").

41 *Ibid.* 25: "Most [of the girls who] wore their hair short and dressed in trousers […] all the same in their pretending men's disguise, smoking cigarettes with a longshoremen attitude and frowning, their legs crossed, one over the other, ankle on knee, feigning a masculine pose."

[42] *Ibid.* 43: "congregation of jerks and tomboys […] who wore crew cut peroxide dyed hair, who wore children size shirts and furry jackets and Bulgarian football player shoes."

[43] Beatriz began by opposing girlish pink to "Azul, […] el [color] de los uniformes de trabajo. Monos de mecánico, trajes de azafata. Azul. Corbatas de ejecutivo, bolígrafos para hacer cuentas" (*Ibid.*, 214–215: "Blue [is] the [color] of work uniforms. Overalls for mechanics, flight attendant suits. Blue. Business ties, pens for calculating."). A few years before *Beatriz...* was published, feminist critic Estrella de Diego underlined the gender dichotomy of dressing which by the way agrees with Beatriz's criticisms: pink is for girls and blue for boys because the former is related to emotions and the latter to work (*El andrógino sexuado*, 48, quoted in Mirizio 136).

[44] Castrejón 16: "The enemies [that were] the past, the Francoism, the heterosexual marriages that were like prisons for the couples and their daughters."

[45] Etxebarria, *Beatriz...*, 61: "[She has] put on for the occasion a grey classic and discreet suit […] and [she] even has eye make-up to lessen the strident effect of [her] crew cut hair."

[46] Mirizio 141.

[47] Etxebarria, *Beatriz...*, 61: "a very masculine chocolate suit whose austerity is sweetened by a pale pink tie, knotted, to provide a touch of casualness, over an open neck."

[48] *Ibid.* 32: "her short blond mane and her impeccable skirt suit give her a Marlene Dietrich air."

[49] *Ibid.* 25.

[50] Bard 264, paraphrasing Marie-Thérèse Basse and Olivier Burgelin in "L'unisexe. Perpectives diachroniques." *Communications*. 46 (1987): 295.

[51] *Ibid.* 38: "Caitlin was not, apparently at least, a sexual woman. She did not show off her body, she never wore clothes that would reveal her muscles or her curves, she did not wear makeup, she did not do her hair, and she wore no tattoos, no earrings, much less piercings. In short: she never tried to highlight any part of her anatomy."

[52] *Ibid.* 31: "At […] the Body Shop […] I stop by a bottle of Activist, the cologne Caitlin used to wear, a man's fragrance that mimics the Antaneus by Chanel. […] I will remember her only through a smell […] for the next two months."

[53] Guzner 253: "The mirror gave me back a telling but casual, elegant and sexy image."

[54] *Ibid.* 289: "[l]esbian and a heavy one, judging from the appearance[:] [… a] dark grey severe outfit of jacket and trousers [which] only needed a diagonal stripe tie to complete the living image of a worker dressed for Sunday."

[55] *Ibid.* 297.

[56] *Ibid.* 289: "a classic men's shirt."

[57] *Ibid.* 371: "tomboy [and] gas station attendant."

[58] Madrigal 115: "fanaticism and exclusion, which functioned privately and in complicity with legitimizing public institutions, such as religion, science, and medicine." See pages 114 to 118 for a detailed comment on the narrative strategy.

[59] Law of Social Dangerousness and Social Rehabilitation.

[60] Guzner 164: "tomboy."

[61] *Ibid.* 155: "wears a crew-cut."

[62] Loc. cit.: "very fashionable in a particular lesbian territory: black jeans (Calvin Klein, if possible), same black or Nebraska lumberjack shirt, brogans, a leather belt that must hang for near five inches after fastening the buckle, no trace of makeup, and a most peculiar way of smoking sideways holding the cigarette with all fingertips."

[63] *Ibid.* 156: "effeminate."

[64] *Ibid.* 252–3: "I felt like trying […] something transgressing, and I chose a pair of black jeans and a mannish blouse in the same color. […] / —María! What are you wearing? —[Eva] cried outraged at seeing me.—Everyone can notice you are a lesbian. / —I am, Eva

[…] / I kept on managing the free fall effect with the belt buckle that added the final touch to the Silvia look. I indulged myself with a generous amount of makeup to contrast with the lezzie effect […] The mirror gave me back a telling but casual, elegant and sexy image."

65 *Ibid.* 253–4.

66 The author has avoided discussing the confrontation of the characters in her novel due to their appearance. In an interview, she referred to masculine and feminine looking lesbians as a symptom of heterogeneity and also as a general practice. She seems to consider the femme / butch division as a given, just as the world has been divided into man and woman. See Ferrera.

67 Castrejón 265–6.

68 Franc 253: "There she was, inspector García dressed in jeans, wearing her hair down and lenses."

69 Corbalán. Her argument is further explained on pages 163–4, 169–70, and 174.

70 Showalter 105.

71 Wittig's *L 'Opoponax* (1964) and *Les Guérillères* (1969) exemplify such strategies. The *on* of the former expresses singular and plural, and the *elles* of the latter stands both for "feminine" and "masculine" and it also agrees with the power of a new lesbian collective. Male characters appear only at the closing of *Les Guérillères*, weak, frightened, and displaced from the ferocious order of the amazons.

72 Jeannelle 259.

73 Franc 27 and 108: "a white button-down shirt with the buttons fastened almost to the collar."

74 *Ibid.* 27 and 108.

75 *Ibid.* 108 and 134.

76 See Bard for a comment about police women and their uniforms on 293–300.

77 Franc 27: "jeans, a boatneck t-shirt and a denim jacket."

78 *Ibid.* 253.

79 *Ibid.* 123: "a linen V-neck dress [,…] a skirt over the knees [... and] a matching capelet."

80 Pertusa.

81 Franc 143: —What are you wearing, Murals?—García asked wrinkling her nose. / —«212» by Carolina Herrera. […] A colleague told me it is good cologne and it gives a touch of elegance to those who wear it—Murals answered proudly. / […García] stared severely at the agent and blurted out: / —It does not match the uniform, to be honest."

82 *Ibid.* 253. "[Murals] was not in her uniform, with no sunglasses on, her beautiful clear eyes looks revealed. / —You're wearing mascara, right?—García was asking. / —I am—the agent smiled. / —Very well, Murals, but whenever you're on duty I don't want to see you wearing mascara, eye shadow, blush, and nothing of the sort. Understood? / —Count on that, boss…"

83 Bard 297.

84 *Ibid.* 160: "without the phallic affirmation, there is no doubt that it would have been impossible [for these women] to realize their uniqueness." Bard quotes Kristeva, Julia. *Les mots. Colette ou la Chair du monde*. Vol. 3. *Le Génie féminin.* Paris: Fayard, 2002. 564.

85 Sloop 49.

86 *Ibid.* 23.

87 Halberstam 142.

88 *Ibid.* 60. See also Millington on the necessity of stable markers for the ideological effect of gender to take place.

89 From different standpoints, Michael Kimmel and Robert Connell have observed that masculinity is always opposed to and above some concept of femininity. For comments on their proposals, see Whitehead and Barrett 1–26, 2, and 31.

90 Reeser 139.

91 Saulquin 175.

92 The term "equiphony" has been proposed by Alicia H. Puleo in "De «eterna ironía de la comunidad» a sujeto del discurso: mujeres y creación cultural," in Carabí and Segarra 65.

## Bibliography

Acosta, Yaiza. "Pelotaris pioneras." *El País* 8 July 2012: n. pag. Web. 9 Oct. 2013. <http://goo.gl/JfmVjj>.

Almendros, Néstor, and Orlando Jiménez-Leal. *Conducta impropia*. Barcelona: Egales, 2008. Print.

Bard, Christine. *Historia política del pantalón*. Trans. Nuria Viver Barri. México: Tusquets, 2012. Print.

Carabí, Àngels, and Marta Segarra, eds. *Nuevas masculinidades*. Barcelona: Icaria, 2000. Print.

Castrejón, María. *...Que me estoy muriendo de agua. Guía de narrativa lésbica española.* Barcelona: Egales, 2008. Print.

Corbalán, Ana. "Abajo el patriarcado: utopía lésbica en *No me llames cariño*, de Isabel Franc." *Letras Femeninas* XXXVI. 1 (Summer 2010): 161–178. Print.

Etxebarria, Lucía. *Beatriz y los cuerpos celestes. Una novela rosa*. Barcelona: Destino, 1998. Print.

———. *Estación del infierno*. Barcelona: Lumen. 2001. Print.

Ferrera, Ruymán. "Susana Guzner: «Mis novelas son muy cinematográficas, escribo imaginando escenas»." *La Provincia.* 2 Aug. 2001. Web. 6 Jul. 2013. <www.susanaguzner.com>.

Foster, David William. *Ensayos sobre culturas homoeróticas latinoamericanas*. Ciudad Juárez: Universidad Autónoma de Ciudad Juárez, 2009. Print.

Frohlich, Margaret G. *Framing the Margin: Nationality and Sexuality across Borders*. Tempe: Asociación Internacional de Literatura y Cultura Femenina Hispánica, 2008. Print.

García, Clara Asunción. *El primer caso de Cate Maynes*. Barcelona: Egales, 2011. Print.

Garritz Ruiz, Amaya and Javier Sanchiz Ruiz. *Euskal Etxea de la Ciudad de México.* Colección Urazandi Bilduma, vol. XIII. Vitoria-Gasteiz: Servicio Central de Publicaciones del Gobierno Vasco, 2003. Print. Also web. 9 Oct. 2013. <http://goo.gl/X3Kki7>.

Guerri, Claudio. "Moda y arte de vanguardia." Interview with Juan Mathé. *deSignis* 1 (Oct-2001): 275–278. Print.

Guzner, Susana. *La insensata geometría del amor*. México: Santillana, 2009. Print.

Halberstam, Judith. *Female Masculinity*. Durham: Duke UP, 2004. Print.

"How to Pass As a Male (For FTMs)." N.d. Web. 8 Aug. 2013. <http://goo.gl/mkqSMB>.

Jeannelle, Jean-Louis. "Heterofobia." *Diccionario Akal de la homofobia*. Ed. Louis-Georges Tin. Trans. Taller de Publicaciones. Prologue Bertrand Delanoë. Spanish ed. Francisco López Martín. Madrid: Akal, 2012. Print.

Lacalle, Charo. "Deconstruir la moda. El universo significativo de Vivienne Westwood." *deSignis* 1 (Oct. 2001): 253–263. Print.

Madrigal, Elena. "Amor lésbico, paradoja y quiasmo en *La insensata geometría del amor*." *Minorías sexuales en España (1970–1995). Textos y representaciones*. Ed. Rafael M. Mérida Jiménez. Barcelona: Icaria, 2013. 109–124. Print.

Millington, Mark. *Hombres in/visibles. La representación de la masculinidad en la ficción latinoamericana, 1920–1980*. México: Fondo de Cultura Económica, 2007. Print.

Minello Martini, Nelson. "Los estudios de masculinidad." *Estudios Sociológicos* xx.60 (Sept.–Dec. 2002): 715–732. Print.

———. "Masculinidad/es: un concepto en construcción." *Nueva Antropología: Revista de Ciencias Sociales* 18.61 (2002): 11–30. Print.

Mirizio, Annalisa. "Del carnaval al drag: la extraña relación entre masculinidad y travestismo." *Nuevas masculinidades*. Eds. Àngels Caribí and Marta Segarra. Barcelona: Icaria, 2000. 133–150. Print.

Pardo, Miguel A. "La pelota, en femenino." *Deia* Iparraguirre 15 Aug. 2013. N. pag. Web. 9 Oct. 2013. <http://goo.gl/R89Jfk>.

Pertusa, Inmaculada. "Video-entrevista: Isabel Franc y la primera agencia de detectives lesbiana en las letras peninsulares." *Grafemas*, Dec. 2009. N. pag. Web. 17 Oct. 2013. <http://goo.gl/HO7AmA>.

Reeser, Tod W. *Masculinities in Theory. An Introduction*. Chichester-Malden, MA: Wiley-Blackwell, 2010. Print.

Salinas, Gilda. *Las sombras del* Safari. *Una ciudad, una década y un bar*. México: Diana, 1998. Print.

Saulquin, Susana. "El cuerpo como metáfora." *deSignis*, 1 (Oct. 2001): 169–85. Print.

Showalter, Elaine. "La crítica feminista en el desierto." *Otramente: lectura y escritura feministas*. Coord. Marina Fe. Trans. Argentina Rodríguez. México: Programa Universitario de Estudios de Género-Fondo de Cultura Económica, 1999. 75–111. Print.

Sloop, John M. *Disciplining Gender: Rhetorics of Sexual Identity in Contemporary U.S. Culture*. Amherst and Boston: U of Massachusetts P, 2004. Print.

Van Guardia, Lola [Isabel Franc]. *La mansión de las tríbadas*. Barcelona: Egales, 2002. Print.

Whitehead, Stephen M., and Frank J. Barrett. "The Sociology of Masculinity." *The Masculinities Reader*. Eds. Stephen M. Whitehead and Frank J. Barrett. Cambridge: Blackwell, 2001. 1–26. Print.

Wittig, Monique. *L 'Opoponax*. Paris: Éditions de Minuit, 1964. Print.

———. *Les Guérillères*. Paris: Éditions de Minuit, 1969. Print.

Zaoui, Pierre. "Alteridad." *Diccionario Akal de la homofobia*. Ed. Louis-Georges Tin. Trans. Taller de Publicaciones. Prologue Bertrand Delanoë. Spanish ed. Francisco López Martín. Madrid: Akal, 2012. Print.

# CHAPTER 8

## *Machos* or *divinas*? A Quandary in Argentinean and Spanish Gay Activism

Jorge Luis Peralta
*Universidad Nacional de la Plata—CONICET*

During the 1970s, homosexual liberationist ideas spread internationally through associations that emerged from different latitudes and from bulletins or newspapers that they published and exchanged.[1] Apart from the historical and cultural particularities of each context, some affinity is observed in some of their fundamental proposals, such as those concerning "sexual roles" and the different ways to embody them. Certainly, this debate goes back much further: in his emblematic treaty of defense of paedophilia, *Corydon*, published in 1924, André Gide established a dividing line between respectable (male) gay and outrageous (effeminates).[2] The discussion, far from being overcome, remains in full validity, as can be seen in the reactions to Pedro Almodóvar's latest film, *Los amantes pasajeros* (*I'm So Excited*, 2012): while some critics believe that the "faggot" figure, central to the film, repeats a well-known and reductive stereotype, others value its revolutionary potential and its challenge to the normative of the regulations, both hetero and homo.[3]

The aim of this chapter is to analyze the variable conceptions of masculinity in the texts of two Argentinean activists, Héctor Anabitarte Rivas and Ricardo Lorenzo Sanz, exiled in 1976 in Spain, where they reside since then. The specific production of these authors is of interest since it evidences the ideological proximity between the discourses of Argentinean and Spanish homosexual activism, both influenced by the theories and debates that were spreading to different parts of the globe from the United States and some European countries (mainly France, Italy, and England). Their visionary interests, also due to the contrast between the situation in Argentina, from where they went into exile due to the military dictatorship (1976–1983), and Spain, which at the time of their arrival began the transition into democracy after the death of Francisco Franco in 1975. Therefore, Anabitarte and Lorenzo Sanz witnessed very different historical and socio-cultural processes despite being contemporary, and this circumstance would affect their perception of gender and sexuality. The dark and repressive Argentina that they had abandoned had little in common with Spain, which was taking its first steps towards democracy and where greater opportunities to challenge gender conventions were possible, as it happened in a paradigmatic way in Barcelona and Madrid. The discussions of masculinity that appear in their texts reflect, therefore, the ambivalent positions taken by homosexuals at the time in both sides of the Atlantic.

In this study I will describe, first, the activists' trajectory, focusing on their political work both in Argentina and Spain. Secondly, I will refer to the main postulates of the gay liberationism around "sexual roles," from key texts and authors. Finally, I will discuss the treatment of these topics in Anabitarte and Lorenzo Sanz's articles and books published between the late 1970s and early 1980s, in order to show that their positions on "masculinity" and "femininity" changed over the years, in tune with the tensions and contradictions that, in general, the emerging Argentinean and Spanish gay communities were experiencing.

## From Villa Gerli to *las Ramblas*: Itineraries of an Activism

The name of Héctor Anabitarte Rivas is significantly linked to the origins of Argentinean homosexual activism. His first political experience came in the context of trade unionism and the Communist Youth Federation, which rejected him when he tried to include the issue of homosexuality in their discussions.[4] In 1967 the first attempt of homosexual association took place: Anabitarte and other young proletarians held meetings in a tenement house in Lomas de Zamora to discuss about police persecution, whose main instrument was a series of edicts that allowed the police to arrest all those subjects suspected of practicing a dissenting sexuality.[5] The first organization, also led by Anabitarte, named *Nuestro Mundo* ("Our World") began operations in 1969. According to reports from Anabitarte, one of the usual meeting places of this pioneering group was a working class man's small house located in the suburban village of Villa Gerli. *Nuestro Mundo* is the most immediate antecedent of the FLH (*Frente de Liberación Homosexual*, "Gay Liberation Front").[6] It was the writer from Tucumán, Juan José Hernández, who contributed to the meeting between working class people and trade union workers in *Nuestro Mundo* and a group of intellectuals, including Juan José Sebreli and Blas Matamoro, whose fusion gave rise, in 1971, to the FLH.[7] Although these dates may suggest a link with the French May of 1968 and the American gay movement, which emerged a year later in the heat of the Stonewall events, Anabitarte says that along with other members of *Nuestro Mundo*, later incorporated into the FLH, recognized another affiliation, specifically with Spain: "El grupo no tenía nada que ver con el Mayo Francés ni con el movimiento gay de Estados Unidos. Antes bien, manteníamos correspondencia con españoles, que vivían atemorizados por la Ley de Peligrosidad Social del franquismo, que incluía a los homosexuales."[8] This observation is crucial because it marks distance between Anabitarte's activism and the intellectual sector of FLH, in which the young Néstor Perlongher stood out, later a recognized poet and essay-writer. The reformism in which Anabitarte and his group agreed with it contrasted with the revolutionary tendency headed by Perlongher, resulting in differences that included, as we will later confirm, the issue of masculinity. The FLH was active until 1976, when it was dissolved following the beginning of the *Proceso de Reorganización Militar* ("Military Reorganization Process"). Their broadcasting means, in which Anabitarte collaborated, were the newspaper *Homosexuales*, which only published one issue in July 1973, and the newsletter *Somos*, whose copies—eight in total—were published irregularly between 1973 and 1975.[9]

Anabitarte met Ricardo Lorenzo Sanz in the context of their membership in the FLH in 1975. When the advent of the military dictatorship put their lives in danger, the activists decided to go into exile in Spain. They arrived there in January, 1977 and quickly contacted the Spanish activists: "En Madrid Ricardo y yo nos incorporamos a un grupo gay y luego cuando nos trasladamos a Barcelona (1979) nos vinculamos al Lambda y al movimiento gay catalán; estas organizaciones son las más pioneras en España. [Tuvimos] íntima relación con Armand [de Fluvià]."[10] Besides participating in these movements, the newcomers published articles, mostly written in collaboration, in different alternative journals like *Bicicleta*, *El Viejo Topo*, *Ajoblanco* o *Triunfo*.[11] Some of these contributions were collected in the volume *Homosexualidad: el asunto está caliente*, in 1979.[12] Two years later, in 1981, a book by Anabitarte entitled *Estrechamente vigilados por la locura*, a sort of personal diary that includes references to the activist work done with his partner both in Argentina and Spain, appeared. In the late 1980s the last co-written book was published, *Sida, el asunto está que arde* (1987).

Anabitarte and Lorenzo Sanz's political trajectory stands out for its ideological coherence and continuity. Their positions did not substantially change when they moved from Argentina to Spain, as it can be seen in their various publications. Even when some of their proposals appear under the clear influence of contemporary activists who stood for radical politics, as in the case of Mario Mieli or Guy Hocquenghem, Anabitarte and Lorenzo Sanz chose a less revolutionary means.

## Gay Liberation and "Sexual Roles"

The gay liberationism had its first impulse in the events occurred around New York's Stonewall bar in June 1969, when gays and transvestites strongly resisted a police raid and, thereby, started, different movements in the defense of the rights of sexual minorities. According to Mérida Jiménez, "los sucesos del *Stonewall* constituyen un acontecimiento que puede considerarse como un símbolo de las luchas por los derechos civiles sexuales en las sociedades occidentales."[13] This same critic warns that, strictly speaking, the first organizations that fought for the rights of gays and lesbians date back to the 1950s and mentions the American paradigmatic examples of the Mattachine Society and The Daughters of Bilitis; and we might add, in the European context, the French organization Arcadie. These pioneering homophile groups differ, however, from the movement emerged from Stonewall, because the principles that supported and inspired them to seek acceptance and social integration were replaced, as of the seventies, by much more radicalized speeches and actions. The Homosexual Liberation Fronts that emerged in Europe and Latin America adopted the same combative policy as the American organizations.[14]

The gay liberationist discourse can be reconstructed from a varied range of texts including manifestos, magazines, newsletters, and books. Among the key titles to be mentioned, books written by three activists of different nationalities and backgrounds, who agree on the substantive aspects of their proposals, must be mentioned; I am referring to *Homosexual: Oppression and Liberation* (1971) by Australian Dennis Altman; *Le désir homosexuel* (*Homosexual Desire*, 1972) by Guy Hocquenghem; and *Elementi di critica omosessuale* (*Homosexuality and Liberation: Elements of a Gay Critique*, 1977) by the Italian writer Mario Mieli. Of the three, possibly Mieli's book was the one that had less impact and international significance, unlike the works of Altman and Hocquenghem,[15] who remain an important reference in the field of LGBT studies.[16]

The analysis and questioning of "sexual roles" assumed a central nature in the framework of the liberationist debate: "la preocupación por la revolución de los roles sexuales es contemporánea a toda una serie de movimientos de liberación homosexual internacionales (liberación de la homosexualidad en una sociedad adversa y liberación de los roles sexuales fijos que la sociedad forma)."[17] The rigid demarcation of the masculine and the feminine contributed, according to the young activists, to a higher value and supremacy of the masculine and also undermined the possibility to explore all those erotic variations that move aside from the established for each of the roles.[18]

For theorists of liberation, sexual roles were organized in an irreducible polarity and included the set of characteristics and attitudes directly derived from biological sexes,[19] in an unappealable continuity that would later be conceptualized by Gayle Rubin as "sex/gender system."[20] Society, and more specifically family, were responsible for reproducing and maintaining rigid unchanging patterns of masculinity and femininity. In a manifesto released in 1969, Carl Wittman said: "We've lived in these institutions all our lives. Naturally we mimic the roles."[21] The idea that these were institutionally promoted and internalized roles were imitated by the subjects is not "natural" had already been developed by Donald West in his book *Homosexuality*,[22] published in 1955: "many of the temperamental characteristics popularly defined as 'masculine' and 'femenine' are the result of cultural training and are not biological sexual distinctions."[23] The liberationists went, however, much further than West, to examine the heterosexual and heteronormative matrix that establishes these distinctions, particularly oppressive in the case of women and homosexuals. If the masculine is associated with action, domination, and strength and the feminine to passivity, submissiveness, and weakness, it is not difficult to understand why women and "feminine" men are inferiorized and socially stigmatized. Altman suggested, therefore, an alliance between women and gays:

> gays and women are oppressed by similar conceptions of masculine and feminine roles, and by the assumption that the nuclear family is the ultimate form of achieving happiness. [...] Each can only benefit from the strength of the other, which is to say that both are concerned to break down the rigidity and narrowness into which sexuality and social roles have been channelled in our society.

Along with recognizing interconnections between roles and sexual behavior in women and gays, Altman analyzed the gender oppression of gays and lesbians in their own specific terms. He considered that the definition heterosexual, by default, of the "feminine" and "masculine" roles had an effect on social consideration and in the gay and lesbian self-image as people who rejected masculinity and femininity respectively. Thus were established the two ends of male homosexual role: "the drag queen who tends to accentuate the image of the homosexual as a man who would be a woman, and the leather type who seeks to overcome it. To a lesser extent comparable stereotypes exist among lesbians."[24]

Guy Hocquenguem's attack of the intelligibility system of sexual roles was based on a sharp critique of psychoanalysis and its "Oedipal imperialism." The activist questioned Sigmund Freud and other psychoanalytic school representatives' heterosexual interpretation of the homosexual world, transposing to this their categories and establishing an irremediable connection between sexual orientation and object of desire. Ferenczi's distinction between "subject homo-erotism," effeminate homosexual that feels as woman and seeks the *macho*, and the "object homo-erotism," the masculine homosexual that seeks an effeminate man, guarantees, for Hocquenghem, "the existence of a microcosmic homosexual world which luckily can be compared point by point with the heterosexual one."[25] According to this logic, the different and the similar operate in contradictory ways, with the sole purpose of reifying heterosexism: the homosexual is *different* but also *similar* to the heterosexual. He has the wrong object, but his behavior around the object is the same. There is, then, no way of acting that escapes heterosexual parameters. However, Hocquenghem indicates, "homosexuality could upset the clarity of this kind of functional subdivision between subject and object, male and female."[26] So, despite the efforts of psychoanalysis, desires, and behaviors of homosexuals surpass hetero binarism and its assumptions about the connection between biological sex, sexual role, and sexual preference.

Also fighting against psychoanalytic presuppositions, Mario Mieli asserted that the reproduction of sexual roles and the inhibition of original bisexuality from all subjects were a result of what he called *educastration*, "the objective [of which] is the transformation of the infant, in tendency polymorphous and 'perverse', into a heterosexual adult, erotically mutilated but conforming to the Norm."[27] Like Altman, the Italian activist found similarities between the situation of women and homosexuals and reclaimed the exploitation of "femininity" by the latter, as a form of rebellion against the inferiority of women and the feminine itself. His analysis called into question the impossible fluidity of roles propelled by sexist thinking. He questioned, for example, the idea that sex between men is a translation of heterosexual intercourse, with the necessary attribution of masculinity to the "top" and femininity to the "bottom." The deconstruction of the top/bottom pairing ran parallel to the masculine/feminine pairing and to all of the oppositions derived from it. Mieli argued for systematic solution of the barriers and restrictions that prevented sexual fulfillment of men and women, homosexuals, and straight people, and gave the name of *transsexuality* to the "polymorphous and 'undifferentiated' erotic disposition in children, which society suppresses and which, in adult life, every human being carries within him either in a latent state or else confined in the depths of the unconscious under the yoke of repression."[28] According to the activist, the *transsexuality*, in the terms in which he conceived it, "overthrows the present separate and counterpoised categories of that sexuality considered 'normal', which it shows up, rather, as a ridiculous constraint."[29]

## Masculinity/Feminity: Opposite Poles in the Argentinean and Spanish Activism Debate

Liberationists fought the pathologisation and psychiatrisation of homosexuals and opposed to various forms of oppression that, according to its main representatives, were originated in patriarchy and its obligatory heterosexuality regime. The need to strengthen community bonds between homosexuals and to unite the demands of this group to other groups, equally oppressed by patriarchal society, mostly women and working class people, is listed as one of the basic goals to achieve sexual and social revolution. According to Dennis Altman, "gay liberation, then, is part of a much wider movement that is challenging the basic cultural norms of our advanced industrial, capitalist, and bureaucratic society and bringing about changes in individual consciousness and new identities and life-styles."[30] At its most radical aspect, the movement promoted not the liberation of the "homosexual," but of "homosexuality." In Mieli's words, "the object of the revolutionary struggle of homosexuals is not that of winning social tolerance for gays, but rather the liberation of the homoerotic desire in every human being."[31]

Liberationists objected, ultimately, the imposition of fixed sexual roles that not only determined the "correct" way to act for heterosexual men and women, but also served to explain and to model the behavior of homosexuals, lesbians, and other sexual transgressive subjects. Although sometimes limited by the same binary logic they were trying to deconstruct, their analysis of "gender roles" had a deep draft and led to a number of important debates, in and out of the liberation movements. Thus, the discussion around the effeminate homosexual, caused divisions between those, like Mieli, who praised his ability to blow up the boundaries of gender and those who, on the contrary, considered him uncomfortable and counterproductive, while obeying the standard norm imposed by chauvinism. Masculinity became a key focus for debate and for the articulated confronted categories between those who acted according to its parameters and those who did not. David Halperin describes thus the division between virile and effeminate styles of performing sex between men and gender roles:

> On one side of the divide are gay-acting men—effeminate or, at least, not 'real' men—who lack the virile credentials that would make them seriously desirable to other gay men. On the other side are straight or straight-acting men, who are able to carry off a butch performance without too much seeming effort but who are nonetheless willing, for whatever reason, to enter into sexual commerce with a queen. Since effeminacy is a turn-off, whereas masculinity is exciting, queens are attracted to trade, but not to each other. So the division between queens and trade involves a whole system of polarized gender styles, gender identities, erotic object and subject positions, sex-roles, sexual practices and sexual subjectivities.[32]

Liberationists faced the challenge of overcoming this dichotomy. In the Spanish and Latin American context this task was, however, very hard, since it had to overcome the obstacle of a macho attitude extended even within the homosexual movement. It was very difficult to reach an agreement on what model of "homosexual," if the "male" or "effeminate," suited to embody and project from political activism.[33]

At that crossroads, Anabitarte and Lorenzo Sanz's texts published in Spain since 1977 are located, what shows the influence of the theorists of liberation to which I have referred to. Both activists say, in fact, that they had read Mario Mieli and Dennis Altman, and that they even hosted the latter in one of their visits to Spain.[34] Interestingly, however, despite having been translated in Argentina, the authors do not mention Guy Hocquehguem among their influences. And yet they put emphasis on the book *Heraclés. Sobre una manera de ser* by Spanish poet and novelist Juan Gil-Albert (1904–1994), written in 1955 and published a mere twenty years later, in 1975. It is an odd reference taking into account that, according to Alberto Mira, this homophile treatise had a very relative impact between Transition homosexuals, who "esperaban (y lo tuvieron) que las ideas se expresaran de manera más contundente."[35] For Anabitarte and Lorenzo Sanz, the reading of Gil-Albert allowed them, in their own words, "reflexionar sobre los orígenes de la homosexualidad en la cultura."[36] In my view, they could have also been influenced by the considerations about masculinity and femininity, a topic that the writer develops extensively in the book. As argued, the effeminate homosexual makes the mistake of distorting itself, "desde el momento en que […] modifica los términos de la ecuación amorosa que le impone su instinto, tratando de parecerse a la mujer [...], se sacrifica a sí mismo, quiere ser lo que no es."[37]

The articles that Anabitarte and Lorenzo spread in Spain are ideologically linked with the publications of the FLH, which they had belonged to. Regarding the specific issue of sexual roles, it should be noted that the article "Homosexualidad y machismo. Análisis desde una perspectiva liberacionista," appeared in the *Ajoblanco* magazine in 1979 and it was also included that same year in the volume *Homosexualidad: el asunto está caliente*, reproduces almost literally the content of the article "Homosexualidad masculina y machismo," published by *Grupo de Profesionales* of the FLH in the only issue of the newspaper *Homosexuales*, in July 1973.[38] Anabitarte does not remember exactly if he was involved in writing the article published in Argentina, but it is evident that he contributed to, or asked the authors for permission to make it public in Spain, signed by himself and Lorenzo Sanz.

This article sustains that the official sexual ethics are based on the overvaluation of what is masculine and the cult of the phallus that places women in an inferior position not only as regards the work arena but also regarding interpersonal relationships. When it is referred to the relations between men, the dominant male chauvinism produces the image of the *loca* or *marica* ("faggot"), the effeminate gay: "Al homosexual no se le otorgan opciones, ya que se los ha condicionado para que su homosexualidad lleve al afeminamiento. No existe, para la cultura machista, el homosexual que conserve su estamento viril."[39] The effeminate homosexuals would assume the feminine role by a system unable to conceive the existence of a "masculine" homosexual: "Ser homosexual para el machista, es ser un varón disfrazado de mujer. La internalización de este modelo, en casos extremos, devasta al homosexual hasta el punto de que su virilidad le resulta incompatible consigo mismo: el 'partenaire' es, entonces, el 'macho', y él, es la 'hembra', con todo lo que, para la cultura oficial, implica de degenerativo esta metamorfosis."[40]

Anabitarte and Lorenzo Sanz endorse, then, that the idea of the *loca* has been introduced by the chauvinist society to have homosexuals assuming the woman's role and feeling guilty for that identification and for their homosexuality. However, the final section of the article transforms significantly the original text published in *Homosexuales*, in which the image of the *loca* is judged in harsh terms:

> Hay homosexuales que han obedecido al esquema machista [...] Entre los que responden al modelo del 'marica' se cuentan los que exageran su afeminamiento, para excitar más fácilmente a los sujetos que les interesan, para los cuales desempeñan el rol de mujeres. Pero esta aberración no tiene nada que ver con la auténtica relación homosexual, que es la relación entre dos individuos del mismo sexo que se identifican con la sexualidad biológica con que cuentan sus cuerpos.[41]

Activists suppressed this paragraph, most likely because of its homophobic tone. Nevertheless, they maintained the idea that homosexuals did not differ in anything from the "normal" man: "se trata de individuos que, después de que biológica y psicológicamente, son varones como cualesquiera otros."[42] The questioning of the masculine and feminine roles within the homosexual relationship has, as a goal, for Anabitarte and Lorenzo Sanz, to debunk the presumption that intermasculine bonds are ruled by the same parameters of those of heterosexual couples. They discuss, in this sense, notions of sexual topness and sexual bottomness and claim a multiplicity of possibilities that go beyond this Manichaean model: "en una auténtica relación sexual, no puede haber 'parte activa' y parte 'pasiva': los dos sujetos -eventualmente, más de dos-, que participan son igualmente activos, hacen algo por el compañero, sea cual fuere su sexo."[43] This defense of the "equality" does not completely hide the quite positive assessment of the masculine performance in the homosexual, and to a certain extent, it contributes to reinforce the stigmatization of the *loca*, who would do nothing else but to mechanically follow a script set by the ruling chauvinism. At this point, Anabitarte and Lorenzo Sanz are closer to Juan Gil-Albert, who rejects effeminacy as a typical trait of the homosexual and affirms, on the other hand, that the masculine homosexual wants to keep being a man because "es característica del hombre el querer ser lo que es."[44]

The image of the *loca* had caused differences within the FLH: the article reproduced by Anabitarte and Lorenzo Sanz precisely originated, according to Rapisardi, "un fuerte debate interno por el cual gran cantidad de activistas del FLH se negaron a repartir el periódico."[45] It should be borne in mind that the FLH was formed by groups of heterogeneous ideological stances. With the incorporation of Néstor Perlongher as their leader of the group "Eros" in 1972, the confrontation between the more moderate faction, to which Anabitarte belonged to, and the more radical one encouraged by Perlongher, deepened.[46] In an interview published in 1974 in *Panorama* magazine, a member of the FLH asserted: "para nosotros, el homosexual escapa tanto del papel masculino como del femenino. [...] [El homosexual afeminado] demuestra la artificialidad de los papeles, que tanto uno como otro son inventos de la cultura. [...] De allí se desprende el color revolucionario que nosotros damos al *marica*."[47] This was exactly Perlongher's position, for whom exaggerating effeminacy did not constitute a mere internalization of the chauvinist oppression but a development that blurs and generates debate regarding the boundaries between what is masculine and feminine.[48] In his analysis of the development of the FLH, Jung Ha Kang and Emilio Bernini assert that *Somos*, the publication subsequent to *Homosexuales*, articulated an "apología de la loca, contraria al modelo *gay* [...] En la loca hay un germen revolucionario que subvierte todos los órdenes."[49]

It becomes evident that when spreading in Spain (around 1979) an article by the FLH whose postulates had been contested within the movement over those years, Anabitarte and Lorenzo Sanz continued keeping certain objections towards the image of the *loca*. Another article called "Los roles sexuales. La mutilación" from the book *Homosexualidad: el asunto está caliente* confirmed it by stating:

> [Los homosexuales] imposibilitados de identificarse con los varones, expulsados luego del mundo masculino de la manera más cruel, tratarán de asumir el rol femenino. En principio aparecerá el modelo de la madre, puro e inmaculado [...], pero pronto serán expulsados, de este otro mundo 'normal y decente'; sucesivamente expulsados, arrojados al territorio del pecado y del delito [...]. No les queda otro camino que asumir de manera grotesca, agresiva, patética, el papel de la mujer fatal, despreciada y codiciada. Se convierte en una *loca*.[50]

This analysis of the effeminate homosexual, in which it is tacitly proposed as more desirable masculine performance, should be understood in the framework of the proper discussions to the Spanish activism. That is to say, the members of the FLH in Argentina assumed opposing positions as regards the question of the *loca*. The same occurred in Spain. Alberto Mira explains that the reticence that the *loca* provokes among the Spanish activists was intensified in the late 1970s, when his presence in demonstrations, together with transvestites, was considered by some members of the group as negative publicity, in the sense that it displayed a distorted image of homosexuality: "El presupuesto de textos militantes [...] es que con la supresión de las leyes homófobas llegaría necesariamente un cambio de mentalidades total que dejaría obsoletos los viejos estereotipos. La loca era producto de la represión y desaparecería con ella."[51] Mira observes that the dilemma between the "masculine" and "feminine" ways of living homosexuality becomes false because it rests on an essentialist vision of gender, and he alludes to Judith Butler's proposition that not only the masculine but also the feminine are constructed imitations in the symbolic, no matter whether it is in men or women. Masculinity, in this sense, would not be essential to men and the horror to effeminacy would constitute only a sign of misogynistic devaluation of everything that reproduces the feminine. However, the Spanish activists—the same as the Argentinian ones—were far from being in a position to think in those terms. Moreover, the debates in which they were involved show the tension unleashed from the conceptions of masculine and feminine as attributes proper to "man" and "woman." The articles by Anabitarte and Lorenzo Sanz commented upon up to this point show a forceful denunciation of "the dictatorship of the sexual roles," but they cannot avoid completely misogynist and homophobic attitudes deeply rooted since the devaluation of the *loca* goes hand in hand with the devaluation of "women."

However, other texts by the activists address the issue from a different viewpoint. I refer, in particular, to the article "Homenaje a las Divinas," published by Anabitarte and Lorenzo Sanz in the anarchist magazine *Bicicleta* in 1981, and to the book by Anabitarte *Estrechamente vigilados por la locura*, from the same year. The article constitutes, as the title suggests, a homage to the *divinas* ("divines"), that is to say, to the *locas*, who were widely credited to have made homosexuality visible when it remained marginalized (and auto-marginalized) by "la civilización hetero-monogámica-patriarcal."[52] According to Richard Cleminson, the text presents the *divina* as a mythical category of the homosexual and it has a humorous tone "que se podría tildar de 'camp'."[53] Certainly, from the stylistic point of view, the article contrasts with other works by the authors; it could be affirmed that it distinguishes from those because of its "literariness." Anabitarte and Lorenzo Sanz draw here a genealogy of the *locas* as disturbing images of the established moral canons. They highlight that it was them who "con un gesto teatral, espectacular, falso, corrieron el cerrojo, el oxidado cerrojo, que permitió a la homosexualidad escapar de su estrecha celda, [...] para coger la calle por los cuatro costados y hacer en ella su catedral."[54] As the emphasis is placed in the "theatricality" of the *divinas*, in the made up temperament of their personality, they express a proximity with the idea of the performativity of gender exposed by Butler. The acceptance of "femininity" on part of the homosexuals is not conceived as a mechanical response of "women" but as an extreme reaction towards heterosexism:

> El deseo homosexual es la representación más exacerbada, pura, nítida, de la heterosexualidad. Es la pasión de la hembra, hembra femenina, por un hombre, por un hombre muy macho (Manuel Puig y su araña andan por estos renglones).
>
> Y [en] esa representación, en donde el Falo es el único punto válido de la relación, el macho es todo Falo, y entonces Las Divinas son las hembras que 'asumen complacidas la castración', y la afirmación del primero y la negación de los segundos, pone en crisis el esquema tradicional. Todo es una representación voluntaria. Se puede elegir ser muy macho, o ser muy hembra.[55]

It can be clearly appreciated that "masculinity" does not constitute for Anabitarte and Lorenzo Sanz the most desirable pole of the homosexual representation. Even though the "feminine" and "masculine" performances can be chosen voluntarily, it becomes questionable from the current theories about gender,[56] this article heads in the performativity direction when it defends "the exaggeration of effeminacy" as a subversive performance and it moves his protagonists from the abject spaces in which they were placed by diverse discourses, including the ones upheld by some homosexual activists.[57] The reference to the novel *El beso de la mujer araña* by Manuel Puig (1976) becomes, in this context, fully justified: its protagonist, Molina, is precisely a *divina* to whom the authors pay homage. A homosexual who refers to himself as a woman and who only establishes relationships with "heterosexual men," although that hierarchical model is questioned and deconstructed throughout the novel.[58]

Another playful and advocative vision of the *loca* can be found in the book *Estrechamente vigilados por la locura* by Anabitarte. It is a collection of memoirs and reflections about his personal life and his political activity in Argentina and in Spain.[59] Many of the stories included in that volume are based on *divina*'s lives, and they offer valuable testimonies of these unique and unclassifiable persons. As an example, I quote an extract of the passage referring to "la Cuca":

> Un día un chongo quiso robarle y la Cuca le dio una soberana paliza: Robarme a mí, que soy tan buena con los chongos. La Cuca una vez, en su pueblo, había visto a Evita y le había pedido una muñeca. Evita le dijo que era un muchacho y le dio una pelota. La Cuca se casó y tuvo un hijo, pero años después, contando su mitológica vida, decía: Evita era un travestí, y esto lo autorizaba a lanzarse de lleno en la homosexualidad.[60]

These hilarious stories of faggots who defied the public morality and made homosexuality visible in spite of the serious risks implied, demonstrate an attitude of acknowledgement by Anabitarte. Therefore, this article written by Anabitarte and Lorenzo Sanz will be set out as "homage," a way to assert those who put homosexuality in the public sphere and questioned the rigid polarity between the "masculine" and the "feminine." This was a look, definitely, far from what in other articles was suggested, implicitly, that is the convenience of "masculinity." If the new generation of homosexuals, in Anabitarte's words, "se identifica menos con lo femenino,"[61] the texts that I have already commented pay the debt we owe to the "faggots from the past," prior not only to the masculine gay identity but also to any attempt at classifying the sexual identities as stable and definite.[62]

As we have seen, the Latin American homosexual activism held diverging opinions about the question of "masculinity" and "femininity." The texts by Anabitarte and Lorenzo Sanz enter this discussion in a significant way since they offer opposing opinions and even, to a certain extent, contradictory: whereas some of their works propose the masculine performance as more appropriate for the homosexual man, in some others they recognize the revolutionary value of the *locas*, who call into question this same postulate. It should be noted that in Spain, as Guasch explains, homosexuals stood up for, initially, the right to be effeminate, to be a *loca*, and only after that, during the 1980s, the virile model, which had already been consolidated in America and some other European countries, was widely disseminated.[63] In Argentina, on the other hand, being a faggot generated controversy: among other factors, it was decisive the fact that the military coup (1976–1983) took place and for that reason many individuals opted for a "masculine" behavior, so as not to be identified as homosexuals.[64] And they would question, in turn, those who openly performed their femininity. There would be the likelihood, then, that the apparently antagonistic positions presented by Anabitarte and Lorenzo Sanz in their texts, are, in fact, complementary, in harmony with some contexts—the Argentinian and the Spanish one—where the "liberation" of the homosexuals not only became subject to hostility and external stereotypes but also the tensions and internal differences within the group.

## Notes

1 The emergence of gay liberation movements on a global scale has been extensively discussed in the volume edited by Adam, Duyvendak & Kreuwel (1999), which contains articles on Canada, the U.S., Brazil, Argentina, UK, Germany, France, Spain, Romania, Hungary & Czech Republic, South Africa, Japan, and Australia. See also Beatriz Preciado's article. This chapter was conducted as part of the research project entitled "Representaciones culturales de las sexualidades marginadas en España (1970–1995)" ["Cultural representations of marginalized sexualities in Spain (1970–1995)"], FEM2011—24064, funded by the Spanish Ministerio de Economía y Competitividad.

2 Gide, *Corydon*, 200–201. For an analysis of the rhetoric of the two types of homosexual that this book addresses, see Mira (*De Sodoma a Chueca*, 208–216).

3 See, for example, the film reviews by Abel Arana and Diego Trerotola's.

4 See the interview with Anabitarte in Fluvià 147–150; a newspaper note from the same author in which he reconstructs his trajectory as an activist (Anabitarte, "Confesiones" and Modarelli), focused on Anabitarte and Lorenzo's activist work.

5 On police persecution to homosexuals, see Bazán.

6 According to Stephen Brown, "the Grupo Nuestro Mundo was founded in November 1969, while Argentina was under a militaty dictatorship. Although informal gay and lesbian social groups had previously existed, this was the first gay political organization in Argentina—and, in fact, in Latin America" (Brown 111). On the history of the homosexual movement in Argentina see Perlongher's work ("Historia"), Rapisardi and Modarelli (140–211) and Bazán (293–342).

7 Bazán 299–300.

8 Anabitarte quoted in Rapisardi and Modarelli 143: "The group did not have anything to do either with the May 1968 events in France or with the gay movement in The United States. In any case, we kept correspondence with Spanish people, who lived in fear due to the *Ley de Peligrosidad Social* ("Law of Social Dangerousness and Social Rehabilitation") of Franco's regime, which included homosexuals." The activist also refers to the link with Spain in an interview (Fluvià 148).

9 On publications by the FLH, see the work by Vespucci and Moscoso.

10 Anabitarte, personal interview, 2013: "In Madrid Ricardo and I joined a gay group and when we moved to Barcelona (1979) we joined Lambda and the Catalan gay movement. These organizations are the most pioneering in Spain. We were intimate with Armand [de Fluvià]."

11 For an analysis of the presence of the homosexual issue in the alternative press of the Transition see Cleminson.

12 I have included in the references Anabitarte and Lorenzo Sanz's articles which are most linked with the subject analyzed here.

13 Mérida Jiménez 9: "The events in Stonewall constitute an event that can be considered to be a symbol of the struggle for civil sexual rights in western societies."

14 It also should be kept in mind that gay liberation could articulate itself and gain space in the public sphere because it joined the opposition space opened by other contemporary struggles, including those lead by women, black people, students, and people opposed to the Vietnam War. For a detailed analysis of the relationship between the gay liberation movement and the black and women movements, see Altman (197–236).

15 Altman's book was not translated into Spanish although some of his ideas were spread by Manuel Puig in the footnotes of his novel *El beso de la mujer araña* , published in 1976. The English version was reprinted in 1993 with a prologue by Jeffrey Weeks and an epilogue by Altman. Guy Hocquenguem's book was translated into Spanish for the first time in Argentina in 1974 with the title *Homosexualidad y sociedad represiva.* A second translation appeared in 2009 in Spain with an introduction by René Schérer and a short study by Beatriz Preciado entitled "Terror anal. Apuntes sobre los primeros días de la revolución sexual." Mario Mieli's book was translated into Spanish in 1979 and into English in 1980. There is also an Italian re-edition from 2002.

16 Regarding the periodic publications related to the liberationist movement, it should be noted, among many others, *Gay Sunshine Journal* and *Come Out!* (USA), *Lambda. Giornale di controcultura del movimento gay* (Italy), *Aghois* (Spain) *Somos* (Argentina), and *Lampião* (Brazil). An important selection of gay and lesbian manifestos elaborated in the United States were collected by Mérida Jiménez in an anthology published in 2009; for the rest of the countries this type of material is difficult to access. In the case of Argentina, a manifesto entitled "Sexo y Revolución" exists, spread by the *Frente de Liberación Homosexual* in 1973 and its reproduction currently circulates on the Internet.

17 Ha Kang and Bernini 74: "The concern about the revolution of sexual roles is contemporary to a whole series of international gay liberation movements (liberation of homosexuality in an adverse society and liberation of the fixed sexual roles that society forms)."

18 The influence of the new psychoanalytic interpretations by Herbert Marcuse and Norman Brown is seen in these proposals, which find in Sigmund Freud's "polymorphous perversity" the key of a new universe of pleasures and relations where the strong barriers that determine how man and women should be and which sexual practices are more or less adequate to them do not intervene (Altman 80–116, Mieli 22–31).

19 José Amícola explains that the English term *gender* "viene a suplantar en castellano al giro no crítico y menos abarcador de 'rol sexual'. Se trata, en cambio, de un término implantado por las feministas norteamericanas que implica una postura vigilante frente a la ideología que cada asignación sexual lleva consigo. [...] El concepto acentúa la dimensión relacional e histórica que no estaba suficientemente presente en el giro de 'rol sexual'" (Amícola 92). "Comes to take the place in Spanish of the non-critical shift and less inclusive of 'sexual role'. It is a term, on the other hand, used by the North American feminists that implies a vigilant position opposite to the ideology that every sexual assignment has within it. The concept accentuates the relational and historical dimension that was not sufficiently present in the term 'sexual role'."

20 Rubin 33–66.

21 Wittman n. p.

22 West's book was, according to Altman, "a major survey of the psychological literature" about homosexuality (Altman 69), that in some aspects departed from the general vision of the homosexual as "deviant" and emphasized his social disadvantages. Manuel Puig used some of the arguments developed by West in his novel "Kiss of the Spider Woman." Puig published *El beso de la mujer araña* in 1976.

23 West 59.

24 Altman 91.

25 Hocquenghem 125.

26 *Ibid.* 122.

27 Mieli 24.

28 *Ibid.* 25.

29 *Ibid.* 28.

30 Altman 244.

31 Mieli 82.
32 Halperin 205.
33 See Calvo's chapter in this volume.
34 Anabitarte and Lorenzo Sanz, personal interview, 2013.
35 Mira 382. "Hoped (and had to) that ideas were expressed more bluntly."
36 Anabitarte and Lorenzo Sanz, personal interview, 2013: "To reflect on the origins of homosexuality in culture."
37 Gil-Albert 91: "From the moment that the homosexual modifies the terms of the loving equation that his instinct imposes upon him, trying to look like women [...] he sacrifices himself and wants to be what he is not."
38 An English translation from this text appeared in 1974 in the magazine *Gay Sunshine*, edited by Winston Leyland.
39 Grupo de Profesionales del FLH argentino 3: "The homosexuals were not granted options since they have been conditioned to take their homosexuality to effeminacy. I doesn't exist, for the chauvinist culture, the homosexual which preserves his virile establishment."
40 *Ibid.* 3: "For a chauvinist person, being a homosexual means to be a man disguised as a woman. In extreme cases, the internalization of this model devastates the homosexual, to the point that his manhood is incompatible to himself. Thus, the 'partner' is 'male' and he is 'female', with all the degenerative metamorphosis that implies for the official culture."
41 *Ibid.* 3: "There are homosexuals who have obeyed the chauvinist scheme [...] Among who respond to the model of 'fagot' are those who exaggerate their effeminacy, to arouse more easily the subjects they are interested in, and for whom they play the role of a women . But this aberration has nothing to do with a genuine homosexual relationship, which is the relationship between two individuals of the same sex who identify themselves with the biological sex their bodies have."
42 Anabitarte and Lorenzo Sanz, *Homosexualidad*, 61: "It is about individuals who biological and psychologically are men as any other."
43 *Ibid.* 61: "In an authentic sexual intercourse, there cannot be an 'active part' and a 'passive part': two persons–eventually, more than two—who take part in it are both equally active, doing something for their partner, no matter his/her sex."
44 Gil-Albert 93: "It is characteristic of men that want to be what they are."
45 Rapisardi 982: "[After] a strong internal debate, a great number of activists from the FLH refused to distribute the pamphlet."
46 According to Néstor Perlongher, "en lo organizativo, el FLH se definía como una alianza de grupos autónomos, que coordinaban acciones comunes entre sí. En el momento de apogeo (setiembre 72–agosto 73) el movimiento llegó a contar con alrededor de diez de tales grupos, constituido por unos diez militantes y una buena cohorte de simpatizantes cada uno. Los más importantes eran: Eros, Nuestro Mundo, Profesionales, Safo (formado por lesbianas), Bandera Negra (anarquistas), Emanuel (cristianos), Católicos homosexuales argentinos, etc." (Perlongher, "Historia del Frente," 79). "Organizationally, the FLH defined itself as an alliance of autonomous groups who coordinated joint actions together. In the heyday (September 1972–August 1973) the movement reached ten groups, having each one around ten militants and an entourage of supporters. The most important were: Eros, Our World, Professionals, Sappho (formed by lesbians), Black Flag (Anarchists), Emanuel (Christians), Argentine Catholic Homosexuals, etc."
47 Quoted in Acevedo 56: "For us, the homosexual escapes from both male and female role. [...] [The effeminate homosexual] demonstrates the artificiality of the roles, both of them are cultural inventions. [...] Hence it follows the revolutionary color we give to the 'fag'."
48 During the 1980s, Perlongher harshly criticized the assimilationist—and masculine—policies of the gay model, which increasingly started to enter the daily life in the Río de

la Plata region. In a well-known article called "La desaparición de la homosexualidad," published originally in 1991, the sociologist laments the negative effects of the institutionalization of gayness, that in his opinion, put down the revolutionary impulse that have characterized the homosexuals, mainly the faggots, since the 1970s (Perlongher, "La desaparición," 89).

49 Ha Kang and Bernini 72: "Apology for the queen model, contrary to the gay model [...] there is a revolutionary seed in 'queens' that subverts all social orders."

50 Anabitarte and Lorenzo Sanz, *Homosexualidad*, 66: "[Homosexuals], unable to identify themselves with a male figure, and expelled from the masculine world in the most cruel way, they will try to assume a female role. In the beginning, the mother model, pure and immaculate [...] will be the first to appear, but they will soon be expelled from this other 'normal and decent' world; successively expelled, thrown into the territory of sin and crime [...]. They have no other way but to assume, in a grotesque, aggressive, pathetic way, the role of the femme fatale, despised and coveted. They become fags."

51 Mira 436: "The presupposition in the militant texts [...] is that with the suppression of homophobic laws a total change in the way of thinking, that would leave obsolete stereotypes aside, would necessarily come. The faggot was a product of repression and he would disappear with it."

52 Lorenzo Sanz and Anabitarte Rivas, "Homenaje," 28: "Hetero-monogamic patriarchal civilization."

53 Cleminson 70: "That it could be called 'camp'."

54 Lorenzo Sanz and Anabitarte Rivas, "Homenaje," 28: "With a theatrical, spectacular, and false gesture they unlocked the lock, the rusted lock, and let homosexuality escape from its narrow cell, [...] to take it to the streets and build their cathedral there."

55 Lorenzo Sanz and Anabitarte Rivas, "Homenaje," 29: "Homosexual desire is the more exacerbated, pure, clear representation of heterosexuality. It is the passion of the female, the feminine female for a man, a very macho man (Manuel Puig and his spider walk these lines). And [in] this representation, where the Phallus is the only valid point in the relationship, the male is all Phallus, and then The Divines are females 'assuming castration pleased' and the assertion of the first and the denial of the seconds puts a strain on the traditional scheme. Everything is a voluntary representation. You can choose to be very male or a very female."

56 Butler holds that "if gender is a king of doing, an incessant activity performed, in part, without one's knowing and without one's willing, it is not for that reason automatic or mechanical. On the contrary, it is a practice of improvisation within a scene of constraint" (Butler 1).

57 He adds a note where an antithetical positioning to the one of some Spanish gays, as in the case of Alberto Cardín in "¿Quiénes son las divinas?," published in the newspaper Asturias on 15 February 1979, is alleged.

58 Echavarren 53. He makes reference to the "faggot" and introduces the character from the novel by Puig as a literary paradigmatic example.

59 Also in an unpublished novel by Lorenzo Sanz, called *Bienvenidos a Sodoma*, a "faggot" would be the protagonist as it is seen in a fragment of this work quoted by Anabitarte ("La situación de las dictaduras," 237).

60 Anabitarte, *Estrechamente*, 119: "One day a *chongo* wanted to steal her, and La Cuca gave him a severe beaten: Steal me, that I am so good with the *chongos*. Once in his hometown, La Cuca saw Evita [Eva Perón] and she had asked her a doll. Evita said he was a boy and gave him a ball. The Cuca got married and had a child, but years later, telling his mythological life, said: Evita was a transvestite, and this entitled her to jump right into homosexuality." *Chongo* was the term used to define heterosexual, masculine man, who occasionally had sex with effeminate homosexuals. (Sebreli 350–352).

61 *Ibid.* 128: “[They] identified less with the feminine.”

62 According to Joaquín Insausti, it would be erroneous to interpret the “faggot” from current theories regarding sex-gender identity: “gays y travestis son formas de vida planteadas identitariamente como inequívocas, la loca ‘es’ equívoca, habla a veces en femenino y otras en masculino, es hombre y es mujer y a veces no es ninguna de las dos cosas, no quiere cambiar su cuerpo pero lo cambia a través de gestos, de vestimentas, lo que la vuelve inaprensible desde la lógica identitaria gay o travesti” (Insausti 7). “Gays and transvestites are identitarian lifestyles raised as unambiguous; a queer ‘is’ ambiguous, sometimes speaking in feminine, sometimes in masculine, [a queer] is a man and is a woman, and sometimes neither of them, [queers] do not want to change their bodyies but they change them through gestures and clothes, what makes them incomprehensible from the gay or transvestite identity logic.”

63 Guasch 79.

64 As regards this point, Anabitarte and Lorenzo Sanz declare: “No tenemos que olvidar que en Argentina éramos clandestinos y teníamos que intentar no llamar la atención” (Anabitarte and Lorenzo Sanz, personal interview, 2013). “Keep in mind that in Argentina we were illegal and we had to try not to attract attention.”

## Bibliography

Acevedo, Zelmar. *Homosexualidad: hacia la destrucción de los mitos.* Buenos Aires: Del Ser, 1985. Print.

Adam, Barry, Jan W. Duyvendak, and André Krouwel. Ed. *The Global Emergency of Lesbian and Gay Politics. National Imprints of a Worldwide Movement.* Philadelphia: Temple University Press, 1999. Print.

Altman, Dennis. *Homosexual: Oppression and Liberation.* 1993 ed. New York: New York UP, 1971. Print.

Anabitarte Rivas, Héctor. *Estrechamente vigilados por la locura.* Madrid: Hacer, 1981. Print.

———. “La situación de las dictaduras argentinas y España.” *Una discriminación universal. La homosexualidad bajo el franquismo y la Transición.* Ed. Javier Ugarte Pérez. Barcelona: Egales, 2008. 225–245. Print.

———. “Confesiones de un militante homosexual y comunista.” *Clarín* Feb. 2012: n. p. Web. 25 Sep. 2013. <http://goo.gl/9kYtl9>.

——— and Ricardo Lorenzo Sanz. *Homosexualidad: el asunto está caliente.* Madrid: Queimada, 1979. Print.

Amícola, José. *Camp y posvanguardia. Manifestaciones culturales de un siglo fenecido.* Buenos Aires: Paidós, 2000. Print.

Arana, Abel. “Los amantes pasajeros: Bienvenido a casa, Pedro.” *La columna de Abel Arana.* Mar. 2013: n. p. Web. 09 May. 2013. <http://goo.gl/dHoZOR>.

Bazán, Osvaldo. *Historia de la homosexualidad en Argentina. De la Conquista de América al siglo XXI.* 2006 ed. Buenos Aires: Marea, 2004. Print.

Brown, Stephen. “Democracy and Sexual Difference. The Lesbian and Gay Movement in Argentina.” *The Global Emergence of Gay and Lesbian Politics. National Imprints of a Worldwide Movement.* Ed. Barry Adam, Jan W. Duyvendak, and André Krouvel. Philadelphia: Temple UP, 1999. 110–132. Print.

Butler, Judith. *Undoing Gender.* New York: Routledge, 2004. Print.

Cleminson, Richard. “La prensa alternativa durante la Transición y la recepción de la cuestión ‘homosexual’: un estudio de *El Viejo Topo* y *Ajoblanco.*” *Minorías sexuales en España (1970–1995). Textos y representaciones.* Ed. Rafael M. Mérida Jiménez. Barcelona: Icaria, 2013. 67–88. Print.

Echavarren, Roberto. *Arte andrógino. Estilo versus moda en un siglo corto*. Buenos Aires: Colihue, 1998. Print.

Fluvià, Armand de. *El moviment gai a la clandestinitat del franquisme (1970–1975)*. Barcelona: Laertes, 2003. Print.

Gil-Albert, Juan. *Heraclés. Sobre una manera de ser*. 1987 ed. Madrid: Akal, 1975. Print.

Grupo de profesionales del FLH argentino. "Homosexualidad masculina y machismo." *Homosexuales* 1 (July 1973): 3. Print.

Guasch, Óscar. *La sociedad rosa*. Barcelona: Anagrama, 1991. Print.

Ha Kang, Jung and Emilio Bernini. "Por qué seremos tan hermosas. Frente de Liberación Homosexual: una política del loqueo." *El Ojo Mocho. Revista de Crítica Cultural* 11 (1997): 70–74. Print.

Halperin, David. *How to Be Gay*. Cambridge, Mass.: Belknap Harvard UP, 2012. Print.

Hocquenghem, Guy. *Homosexual Desire*. 1993 ed. Trans. Daniella Dangoor. Durham: Duke UP, 1972. Print.

Insausti, Joaquín. "Apuntes para un análisis genealógico de las identidades genéricas y sexuales." *IV Jornadas de Jóvenes Investigadores/IIGG*. (2007): n. p. Web. 21 Sep. 2013. <http://goo.gl/gJdYfC>.

Lorenzo Sanz, Ricardo and Héctor Anabitarte Rivas. "Homenaje a las divinas." *Bicicleta. Revista de Comunicaciones Libertarias* 38 (1981): 28–29. Print.

———. *Sida: el asunto está que arde*. Madrid: Revolución, 1987. Print.

Mérida Jiménez, Rafael M. Ed. *Manifiestos gays, lesbianos y queer. Testimonios de una lucha (1969–1994)*. Barcelona: Icaria, 2009. Print.

Mieli, Mario. *Homosexuality and Liberation: Elements of a Gay Critique*. 1980 ed. Trans. David Fernbach. London: Gay Men's P, 1977. Print.

Mira, Alberto. *De Sodoma a Chueca. Una historia cultural de la homosexualidad en España en el siglo XX*. Barcelona: Egales, 2004. Print.

Modarelli, Alejandro. "Íntimas escenas del horror." *Suplemento Soy* Mar. (2012): n. p. Web. 05 Sep. 2013. <http://goo.gl/k3c8HR>.

Moscoso Cadavid, Javier. "De Somos a Soy. Fragmentos de representaciones de la homosexualidad masculina en los medios gráficos desde los 70' hasta la actualidad." 2011. TS.

Perlongher, Néstor. "Historia del Frente de Liberación Homosexual." *Prosa plebeya: Ensayos 1980–1992*. Buenos Aires: Colihue, 2008. 77–84. Print.

———. "La desaparición de la homosexualidad." *Prosa plebeya: Ensayos 1980–1992*, 85–91. Buenos Aires: Colihue, 2008. N. p. Print.

Preciado, Beatriz. "Terror anal: apuntes sobre los primeros días de la revolución sexual." *El deseo homosexual*. Guy Hocquenghem. Trans. Geoffroy Huard de la Marre. Barcelona: Melusina, 2009. 135–174. Print.

Puig, Manuel. *El beso de la mujer araña*. 1976 ed. José Amícola & Jorge Panesi. Nanterre: Archivos de las literaturas latinoamericanas, del Caribe y africanas, 2002. Print.

Rapisardi, Flavio and Alejandro Modarelli. *Fiestas, baños y exilios. Los gays porteños en la última dictadura*. Buenos Aires: Sudamericana, 2001. Print.

Rubin, Gayle. "The Traffic on Women. Notes on the Political Economy of Sex." *Deviations. A Gayle Rubin Reader*. Durham: Duke UP, 2011. 33–66. Print.

Sebreli, Juan José. "Historia secreta de los homosexuales en Buenos Aires." *Escritos sobre escritos, ciudades bajo ciudades*. Buenos Aires: Sudamericana, 1997. 275–370. Print.

Trerotola, Diego. "Gracias por volar torcido." *Suplemento Soy* Aug. (2013): n. p. Web. 12 Sep. 2013. <http://goo.gl/BMZUE7>.

Vespucci, Guido. "Explorando un intrincado triángulo conceptual: *homosexualidad, familia* y *liberación* en los discursos del Frente de Liberación Homosexual de Argentina (FLH, 1971–1976)." *Historia Crítica* 43 (2010): 174–197. Print.

West, D. J. *Homosexuality*. 1974 ed. Harmondsworth: Penguin Books, 1955. Print.
Wittman, Carl. “Refugees of Amerika: a Gay Manifesto.” *Gay Homeland Foundation*. 1969. (2013): n. p. Web. 15 Sep. 2013. <http://goo.gl/Ob5Lpy>.

# CHAPTER 9

## Demasculinizing: Challenging Hegemonic Masculinity in Spanish Art and Culture

Juan Vicente Aliaga
*Universitat Politècnica de València*

This chapter explores the group of cultural movements (musical, photographic, pictorial, performative...) that were born in Spain from the end of Francoism and the establishment of the democracy—the historical period known as the Transition.[1] The identification and the analysis of these esthetics and political experiences allow consideration of the changes Spanish society experienced regarding the gender rules and codes as well as, and especially, the dominant masculinity. This predominant situation spread not only through the patriarchal hierarchy within family life, where women and the feminine were underestimated, but also through a diverse group of power mechanisms and gender technologies: the presence of the police and the army, the impact of sports (especially soccer players), film stars, television and music.

For those who had different sexual desires from the heterosexual ones, and who did not behave according to the rules of the Spanish macho, 1970 was a decisive year. Five years before Dictator Francisco Franco's death, the *Ley de Peligrosidad y Rehabilitación Social* ("Law of Social Dangerousness and Social Rehabilitation") was passed. That was a time of clear repressive atmosphere whose aim was to end up with the progressive resistance, a ressistance which during a long time struggled in order to express its urge of freedom. In that climate, the law chased to accentuate the principles of a former law—the 1954 Vagrancy Act, following the one passed in 1933, known as *La Gandula*[2] ("The Lazy"). It is true that during that period, homosexuals were not identified as questionable subjects, although in the 1954 Act, homosexuals were added onto the list. These individuals could be taken to work camps; they also were forced to reside in specific places having to declare their home addresses, in addition to being kept under surveillance. What did the Law of Social Dangerousness and Social Rehabilitation add? Besides the prison sentence—up to five-year internments—the objective of the new law was to deal with the prisoners considered dangerous. However, reality was very different. The case of Antonio Gutiérrez Dorado who was in the Modelo Barcelona prison, is an example: "Aunque justificada como una norma cuya meta era la reeducación del peligroso social, en la Modelo ni siquiera se cumplió el trámite de que reconociera un médico para diagnosticar su caso—de acuerdo con los elaborados esquemas clasificatorios de los diferentes tipos de homosexualidad que se pusieron de moda a finales de los años sesenta—y proponer la curación correspondiente"[3] (Arnalte 13).

This quote recalls the existing literature with a denigrating and homophobic basis, handled by some jurists and some medical sectors, that also abounds in a delirious classification about the assumed different typologies of homosexuality. The main cut was based on the anal intercourse symbolism and the role performed in that coitus—that is, the distinction between tops and bottoms. That is the reason why, in the enforcement of the law, different spaces were habilitated: the prison in Huelva was the place for those who were the assumed men—being tops—and the jail in Badajoz was the spot for the men who "acted" as women as they were the bottoms. It did not take into account the versatile or those who did not have anal intercourse, among many other variations of sexuality among biological men. Both sodomitic behaviours were punished and the Francoist way rejected both in order to make real men from the prisoners. That is, heterosexual men with an irreproachable masculinity.

I would like now to bring up a valuable testimony of Rampova, who was committed to prison different times. The first time he was fourteen-years-old and he was jailed "por ser maricón" ("for being a fag"), as the police officers who arrested him in València told me. Rampova, whose work as a member of Ploma 2 I will refer to later on, is a comrade of the *Asociación Ex Presos Sociales* ("Former Social Prisoners Association"): "En la prisión de Barcelona me enviaron a un pabellón de invertidos para menores. Los presos pagaban a los vigilantes para colarse y violarnos. Luego nos pegaban palizas para demostrar que ellos no eran gays. Venían cinco, seis veces al día. A veces hasta ocho. [...] He tenido más violaciones que relaciones consentidas"[4] (Junquera n. pag.). This piercing testimony from 2006 proves that hegemonic masculinity was built and exposed in the public shared sphere through homophobic blows and other attacks. In confined spaces, as in a prison, power relationships are transferred and expressed through body language, oral communication, and the permanent demonstration of manhood. A weak man is equal to a feminine subject, someone who resigns to the virile man, a non-entire individual who is less man and, from there, that strength must prevail especially through blows, kicks, and beatings. However, these violent practices do not prevent the existence of the desire or the liberation of the sexual tensions; that is brutally shown in the example given above. In short, the non-consensual sexual relations, the rape of a young body—denigrated when it is publically interpellated as a queer body,[5] a fag body who in his passivity, is turned into a feminine, penetrable, and usable body.[6] How many of those rapists would have a heterosexual life according to the regulation and heterosexist respectability? To whom do those prisoners have to show they were not gays?

The answer points to the others, to the cell or pavilion mates but not to themselves, or does it? It is in the shared space where any track or suspicion of homosexuality—therefore, effeminacy as it is an offense for masculinity—cannot be found. It is, moreover, in the context of confinement where individuality and privacy do not count or it is much diminished. It is important to wonder—extramural, in the city, in the countryside, and in the collective imaginary of the citizenship who could not act freely due to obvious political reasons—which visions prevailed over the hegemonic masculinity in the 1970s and who represented the antinomy of that masculinity.

In a strongly hierarchized patriarchal society as is the Spanish one, the masculine power was especially represented by the different stratums: the army, *La Guardia Civil* ("The Civil Guard"), the riot police officers... Besides, in a country that was increasingly influenced by the media and in contact with tourists,[7] other images of the normative masculinity (fit, decisive, and determined men) emerged. Sport was the place that shaped bodies and minds such as the soccer players Johan Cruyff, Ulrich Stielike, and Pirri (whose standard family life—married to Sonia Bruno and had two kids—was frequently featured on magazines such as *Semana*, *Lecturas*, and *Hola*) or the boxer José Manuel Urtain (boxing was fashionable during the 1970s). The roles played by Hollywood actors (tough men such as Al Pacino, Clint Eastwood, Robert Redford or Robert de Niro) introduced the ideal of masculinity, which was also spread by magazines and television. In Spanish cinema and television, bandits, rogues, and seductive characters thrived: Sancho Gracia, Juan Luis Galiardo, José Luis López Vázquez, José Sacristán...[8] After Franco's death, the development of the phenomenon named as the *destape* ("The Reveal") brought old-fashioned and male chauvinist films through actors as José Sazatornil ("Saza"), Antonio Ozores or Alfredo Landa.[9]

Nevertheless, media contributed enormously to promote the disdain towards homosexuals and transsexuals—and, paradoxically, it encouraged its visibility at the same time.[10] They were presented as degenerated and perverted individuals, who usually were turned into transvestites, in a permanent party, made up as women with inmoral life and, therefore, effeminate: the anti-manliness. The publication of the magazine *Party*,[11] in the mid-1970s, helped someway as a counterweight to magazines that were more conservative. In the following decades, despite the AIDS blow and the negative burden that entailed the political and media use of the pandemic, other publications came out with a more open orientation (*Mensual*, *Entiendes*, *Zero*…). In the musical sphere, despite some foreigner exceptions such as David Bowie, Marc Bolan, Roxie Music, New York Dolls, Iggy Pop, and the languid and childlike beauty of national singers who whispered passionate love songs to teenagers (Pedro Marín, Miguel Bosé, Los Pecos…), heterosexist masculine representations kept proclaiming the perfect manliness.

Considering some artists and producers lived in a country which, in addition to a patriarcal world, was plagued by its behaviours and military reactionary traditions, which strategies did they transmit? The first resistances to the dominant male order occurred in private. Almost nobody could see them, as they were not publicly shown. Juan Hidalgo made on the sly a series of twelve pictures where a well-dressed man, whose face was not visible, was undressing slowly. I am referring to *Flor y hombre* (1969) in its two versions: coloured and black-and-white. The underlying questioning to the Hidalgo proposal was addressed to the morals and interdicts that impeded showing the naked body of a man. Furthermore, that work—among others—implied the prohibited manifestation of desire between men. That being said, the men's bodies photographed by Hidalgo do not stand up for sexual flexibility or ambiguity. He does not seem to be interested either by representations of mannered, effeminate or queer men. Demasculinizing was not his goal, except for one: the photograph montage named *Biozaj apolíneo, Biozaj dionisíaco* (1977). That production was formed through the superposition of four females and male bodies that turned out a new being called Biozaj.[12] That said, in many of the Hidalgo puzzling texts—named *etceteras*—written in the mid-1960s, there are frequent allusions to anal sex, which is another of the big taboos of the sex-phobic regime built by

Francoism based on a clear ultra-catholic religious groundwork. Among those works, there are *Mister Destrucción* (1966) and *L'uno, il suo cazzo, il suo ano*, which was presented in Milan in 1974.[13] By mentioning the anal issue, it is proclaiming an attack against the dominant masculinity: a real man's body is equal to a cuirass that cannot be penetrated. The artistic material I am about to analyse comes out in the second half of the 1970s with an unusual effervescence after the Dictator's death and it is made with a different nature. It cannot be fairly figured out without taking into account the social and political context that blew up in Spain after decades of affected piety and repression. In addition, it does it through an effeminate language, including a great camp display, showing to the different audiences where it turned out that a man's body could achieve a variety of appearances, shapes, and behaviours, which move away from the canonical expression of masculinity.

The most analysed case in the recent historiography has been José Pérez Ocaña in the late 1970s in Barcelona, parallel to the emergence of the homosexual liberationist movements.[14] Despite the fact that he was a very well-known person in some of the counter-culture Barcelona spheres—the magazine *Ajoblanco* dedicated to him some articles—it was the Ventura Pons' film *Ocaña. Retrat intermitent* (1978) the one that turned him into a known individual. Ocaña's transgressor value lay in his street performances and in his boldness for making public his individualist and libertarian vision of life. A vision where effeminacy and its signs occupied his biologically male body. A body that was no longer destined to move in an enclosed area, as the festive space where transvestites acted,[15] but that it would thoughtlessly invade the street as someone living freely without feeling the threat from the established order, despite the long-suffering detentions. A phallic-centered and male chauvinist order that leaked not only in the public spheres controlled by the police but also in the restricted and used spaces by the assumed sexually open libertarians. Suffice it to say that the experiences told by Ocaña regarding the *Jornadas Libertarias de Barcelona* ("Barcelona Libertarian Conference") held in Parc Güell in 1977. He was not welcomed by some CNT members. What really upset some of the libertarians? Effeminacy insolence? The fact that the manliness of some anarchists was demasculinized? Regarding gender flexibility and transferring femininity and masculinity within the same body and individual, the acting left wing in Spain still had much to learn. Moreover, Ocaña's disconcerting body language, where the clothes played a distinguished and eccentric role—it was not just about cross-dressing as he performed Charlot, an angel or a hunchback woman—irritated some individuals, although they did not stop him from participating in popular carnivals as the ones in Vilanova i la Geltrú, Sitges, and Sevilla.

Ocaña's esthetic is complex—his naïve paintings, wire dolls, handmade paper flowers, cardboard Macarenas—and it comes from his native Andalucía.[16] He considers himself as an Andalusian in the admiration of cemeteries, static angels, Baroque shapes, and the virgins with tormented and bereaved faces. Shortening his work to a painter's activity, it would distort and limit a broad group of issues—the importance he gave to the exhibitions or *gazpachos*—an expression used by Beatriz Preciado in a lecture at Macba's Campceptualismos del sur. Ocaña y la historiografía española, 19th November 2012—he showed in his showings, among others—as the exhibit that took place in the Mec-Mec gallery in Barcelona in 1977. The different pieces, using current terminology, filled up the floor and the walls as an installation, turning the space into a mean and miraculous copy of the Sevillian *Feria de abril*. The great number of references to the religious iconography and the esthetic set, which bothered some priests, was defined by Ocaña himself in an interview conducted by Paloma Chamorro as a "cheap folk picturesque." However, allusions to the cultivated paintings—the colorful works of the Ocaña's admired painters Chagall and Matisse—were not missing. As well as the mad scenographies by the dancer Lindsay Kemp, who set up *Flowers* (1974), a queer show based on *Notre Dame des Fleurs* (1944) by Jean Genet, who had a terrific success in his tour around Spain.

Ocaña's unfaithfully naive and transgressive paintings in which he treated religious themes in an irreverent, uninhibited, and necrophiliac way were important. Nevertheless he would not have the echo he had at that moment, and many years later, without his street activity—a double political action.[17] It is shown in Ocaña's pictures of the first homosexual demonstration in Barcelona in June 1977, where people demanded the repeal of the Law of Social Dangerousness and Social Rehabilitation. It is also visible in the salacious walks he performed in *Las Ramblas* and Real Square, where he clearly shows his manly biological features while he is dressed as a woman. In an extract of Ventura Pons' film, Ocaña walks holding Nazario and Camilo's arms while they energetically move their fans. Ocaña shows off a wide blue hat with a feather on it, a flowered dress, white stockings and shoes, dark glasses, and he has his lips painted in crimson and his face white powdered. Throughout these images, it is inferred an empathy from the public and towards someone who resigns to play the manliness that is supposed to a biological man. Were the fair and understandable longings to freedom of a castrate country, the ones that warmly welcome the gestures and the movements of an Andalusian artist by many of whom went along *Las Ramblas*?[18]

In his festive wandering, provocative gestures such as when he pulled his skirt up and showed his genitalia, did not stop. There is an attentive young and not very tall man with a yellow t-shirt who watches them while standing idly by. The man, whose pose and way of walking looks masculine, seems to be excited with Ocaña's daring revelation. That is, an irreverence built on the self-confidence he embodies, an unknown gender flexibility until then in the Spanish public space. "Me visto de mujer para provocar, para divertirme, para reírme con la gente, para pasármelo bien,"[19] he stated to Paloma Chamorro. Ocaña sometimes paid for that provocation, as he got beat by some offended defenders of the masculine moral that means guards of the hegemonic virility. That order was also attacked by Ocaña when he appeared with make up on, with earrings, and a curl over his forehead—according to Estrellita Castro style—as it can be seen in a recording named *Actuació d'Ocaña i Camilo* (1977), made by the association Video-Nou, where Ocaña shouts his head off when singing flamenco background songs. After the performance, Ocaña is visible among half-naked friends in a kind of a dope smoker spree.[20]

There were many people in Ocaña's world: the Andalusian artist Nazario lived in it. He talked this way:

> Me vine a Barcelona, como mucha gente, porque ésta era la ciudad más cosmopolita de España. Acá, en los últimos años de Franco, había montones de bares gays, había como veinte, más que en París. Estaba minado de bares gays con cierta tradición, a lo Genet, todo un ambiente de mariconeo, de travestis. Y Madrid, al ser la capital, siempre ha sido más facha que Barcelona, donde había una tradición anarquista durante la República. Aquí empezaron los movimientos de gays, el movimiento feminista y el libertario.[21] (Trerotola n. pag.).

From 1975 to 2001, Nazario drew in his new graphic novels (some of them are compilations) an invented, colorful, and transgressive Barcelona. The first one, a clandestine self-edition, was *La piraña divina*. On the one hand, that reality was true and on the other hand it was fiction, where there were characters with a bad reputation but, above all, hustlers, queers of different ages, transvestites, and transsexuals. Moreover, in his main work, *Anarcoma* (1980), the main characters of his creation passed by: Anarcoma himself,

Jamfry, Herr Brothers, XM, Professor Onliyú, Count Black, and the Knights of the Saint Reprimonio Order. A very far world from the warring *El guerrero del antifaz*, which had such a success during the Francoism. His graphic novels made some voracious readers curious and rebel making. For them Anarcoma is the most outstanding character and the most interesting one for this analysis about crosscurrent masculinities.

Anarcoma is, in some way, Nazario's alter ego: a transsexual private investigator who goes around Barcelona's night and its dives looking for clues but who is usually mixed up with desire and sexual passion issues. Anarcoma is presented with long hair, sharpened red nails, spectacular neckline in a body showing impressive breasts by a tight zipped leather jacket, without disguising a huge penis. In the two books Nazario published through *El Víbora*, there are plots and subplots that are threaded. However, the main plot is the one that connects the bondless sexual heat between Anarcoma and the robot XM2, a bold and hairy character. If the stereotype says that every transsexual has to become a prostitute, that is not Acarcoma's case, as he simultaneously works as a private investigator and as an artist in the Club Torpedo. Femininity and masculinity are intertwined in an upset character due to his sexual voltage and his surroundings of a hyper-phallic iconography of huge penises. It looks like there is no place and space for other bodies nor penises.[22]

Madrid was, together with Barcelona, a city where immigrants arrived from other parts of the country. Among others, the couple known as Costus and made up by Juan Carrero Galofré (Palma de Mallorca, 1955–Sitges, 1989) and Enrique Naya Igueravide (Cádiz, 1953–Badalona, 1989).[23] Their work was mainly pictorial, but the sculpture was not something alien for them. They worked with bunches of lively spirits who built what is known as *La Movida*, and among them, Alaska, Pedro Almodóvar, Bibiana Fernández… In their colorful, electrifying, and pop paintings, it is notorious the influence of a religious Baroque esthetic: pietas, crucifixions… Besides the feminine figures, some of them came from frivolous gossip magazines (Lola Flores, Duchess of Alba, Pitita Ridruejo, Persia's Sha, and Farah Diba), representations of indolent men with long hair abounded. Those men—their long hair was a repetition among artists—lay down in an erotic, waiting, and surrendered pose with a languid and ambiguous body language that did not match with the masculine straightened standards. In the body's representation, Costus mainly chose to do not make genitalia visible, except in the series entitled *Chulos* (1981). Juan Carreño, using exclusively fluorescent acrylic, painted that series set in the Caños de Meca beach in Cádiz. Erogenous zones are present in the paintings, through half erections or almost flaccidity. The hunks, a very common term for a gay porn magazine, show off mannered poses.

Some of their friends posed for one of their most explosive and controversial series, *El valle de los caídos*, carried out between 1981 and 1985. Some of them are Olvido Alaska, Fabio de Miguel (Fanny McNamara), Ana Curra (member of the music band Parálisis Permanente), and Pedro Marín, who had a terrific success among teenagers with the song "Que no" (1980). Marín sang it in Televisión Española with a great display of energy, jumps, and leaps while he shook his hips in a not very masculine way, according to the manners of that time. In this esthetical kitsch series—no offense meant—and flashy colors, Costus introduced themselves in the sanctuary where Francoism and its fallen are worshiped and glorified. They are so, no matter the republicans who built the basilica, the religious figures (saints, evangelists) and the cardinal virtues (justice, temperance) taking as models the couple's friends, therefore, a diverse group of involved punk and pop individuals. In one of the paintings, insolence is huge: a portrait of Tino Casal, with a make-up face, a smooth punk esthetic, and long red hair holding a red banner over a valley landscape. Costus brought their psychedelic daily routine to a type of postmodern painting—at that time there was a peak of the Italian trans-vanguard and the German neo-expressionism—that claims to (falsely and fraudly) be about history and religion. Men do not hold the power of a patriarchal society, and women show strength and courage, that is another way of demasculinizing. Costus carried that social activity that clearly separated them from the victorious masculinity, always active and present in the power's space, by giving up to what men do in order to be and show that they are men.[24]

The figure of Pablo Pérez Mínguez (1946–2012) emerged in the context of the painters' apartment in Madrid. He was the cofounder of the magazine *Nueva Lente* in 1971 and developed a great photographic career, even though he stood up for his pop and colorful pictures of Madrid's nightlife. Men, women, and transgendered individuals passed by in front of his camera. Regarding his glance to masculinity, hustlers and models cohabitated in his production. Luis Antonio de Villena talks about those men, who clearly appear as carnal beings and objects of desire, as Pérez Mínguez's friends.[25] In that sense, some portraits of Fanny McNamara and Pedro Almodóvar stand out for its audacity. In fact, those are some of the most known by the public and the ones that deserve it by making visible a reality that Spanish Establishment ignored systematically.[26]

In some cases, Pérez Mínguez's eye holds back the process of esthetic and gender transformation of the portrayed models when they were about to go out on stage, such as it is seen in the film *Laberinto de pasiones* by Almodóvar (1982) where the director and McNamara performed the songs "Suck it to me" or "Gran ganga." In an untitled picture of 1983, which leaks a relaxed atmosphere, Fanny puts lipstick on while watching himself at the mirror and Almodóvar smooths a pair of thick fishnet stockings. Men dressed as women, or better to say a certain kind of women as femininity is not univocal, but it brings more multiplicity that it is usually understood. In another picture, of 1983 too, the dressmaker Antonio Alvarado poses with an abstract painting as the background. His thin body has been captured in a three-quarters position in order to stamp movement, besides the fact that it recalls the famous classicism *contraposto*: Alvarado shows his chest—partially covered by a dark wig—and the black stockings leave the gluteus uncovered. By showing the butt, a body's part that *real* men protect no matter what because their masculinity would be at risk of a possible penetration,[27] Alvarado does not only confirms his self-confidence but also encourages an anal lewdness.

Pérez Mínguez portrayed outstandingly, among all characters from Madrid—which is also the title of a group of pictures from 1984—Fanny McNamara, not to be mistaken for Patty Diphusa,[28] an extravagant star of porn stories illustrated with photos, created by Almodóvar who suggested him to be featured in *Laberinto de pasiones*. Pérez Mínguez named one of his most well known pictures after Almodóvar's character. McNamara appears in the photo as an odalisque lying horizontally, crowned and covered with jewels, including a heart shaped diamond covering his genitalia. It is something necessary to emphasize that the jewels are not valuable but *cutrelux* imitation jewelry, a highly used neologism by the photographer meaning cheap objects. With that picture, an apparently male body poses in one of the historical lineage pose: the one that Manet painted, among many others, where concubines were at the service of men. Is not that work a challenge sufficiently audacious for those who support the immobility of gender? I will give some more examples that abound in the representation of a weird individuality closer to a femininity built on trash literature, punk, and *cañí* transvestism. According to queer theory postulates (Judith Butler, Eve Kosofsky Sedwick…), and previously Gayle Rubin, every expression of gender is a construct, a cultural, social, and political invention because it answers and satisfies certain claims about how subjects must behave and act. At this point, I would like to recall that McNamara's esthetic and conduct were met sometimes, with animosity. In 1981, for example, during a performance of the band Pegamoides in Ventas bull ring in Madrid, the fans of a heavy metal band who also participated in the same concert, threw different objects at McNamara when he appeared wearing a flamenco dancer dress. The performance stopped, and Carlos Berlanga, the guitarist of the band, needed medical attention. The exacerbated machismo and heterosexism of the heavy metal world could not stand a man dressed as a woman and who incarnated, in his theatrical performativity, cultural models far from the biker, necrophiliac, and virile universe.[29]

*Fanny en la columna* (1985) is a picture that exudes a crosscurrent esthetic of the masculine normalcy. McNamara appears seated and watching in the distance, with one of his hands on the hip, the other on the knee, in a pose of a shameless star. He appears on a plaster column, which is an allusion to the ancient culture that exalts and magnifies whoever gets closer to the column that, at the same time, is a cheap material. His clothes and accessories (a moiré jacket, a pair of tight trousers, a pearl necklace, and high heeled shoes) suggest luxury and a break up in gender conventions—a Costus'wish as it is inferred in their *chochonismo ilustrado*, a name that was used to name the 1981 exhibition in the Fernando Vijande gallery in Madrid. In *Fanny, agente secreto* (1985), in color, as another side of the same character, is important. The dark crimson colored hair—Tino Casal style—a glam influence, the red shoes and the blue blackground build the tone of the picture. The gesture that invites us cannot be more stereotypically feminine: in fact, more than thinking of a specific woman, the hand on the hip drives us to the mannequins and their impossible poses. Fashion designers and window dressers conceive them by creating a vision about what is supposedly feminine or a queer version of James Bond. The assumed masculine echo of the jacket, that could recall Marlon Brando's trail in *The Wild One* (1953), stays lackluster—or, depending on the approach, the opposite—because of the showy cartridge belt on the upper tights and the black synthetic woolen tights made probably by Lurex. That place of paradoxes and fascinations reaches the peak with the toy pistol: a manliness of little white lies loaded with blank bullets or even without them.

In 1980, on the Mediterranean coast—more precisely in València—the musical and cabaret group Ploma 2 was born. Their members were Rampova,

Clara Bowie, Greta Guevara, Amador, and Toni Ruiz. During the same decade, the international market welcomed the return of the neo-figurative painting mainly practiced by men (Miquel Barceló, Enzo Cucchi, Jörg Immendorf, Julian Schnabel…) and, at the same time, underestimated the work of the artists I mentioned before due to homophobic prejudices. Throughout its eighteen years of existence, up to fourteen different people became part of Ploma 2 and, among them, biological women such as Celia, Teresa, Carmen, and Herminia. Some of them questioned masculinity as a natural manly fact by acting as a drag king (bulge included) before MACBA and Arteleku organized seminars about transfeminism by the end of the 1990s and the beginning of the twenty-first century. In some cases, male characters such as Charles Chaplin, Louis Armstrong or Harpo Marx were impersonated. In some others, Bertolt Brecht texts took up again the stage, or there were imitators who performed Concha Velasco or Marisol without forgetting the political background with gibes about the incorporation of Spain in 1986 into NATO. The political openness of the group, covered by a cabaret confection, had already came out in 1981 during a performance in Furs Square, next to Torres de Serrans in València, along with the singers Pep Laguarda and Remigi Palmero due to the presence of the Irish republican activist Bernadette Devlin. Another example of the politicization of the group, particularly in fighting against the discrimination against gays, lesbians, and transsexuals, was their participation in the *Moviment d'Alliberament Sexual del País Valencià* (MASPV, "Sexual Liberation Movement of València") and the *Moviment d'Alliberament Gai del País Valencià* (MAGPV, "Gay Liberation Movement of València"). In fact, they participated in the gay pride demonstration in 1981 and 1982 along with Encarnita du Clown, a disturbed person like them,[30] who imitated the radio journalist Mrs Elena Francis with sarcasm and a great confidence.[31]

In fact, the origin of the group's name is a wicked allusion to the Spanish dynamite explosive called *goma-2* ("plastic explosive"). They did not have any violent behavior at all since their aspiration was to be explosive per se and to spoil the gender, sexual conventions, and hegemonic esthetics. They did it in Spanish and in Valencian (a dialect of Catalan), two languages that they would use in ironic, funny, rude, and the same time, slummy lyrics. These were inspired on *cuplé*s and they added antifascist contents.[32] The term *ploma* ("camp") is a clear reference to the happy assumption of the feminization and the queerness as a tool and an effective tactic to talk about indeterminate horizons that are against gender binarism. That is, crosscurrent, slippery, promiscuous, and transgender worlds during the years where that term—gender binarism—was not even legal tender in LGBT spheres. Ploma 2 questioned the hyperbolic-masculinity of martial roots that is admired in so many Francoist and post-Francoist public and private domains. It partially comes from the embodiment made by its protagonists in the musical act of Marlene Dietrich, besides quotations and recall signs to the movie *The Blue Angel* and others such as *Cabaret* by Bob Fosse or *Lili Marleen* by Rainer Werner Fassbinder. These influences cohabitated with others coming from *cuplé*'s world where the queen was Raquel Meller—the singer of *La violetera*. Ploma 2 sang those kinds of songs without any longing of virtuosity or stylistics fidelity, putting distance from pure languages in their body language as well as in their witty choreographies. Their influence (1980–1998) stretched throughout many underground and association places and venues.[33]

Different talents merged in Ploma 2. Among others, it pointed out Rampova's piercing experience[34] who was three times in prison due to the Law of Social Dangerousness and Social Rehabilitation. Rampova not only could draw but also made all Ploma 2 costumes for their cabaret. There was also Amador's mad talent and Clara Bowie's interpretative qualities—sarcastic and tender at the same time—whose voice indicated singing studies. In this transgressive and performance universe, the men-to-women and women-to-men role changes were basic. They went beyond clothing transvestism of nightclubs or carnival drag queens because within their performances, the marvelous imagination of the surrealistic props used in their clothes and on the stage stand out. Some examples, conceived by Amador, are draining boards, tiger-nut milk straws, records, octopuses, a long tailed gown made by *El País* newspapers, or accessories such as cardboard kiosks where porn magazines were hanging from it. However, this radical and precarious film esthetic—with a sarcastic and delirious root and sometimes decadent (saying it tongue-in-cheek to Cleopatra and Mata Hari)—did not give up to the political punch in order to bother the conservatives from the right and the accommodating from the left. That allowed them to criticize communist and fascist totalitarianisms without circumlocutions as well as to exalt refined and caustic effeminacy demand, which is a clear example of demasculinizing.[35]

The 1980s were also the decade where mass media (especially the sensationalist one) and medical and political stratums turned AIDS into a social disease. I am referring, by using the adjective "social," to the conversion of an epidemic to a plague built on ideological reasons (many of them of religious substratum). The fact that AIDS' transmission is through the vagina and anus and intravenously, woke up all puritan's devils. The Spanish synod and the ultra-conservative CONCAPA (*Confederación nacional de padres de familia y alumnos*, "National Confederation of Parents and Students") heavily attacked the timid prevention campaigns—the National High Court repealed a national campaign in 1993 named *Póntelo, pónselo* ("Put it yours on, put it his on") because it encouraged promiscuity among youth and infancy. The panic spread among population and homophobia was present up to the point that many gays got back into the closet. This was not a good time for diversity since it was related with promiscuity, infection, and sexual perversion. The fragile body was a death sign. In fact, muscular and virile body worship raised in gyms and in popular culture. There was an urgent need to be fit, and at the same time, a longing to hide the disease's symptoms that denounced the AIDS infected person in front of a exclusive society that got re-masculinized.

In the second half of the 1980s and in the beginning of the 1990s, when AIDS wreaked havoc, and the mass media—besides medical stratum—openly and discriminatorily talked about high-risk groups, heterosexuals were omitted among them; therefore, Ocaña did not exist anymore, Costus died in 1989, and Fanny McNamara and Pablo Pérez-Mínguez were out of the picture. The artists who broke up with the sexist prejudices by creating images and actions where normative masculinity was under judgment, vanished except Ploma 2, who never got the blessing of the cameras. The panic had deeply got through and the heterosexist order strengthened through the exaltation of a monogamous-marital life, an assumed and false antidote to avoid AIDS. It was not until the mid-1990s that approaches questioning the masculinity in the cultural and artistic Spanish context did emerge. Biological women integrated many of them, as the LSD collective and the duet Cabello/Carceller, which was a clear sign of a new time.

## Notes

1 This chapter was conducted as part of the research project entitled "Representaciones culturales de las sexualidades marginadas en España (1970–1995)" ["Cultural representations of marginalized sexualities in Spain (1970–1995)"], FEM2011—24064, funded by the Spanish Ministerio de Economía y Competitividad.

2 This adjective referred to the group of persons with relaxed tastes and reprehensible professions from a moral perspective. These attitudes, according to the conservative

mentality of the government of the Second Republic during the Black Biennium, deserved to be punished.

3 "Although the law explained that its main goal was the re-education of the socially dangerous individuals, in the Modelo prison the act did not follow the step where a doctor had to diagnose the case–according to the complex classificatory organization of the different types of homosexuality, which were fashionable at the end of the 1960s—and propose the pertinent recovery."

4 "I was sent, within the prison of Barcelona, to a pavilion for underaged queers. The prisoners paid the guards to sneak in and to rape us. Then, they beat us to show they were not gay. They came five or six times per day. Sometimes up to eight times. […] I had more rapes than agreed intercourses."

5 About interpellation, the destructive strength of the insults and the hate speech, see Butler, Eribon, and Borrillo.

6 Aliaga 17–37.

7 This is, maybe, one of the reasons of the application of the Law of Social Dangerousness and Social Rehabilitation: Francoist authorities' fear to the sexual promiscuity that, as they believed, was brought from foreigners to places such as Torremolinos, Barcelona or Madrid.

8 The premiere of the tv series *Curro Jiménez*, featured by Gracia, was in 1976. The roles played by Sacristán show an evolution in the appearance of specific areas of ambiguity. That would question the hegemonic masculinity. See Martínez Pérez and Mérida's chapter in this volume.

9 Landa played a fake gay role in a film that gathers all homophobic clichés: *No desearás al vecino del quinto* ("Do not desire the fifth floor neighbor") by Tito Fernández in 1970.

10 See the example given by the sensationalist magazine *Por qué* 1973: 652 or *La Gaceta Ilustrada*.

11 Many *Party* covers reproduced pictures of women that were used to cover up a magazine for gay readers, as it could be seen later with some covers: the singer Miguel Bosé (in 1980) or José Luis Manzano (in 1984)–actor in some of Eloy de la Iglesia's movies–were featured on the cover of the magazine. About the actor, see Martínez-Expósito's chapter in this volume.

12 This name refers to the five iconographies that the doctors formerly labeled as hermaphroditism and that now we would define it more precisely as intersexuality.

13 See Buxán 147–178. To see Juan Hidalgo's production, visit: <http://goo.gl/6Beq7S>.

14 See the catalogue *Ocaña, 1973–1983*, a project inspired by Pedro G. Romero. The catalogue collects texts—among others—by Beatriz Preciado and Pere Pedrals and an interview with Nazario. The exhibition was shown, besides Barcelona, in Vitoria.

15 See Alcalde and Barceló.

16 In order to see Ocaña's work, visit: <http://goo.gl/4nbpjq>.

17 On 6 October 1983, Paloma Chamorro honored him in her tv show *La edad de oro*, where Nazario and Camilo participated. See also Romero.

18 That is, maybe, one of the explanations why Ocaña's relations with some of the passers-by were affectionate. That is what happens with an old man approached by Ocaña who kisses him on his forehead. Or the case with a woman whom he substitutes by pushing a baby carriage with a girl in it.

19 "I dress as a woman in order to provoke, to have fun, to laugh with people, to have a great time."

20 In a different recording by the same association entitled *Ocaña. Exposició a la galeria Mec-Mec* (1977), the camera goes over Ocaña's exhibition, in the mentioned gallery, escorted by the same artist who rejects the idea that the exhibit is about "his paintings." It is true that there is a kind of setting all around the space: in the exhibition, besides the

different works, there was Ocaña's personal furniture, his red covered bed, among others. That was an attempt of bringing his intimacy, private life, and personal routine to the public space. Ocaña's insolence had no limits: when talking to him about a painting of the Macarena, who was dressed with a sash, a muslin, and a shawl that is "drunkenness, sperm, happiness, and beauty," Ocaña states "[She] is a marginalized woman who can either be Maria or a whore from *La Rambla*." With all these statements, it does not seem to be odd that the most puritans rejected his works. In another extract of the recording, a naked Ocaña puts on a flamenco dancer dress and starts to move gracefully around showing his lack of inhibition and his continuous play with a flamenco music background.

21 "I moved to Barcelona, as many other people, because this is the most cosmopolitan city in Spain. Here, during the last years of Franco, there were many gay bars, around twenty, more than in Paris. It was filled with gay bars with a certain tradition, as Genet, a really queer and transvestite atmosphere. Madrid, being the capital, has been more fascist than Barcelona, where there was an anarchist tradition during the Republic. Here it is where all gay, feminist, and libertarian movement started."

22 The title of a text published by Alberto Cardín in 1983 is more than eloquent: "Being delighted in cocks." To get to know Nazario's graphic universe: <http://goo.gl/mJlFD3>.

23 To see Costus visual world: <http://goo.gl/4rAohS>.

24 I am referring to *chochonismo*, a term used by Costus that was inspired in a documentary about a Native American tribe called Chochonis. The couple associated it with the punk esthetic their friends Alaska and Carlos Berlanga discovered in London. *Chochonismo* was carried in the famous house Costus had in La Palma Street, in the Malasaña neighborhood. Therefore, the homage to gossips and rumors, the long conversations where the epicenter were shags or boyfriends. They did so while they were sitting around heated tables, a behavior that according to the male chauvinist cliché, heterosexual women practiced.

25 See Villena.

26 See Sanz for analysis on some artists from *La Movida*.

27 Nowadays, some tv programs use sex as a tactic, the hatching of porn on the Internet, and some films have partially trivialized naked men. However, anality keeps being a taboo issue regarding heterosexual men and it is not analyzed either in other individuals.

28 See Almodóvar.

29 It is important to check the date because prior to that concert, the singer of Judas Priest, Rob Halford came out of the closet. He did it in 1998 in MTV News. However, that does not mean homophobia has disappeared among heavy metal fans, as well as among fans of other types of music.

30 *Gente trastornada* ("disturbed people") was an nickname assumed by the members of Ploma 2 and by Encarnita Clown. They did not feel represented with the transvestite term because, among other issues, they did not use fake breasts although they imitated female voices when they sang.

31 Years later, Ploma 2 kept a firm political commitment in regards to LGBT issues. That happened through the parties organized by COGAM (*Colectivo Gay de Madrid*, "Gay Association of Madrid") and *La Radical Gai de Madrid* ("Gay Radical of Madrid") between 1989 and 1993, and in Barcelona by the FAGC (*Front d'Alliberament Gai de Catalunya*, "Gay Liberation Front of Catalonia) and the CGB (*Col.lectiu Gai de Barcelona*, "Gay Association of Barcelona") in Diamant Square on the Gay Pride in 1995.

32 For example, they changed the lyrics of the song "Y viva España," that was interpreted by their high-pitched and harsh voices, into an antimilitary and antiracist poem. They did not miss the feminist element in any of the songs they sang, especially references to

gender violence. In addition, the political Establishment was the bull's-eye of their invectives, cutting remarks, and mockery, particularly Valencian conservative politicians.

33 They lavished in many occasions in the Covarrubias or Meliès rehearsal rooms, both in València. They also performed in other places around Spain, such as the Salón Cibeles and the Gràcia's Ateneu in Barcelona, the Spanish Communist Party Festival in Casa de Campo in Madrid, and in different places in Girona, Figueres, Hospitalet, Bilbao, and Seville.

34 After Ploma 2 disappeared, Rampova kept performing. See *El mundo de Rampova Cabaret* and <http://goo.gl/NN9DHt>.

35 Ploma 2 lived during the end of Francoism, the 1980s, and the arrival of the democracy with the overwhelming victory of the PSOE (*Partido Socialista Obrero Español*, "Spanish Socialist Laborer Party") in October 1982. However, the raids did not disappear, and some of its members suffered them.

## Bibliography


Aliaga, Juan Vicente. "Saut d'homme. De identidades conflictivas, paranoias misóginas y penetraciones anales." *Bajo vientre. Representaciones de la sexualidad en la cultura y el arte contemporáneos*. Valencia: Generalitat Valenciana, 1997. 17–37. Print.

Alcalde, Jesús and Ricardo J. Barceló. *Celtiberia gay*. Barcelona: Personas, 1976. Print.

Almodóvar, Pedro. *Patty Diphusa y otros textos*. Barcelona: Anagrama, 2000. Print.

Arnalte, Arturo. *Redada de violetas. La represión de los homosexuales durante el franquismo*. Madrid: La esfera de los libros, 2003. Print.

Buxán Bran, Xosé M. "Un Juan Hidalgo más. Algo queer y etcétera." *Lecciones de disidencia. Ensayos de crítica homosexual*. Barcelona: Egales, 2006. 147–178. Print.

Butler, Judith. *Excitable Speech: A Politics of the Performative*. New York: Routledge, 1997. Print.

Borrillo, Daniel. *Homofobia*. Barcelona: Bellaterra, 2001. Print.

Cardín, Alberto. "Delectándose en las pollas." *Anarcoma*. Nazario. Barcelona: La Cúpula, 1994. 7. Print.

*El mundo de Rampova Cabaret*. Curator Graham Bell Tornado. Xàtiva: La erreria (House of Bent). 2009. Web. n. d. <http://goo.gl/OASqtu>.

Eribon, Didier. *Una moral de lo minoritario: Variaciones sobre un tema de Jean Genet*. Barcelona: Anagrama, 2004. Print.

Junquera, Natalia. "Homosexuales peligrosos." *El País*. 27 Dec. 2006. Web. n. d. <http://goo.gl/EzlA9R>.

*La edad de oro* (October, 6th). Dir. Paloma Chamorro. 1983. Web. n. d. <http://goo.gl/PkoJQC>.

Martínez Pérez, Natalia. "Modelos de masculinidad en el cine de la transición: José Sacristán." *Revista Icono* 14 (2011): 275–293. Print.

Preciado, Beatriz. "Campceptualismos del sur. Ocaña y la historiografía española." 19 Nov. 2012. Lecture. Barcelona: Macba. Web. n. d. <http://goo.gl/XcA62a>.

Romero, Pedro G. *Ocaña, 1973–1983: Acciones, actuaciones, activismo*. Barcelona: Polígrafa, 2010. Print.

Sanz Castaño, Héctor. "Institucionalización y marginalidad del arte *desviado* en la Transición española." *El sistema del arte en España*. Ed. Juan A. Ramírez. Madrid: Cátedra, 2009. 335–373. Print.

Trerotola, Diego. "La anarquía de las maricas." *Revista Soy*. 6 Aug. 2010. Buenos Aires. Web. n. d. <http://goo.gl/cV8WvV>.

Villena, Luis A. de. "En la muerte de Pablo Pérez-Mínguez." 24 Nov. 2012. Web. 7 Nov. 2013. <http://goo.gl/owAEPD>.

# CHAPTER 10

## Female Masculinity on Stage: *Young Man!* and the Subversion of Gender Roles

Richard Cleminson
*University of Leeds*
&
Carlos Pons
*DeNada Dance Theatre*

The inversion of gender roles as an entertaining yet often critical device in Spanish theatre enjoys a long history.[1] Transvestism, notably in Golden Age drama, was often employed as a deceit, as a means of gaining justice, or as a temporary embodiment permitting access to a loved one as the plot developed. Any hint of same-sex desire, however, was usually eventually obliterated by the end of the play as the "proper" male and female roles together with heterosexuality were restored to their "natural" position of dominance.[2] More recently, the reaffirmation of both heterosexual relations and traditional gender norms has become less clear-cut in international theatre than in Spain's Golden Age and can be seen in innovatory productions such as Matthew Bourne's *Swan Lake* and, in the Spanish case, Calderón's *La vida es sueño* (*Life is a Dream*), which cast Segismundo in a female role.[3]

It has been argued successfully by Judith Butler among others that all genders, sexes, and sexualities are consolidated, to some degree, by their performative iteration.[4] Their theatrical representation can give rise to productive interpretations and bodily performances on stage, meaning that theatre has become, as Penny Farfan has observed, "an acute site for queer subversions, critiques, and ways of knowing" for diverse kinds of publics.[5] The transfer between the players, the set, and the audience in any performance which is "located, relational, textualized, vocalized, costumed, choreographed," can also in fact serve to produce "queer significations, experiences, feelings, desires, and communities."[6]

The three founding members of the DeNada Dance Theatre Company, Sabrina Ribes Bonet, María Victoria Da Silva, and Carlos Pons, moved to the

United Kingdom to train in contemporary dance in the year 2005. DeNada, which describes itself as devoted to the "adoration for kitsch," was born out of the desire to study the idea of "Spanishness" and the "distortions of Spanish culture" in a foreign setting,[7] subjects that have received multiple interrogations both inside and outside of Spain in the last two decades.[8] One of the central issues in their work has become the exploration of the extent of existing clichés on things Spanish in contemporary Britain. Powerful motifs of gender and sexuality, particularly the Spanish macho, resonate within British popular culture and are explored on stage in DeNada's productions.

In addition to discovering a broad repertoire of stereotypes of this kind, other differences between the cultures of the two countries came to light for the company's members, notably in respect of the kinds of choreography practised in Spain and England. Choreography in England was more abstract in nature, had a more developed taste for conceptual work and was less melodramatic than its Spanish variety. The world of Calderón, Valle-Inclán, and, to a lesser degree, Lorca—the staples of Spanish theatrical schools—seemed far removed from the experience found in England, despite the huge popularity of other Spanish cultural expressions such as the films of Pedro Almodóvar and Bigas Luna. How could one be faithful to a tradition that innovated but carried on a distinctly dramatic Spanish voice in this context? The exploration of this conundrum was what inspired DeNada to bring these writers' legacy to the British dance panorama, to share the origins of the company and to play with the clichés about Spain that the British apparently knew so well—*jamón*, *sangría*, the *toro,* and machismo—in order to examine the culture that the group had inherited and which, for all its famed passion and untamed sensuousness, clearly possesses some of the same basic emotions in common with other cultures.

## Roland Petit's *Le Jeune Homme et la Mort*

Given the persistence of Spanish motifs and stereotypes, it seemed to DeNada that by searching the theatrical past these themes could be productively explored for audiences today. A recasting of Roland Petit's 1946 ballet, *Le Jeune Homme et la Mort*, offered this opportunity. The libretto for Petit's original ballet was provided by Jean Cocteau and it was set to music by J. S. Bach. The translation of an interview of the choreographer by dance journalist Emma Manning, originally undertaken in 1999 but republished as an obituary after Petit's death in 2011, provided the inspiration for further exploration.[9] A few months later, the same international dance magazine, *Dance Europe*, published a special feature on *Le Jeune Homme et la Mort*, which at the time (November 2011) was being rehearsed by the English National Ballet.[10] Several aspects covered by these articles, amongst them, the actual plot of the ballet and the iconic status of the role of the Young Man, which has been performed by most of the male exponents of twentieth-century ballet, and Petit's approach to love and death in his oeuvre, provided motifs to explore these themes further. The significance of characters similar to the "jeune homme" in many European literatures should not be overlooked.[11] In 2013, DeNada made its own production of the play under the title *Young Man!*, first appearing on stage in Leeds in May of the same year.

*Le Jeune Homme et la Mort* takes place in the eponymous man's Parisian attic, amid the accoutrements pertaining to his profession as an artist. A stunning woman in a chic yellow dress seduces him into committing suicide. Once the Young Man has hung himself, she returns in a white gown and red cape, her face covered by a death mask, to lead him to the other world—an ascent they commence against a backdrop of the Parisian skyline. This romantic but tragic tale, a little like a sleek, femme fatale version of Goethe's *The Sufferings of Young Werther*, left many questions unanswered. The beguiling character of the Woman in Yellow and the representation of the character of Death undergoes very few changes in the performer's emotional range throughout the piece. She remains the evil seductress that is often found in Petit's ballets—but what was it that made her drive this young man to an early death? What pleasures, if any, did she obtain from his torment? How could her gaze remain as steely as her *arabesques* when this man is clearly being driven to his calculated demise?

For a work that is nowadays relatively unknown outside of the dance milieu, it is surprising to note how many great male dancers have taken the role of the Young Man. Jean Babilée created the role in 1946; from there, it has been danced by Rudolf Nureyev, Mikhail Baryshnikov, Nicolas le Riche, and, more recently, Ivan Vasilliev and a short film has been made of the Young Man.[12] In ballet, the passing on of the classical repertoire from generation to generation has resulted in the iconization of certain roles. Unlike in contemporary dance, where roles are often not gender specific, ballet has set character roles for each gender—Odette/Odile, the swan, is a female role, and Prince Siegfried is a male role. The Young Man, a relative infant in the classical repertoire, soon achieved this iconic status, which leads us to examine each of the famous exponent's reading of the role. However similar in terms of choreography, nevertheless, every dancer professed a unique type of masculinity expressed through the physicality and theatrics of the dancer. By studying how each approached the role of the Young Man, DeNada could begin to consider how it would approach studying masculinity and its performance from a choreographic perspective.

DeNada wished to push these boundaries further, however, into the realm of the subversion of gender roles and the heterosexuality implied in the original in order to recast these gendered certainties. In addition to this queering of the ballet, DeNada chose to move the story to Spain, to a context with which the group was familiar and which it wished to explore in a locality that was for its members a foreign country. The references to death, for example, in the title of the original ballet seemed to point the production in the direction of Spain. Death is a motif repeated in all national literatures and cultural productions, but in Spain, if we are to believe cinema directors such as Pedro Almodóvar, it connotes some special qualities in this country, not least in Lorca's poetry.[13] Petit himself had a death in almost each of his ballets, as he stated to Manning:

> ...If you see the *Swan Lake* version with death at the end, or you see the version with a wedding, which one is the best? ... It's [death] in every Shakespeare play - and in Goethe everybody dies at the end. And it's because it's the best ending. It is the strongest thing that can happen to you when you are alive is to die. It's the worst accident that can happen![14]

The drama of Petit's work—with its death at the end—seemed very suitable to the drama of Spain, where the death of Christ, of bulls, and family members is commemorated or celebrated. And to end *Young Man!* with a death, "the strongest thing that can happen to you," enacted by two *female* protagonists, seemed, although melodramatic, the best way to mourn the tragedy of the lives of hundreds of gay men and women, trapped inside the veil of invisibility under Francoism and, indeed, despite a greater presence and the legality of same-sex marriage, a lack of visibility today.[15]

## Youth, Death, and Machismo

The first words of the title—a *Jeune Homme*—given the cultural models of masculinity still currently available in Spain, evoke the typical Spanish *macho*. The *macho* is a figure populating a limited range of historical and more recent masculine styles current in the post-dictatorship period, the years in which members of DeNada grew up. The adults that were around during the infancy and adolescence of the DeNada members, had machismo and prevailing strict Catholic values imbued in their lives over the last two decades of the dictatorship. Even in the 1990s, in certain circles to be a *macho* or proper man, one had to be both a Francoist and a homophobe.[16] The political and religious implications of the macho dictatorship seemed to take second place, however; the new macho was made up of a mix of homophobia, misogyny, and idolatry of the *Generalísimo*. This role was contrasted with the effeminate *marica*, both in the past as a folkloric reference and in the "gay lib" days of the 1970s and 1980s. It also contrasted with other expressions of masculinity that did not conform to what were represented as historical or age-old ways of being male which were often violent, reactionary forms.[17] As stated, gender is a performative act and the group dynamics of any particular social structure can permit the performance of this hyper masculine role. Such a diversity of gendered positions literally lent itself perfectly to the stage. And perhaps this was the way to answer another question that came up—what would happen if, due to some terrible mistake of nature, two of these *machos* were to feel desire towards each other?

When Pons Guerra's rehearsals with the female dancers began, they too had had their own negative experiences with the macho. In their case, they spoke of misogyny, and of a feral kind of sexuality that, half in jest, was related to food—the scent of garlic, the coarse texture of ham, the biting of a length of chorizo (and spitting out its skin). This is when the use of food as props came into *Young Man!*, which of course later took on a more symbolic significance.

Given these considerations, two female dancers were chosen to perform the roles of these men—the Young Man and what became the Man in Yellow. Just as other practitioners had done before in order to reflect on the performance of gender, this choice was made to highlight the fact that the Spanish *macho* is as much a construct of a particular time in history as any other character in the dance repertoire. DeNada's production also played with the fact that masculinity, in itself, is a culturally conditioned construct and can be appropriated by women, as it has been in the past. As Judith Halberstam has argued, such "other" expressions of masculinity, including "female masculinity," pry apart maleness and masculinity and function to "explore a queer subject position that can successfully challenge hegemonic models of gender conformity."[18] Like other queer theatre in the past, however unintentionally in this case, it also had the effect of speaking to a lesbian audience; to paraphrase Farfan, it functioned as a queer performance for queer spectators.[19] It did not, by contrast, set out to "deliberately [resist] legibility by straight spectators."[20] Finally, it also may have "functioned to foster queer community and gay kinship" between audience and performers.[21] The next section analyses these questions.

**Playing with Masculinity**

To come up with the two male characters in *Young Man!*, choreographer Pons Guerra designed several improvisational tasks where he asked the two female dancers to physically embody their idea of the *macho*. The different tasks—one of which was a sort of a fashion catwalk, in which the two dancers had to walk, gesticulate, and talk across the dance studio like the men they had in mind—resulted in a very concrete stereotype, although for each of the participants, including the choreographer, the *macho* took on a different appearance that was directly related to each participant's geography. For Pons Guerra, originally from Gran Canaria, the idea was that of a "señorito andaluz," a landowner who tried desperately to hold on to former glories, whereas for Sabrina Ribes Bonet and Victoria Da Silva, from Castellón and Barcelona respectively, the male came from "la España profunda," and was more brutish. The three, however, coincided in that the character was highly misogynist, homophobic, violent, and very sexual (as well as unable to control any flatulence). Interestingly, although the improvisation was designed as an individual exercise, the two dancers eventually ended up competing against each other during their catwalk runs, shouting out comments, making gestures and noises to assert one's masculinity over the other.

For Victoria Da Silva, becoming the Man in Yellow was a difficult task as it separated masculinity from maleness.[22] To physicalize male behaviour as a performance was something she had to work on steadily throughout the three weeks of creation. It was thanks to the character Da Silva created that it was possible to achieve this aim. She had seen the man she envisioned—from the depths of Castile—all her life; for her, it was the "typical Spanish man," so she had many references to go by. Her relationship with this construct was also interesting. Da Silva felt that, were she to meet this man in the street, she would feel a great aversion towards him. *Young Man!* tried to answer what was behind the hyperbolic display of masculinity in these men.

Her character was plagued by guilt over his homosexual desire—so much so that he would lead his lover to death by a heroin over-dose, to rid himself of these feelings. Initially, Victoria could not find the logic to this, as she believed the macho to be incapable of experiencing any emotion other than lust, possessiveness, and aggression—much less love, particularly towards another man. She had to build a story around him, had to force the guilt into the character, and eventually began believing that it could be possible for this man to have some sort of emotional conscience (this process took several weeks, and she had to try out different scenarios in her head). Eventually, Victoria felt pity towards the character, and this feeling allowed her to embody his masculinity. So, for Victoria, to perform machismo for its own sake was a harder task, as she had no emotional connection to what was behind such behaviour, but once she had found what could have caused it, in this case, self-hatred, she was able to connect with the character on a different level, and could thus embody its masculinity both physically and mentally.

For Sabrina Ribes Bonet, the role of the Young Man was easier to approach. The character, created both by Pons Guerra and Ribes Bonet, also came from Castile, but was distinctively of working-class origin. As a parallel to Petit's *Jeune Homme*, he also painted, in this case, cars; it was felt that his character had a different kind of emotional intelligence, and possibly had artistic sensibilities that he was not fully capable of realizing, seeing them as a threat to his masculinity. This young man was also inspired by the character of Alec Scudder, the under-gamekeeper in E. M. Foster's novel, *Maurice*, who, although nowhere as educated as the novel's eponymous protagonist, is more accepting of his homosexual desire and does not appear any less virile for doing so—in fact, measured by Spanish standards of machismo, he is perhaps more masculine than Maurice. Sabrina could easily relate to the feelings the young man experiences throughout the work: the anxiety caused by waiting, the anger, the lust, and the desperation. For her, the challenge was to adopt a masculine vocabulary of movement rather than to relate to the psyche, as for her, the man's emotions instinctively suggested a more stereotypically female physical lexicon. It seemed that the limited emotional and psychological range of the *macho ibérico* made him easier to embody, but harder to understand; whereas to express an ample range of emotion through the body of a macho seemed almost contradictory.

The press reaction to *Young Man!* coincided in the honest adoption of masculine behaviour from both performers. Josephine Leask comments:

> Through a seamless language of symbiotic contact work, crutch-rubbing, chorizo-nibbling and even masturbation involving a flank of ham in this unapologetic display of teasing arousal, the women astound and disturb, not least through their beguiling appropriation of masculine physicality and the phallus.[23]

And Gerard Davies, writing for *Dance Europe*, adds:

> ...Crucially, *Young Man!* had especially strong characterizations... which meant that the slow burn to the fatal heroin-induced conclusion was believable and moving.[24]

Different audience members—both male and female—have commented on the androgyny of the performers, and their general impression was that which was intended; that the macho is indeed a construct, a role that is performed in real life just as both dancers performed onstage. Imbuing masculinity with femaleness, or with "female masculinity"—a construct in itself—facilitated this move. Other audience members, such as lesbian-identified spectators, made very different readings as they believed that the piece spoke directly to them and they too felt that there was a lack of theatre/dance works that catered to them.

**Conclusion**

Kim Marra has argued that the emotional and the corporeal on stage can provide for an embodied performance that in turn can function as a queer methodology for historical research.[25] The direction and staging of *Young Man!* by DeNada Dance Theatre Company, in its examination of gender stereotypes from the past and in its suggestions for a queer perspective on them in the present, has performed a similar kind of task as a piece of practice from which ideas and theory have emerged.[26] This can produce surprising results in speaking to a queer-identified audience in secret codes and can open up dialogical conversations with straight-identified audiences; performance, as Jill Dolan has pointed out, has a capacity for generating transformative affects in the public and even hope.[27] The result, as other studies have suggested, is not only a form of entertainment through "quirky physicality and extravagant theatricality,"[28] but one which can perhaps more importantly help to resolve social identity conflict, especially for those questioning their sexuality or those who identify as LGBTQI. The arts, and the performing arts in particular, as the authors of a study on alliances against homophobia have recently argued, can form part of the empowerment process by asserting that "positive outcomes are indeed possible using theater and dialogue and theater strategies."[29]

## Notes

1 This chapter was conducted as part of the research project entitled "Representaciones culturales de las sexualidades marginadas en España (1970–1995)" ["Cultural representations of marginalized sexualities in Spain (1970–1995)"], FEM2011—24064, funded by the Spanish Ministerio de Economía y Competitividad.

2 See, for example, McKendrick, *Woman and society*.

3 <http://goo.gl/nOpOvS>.

4 In a theatrical context, see Muñoz, *Disidentifications*; Sinfield, *Out on Stage*; Dolan, *Theatre and Sexuality*.

5 Farfan, "Editorial Comment', 1.

6 *Ibid.* 1.

7 <http://goo.gl/kpOud5>.

8 A recent example includes Pérez Isasi, "The Limits of 'Spanishness'." Specifically, with respect to the representation of Spanishness and the stage, see Thompson, *Performing Spanishness*, and, for the written word and cinema, see Sánchez-Conejero (ed.), *Spanishness in the Spanish novel*.

9 Manning, "Roland Petit."

10 Foyer, "Focus," 32.

11 It hardly needs to be pointed out that the mention of a "young man" in the titles of European literature over the twentieth century has been an enduring motif. James Joyce published his *A Portrait of the Artist as a Young Man* in book form in 1916. Cf. for French examples: René Boylesve, *Le dangereux jeune homme*; François Mauriac, *Le jeune homme*; Edmond Jaloux, *Le jeune homme au masque*. Gustave Moreau's painting of "Le Jeune Homme et la Mort" was finished in circa 1881 in honour of his friend Théodore Chassériau.

12 See, for example, the film in which Nureyev starred in 1966 (<http://goo.gl/4Fc4cy>). Another film that uses the "Jeune Homme" is Taylor Hackford's 1985 film, *White Nights*; the opening sequence has Mikhail Baryshnikov dancing the role.

13 See Ciment and Rouyer, "Entretien avec Pedro Almodovar." For an appreciation of Almodóvar's own disruption of Spanishness, see Comuzio, "Transgression and Spanishness."

14 Manning, "Roland Petit," 33.

15 The literature in this area is growing. For an important contribution, see the monographical issue, "Represión franquista," *Orientaciones: revista de homosexualidades*, 7, 2004.

16 A landmark text in the examination of homophobia in Spain is Borrillo, *Homofobia*. A year later, Olga Viñuales published *Lesbofobia*.

17 On the role of violent masculinity as a foundation aspect of the military uprising against the Republic in July 1936 and within later Francoism, see Vincent, "The Martyrs and the Saints."

18 Halberstam, *Female Masculinity*, 9.

19 For a broader discussion, see Doty, *Making Things Perfectly Queer*.

20 Farfan, "Editorial Comment," 1.

21 *Ibid.* 1.

22 See the discussion on the problems and pitfalls of doing so in Halberstam, *Female Masculinity*, 14.

23 Leask, review of "Young Man!."

24 Davies, "Resolution!," 61.

25 Marra, "Riding, Scarring, Knowing," 490.

26 As Marra points out: "in PaR [practice as research], as Estelle Barrett has noted, ideas and theory emerge from practice and not the other way around" (490). Cf. Barrett, "Introduction." This is a task that DeNada continues to undertake within the context of the Liverpool Homotopia festival, where *Young Man!* was performed once more (October 2013).

27 See the discussion in Walsh, "Queer Publics, Public Queers," 92, where Dolan, *Utopia in Performance* is discussed.

28 <http://goo.gl/LbI95a>.

29 Wernick, Dessell, Kulick, and Graham, "LGBTQQ youth creating change," 1577.

## Bibliography


Barrett, Estelle. "Introduction." *Practice as Research: Approaches to Creative Arts Enquiry.* Ed. Estelle Barrett and Barbara Bolt. London: I. B. Tauris, 2007. 1–13. Print.

Borrillo, Daniel. *Homofobia.* Barcelona: Bellaterra, 2001. Print.

Boylesve, René. *Le dangereux jeune homme*. Paris: Calmann-Lévy, 1921. Print.

Ciment, Michel and Philippe Rouyer. "Entretien avec Pedro Almodovar - La vie, la mort, les femmes et la Mancha." *Positif – Revue mensuelle de cinéma*, 2006: 17–21. Print.

Comuzio, Ermanno. "Transgression and Spanishness: The Cinema of Pedro Almodóvar." *Cineforum*, 1999: 94–95. Print.

Davies, Gerard. "Resolution!" *Dance Europe*, March 2013: 59–61. Print.

Dolan, Jill. *Utopia in Performance: Finding Hope at the Theater.* Ann Arbor: U of Michigan P, 2005. Print.

———. *Theatre and Sexuality*. Basingstoke: Palgrave Macmillan, 2010. Print.

Doty, Alexander. *Making Things Perfectly Queer: Interpreting Mass Culture.* Minneapolis: U of Minnesota P, 1993. Print.

Farfan, Penny. "Editorial Comment: Queer Research in Performance." *Theatre Journal* 4 (2012): 1–3. Print.

Foyer, Maggie. "Focus on Roland Petit's *Le Jeune Homme et la Mort." Dance Europe* December 2011: 32–37. Print.

Halberstam, Judith. *Female Masculinity.* Durham: Duke UP, 1998. Print.

Jaloux, Edmond. *Le jeune homme au masque*. Paris: Plon, 1928. Print.

Leask, Josephine. Rev. of *Young Man!,* by DeNada. *The Place Review*, <www.theplace.org.uk>, 08 Feb 2013.

Manning, Emma. "Roland Petit." *Dance Europe* August/September 2011: 32–33. Print.

Marra, Kim. "Riding, Scarring, Knowing: A Queerly Embodied Performance Historiography." *Theatre Journal* 4 (2012): 489–511. Print.

Mauriac, François. *Le jeune homme*. Paris: Hachette, 1926. Print.

McKendrick, Melveena. *Woman and Society in the Spanish Drama of the Golden Age: a Study of the Mujer Varonil.* London: Cambridge UP, 1974. Print.

Muñoz, José Esteban. *Disidentifications: Queers of Color and the Performance of Politics.* Minneapolis: U of Minnesota P, 1999. Print.

Pérez Isasi, Santiago. "The Limits of 'Spanishness' in Nineteenth-century Spanish Literary History." *Bulletin of Hispanic Studies* 2 (2013): 167–187. Print.

Sánchez-Conejero, Cristina, ed. *Spanishness in the Spanish Novel and Cinema of the 20th-21st Century.* Newcastle: Cambridge Scholars Publishing, 2007. Print.

Sinfield, Alan. *Out on Stage: Lesbian and Gay Theatre in the Twentieth Century.* New Haven: Yale UP, 1999. Print.

Thompson, Michael. *Performing Spanishness. History, Cultural Identity and Censorship in the Theatre of José María Rodríguez Méndez.* Bristol: Intellect, 2007. Print.

Vincent, Mary. "The Martyrs and the Saints: Masculinity and the Construction of the Francoist Crusade." *History Workshop Journal* 47 (1999): 68–98. Print.

Viñuales, Olga. *Lesbofobia.* Barcelona: Bellaterra, 2002. Print.

Walsh, Fintan. "Queer Publics, Public Queers." *Performing Ethos* 2 (2011): 91–94. Print.

Wernick, Laura J., Adrienne B. Dessell, Alex Kulick, and Louis F. Graham. "LGBTQQ Youth Creating Change: Developing Allies against Bullying through Performance and Dialogue." *Children and Youth Services Review* 35 (2013): 1576–1586. Print.

# CONTRIBUTORS

**Juan Vicente Aliaga** is Associate Professor of Art Theory at the Universitat Politècnica de València (Spain). He has published, among other books, *Bajo vientre. Representaciones de la sexualidad en la cultura y el arte contemporáneos* (1997), *Arte y cuestiones de género* (2004) and *Orden fálico. Androcentrismo y violencia de género en las prácticas artísticas del siglo XX* (2007). He has been curator of many exhibitions: *Genealogías feministas en el arte español: 1960–2010* (MUSAC, León, 2012), *Claude Cahun* (Jeu de Paume, Paris, 2011), *En todas partes. Políticas de la diversidad sexual en el arte* (CGAC, Santiago de Compostela, 2009), *Valie Export* (Camden Arts Centre, London, 2004), and *Pepe Espaliú* (Museo Reina Sofía, Madrid, 2003).

**Kerman Calvo** is Associate Professor of Sociology at the Universidad de Salamanca (Spain). Previously, he has worked at the Centro de Estudios Políticos Constitucionales (Madrid), Universitat Pompeu Fabra (Barcelona), and Universidad Carlos III (Madrid), as well as in the "Human Rights Centre" at the University of Essex. He has co-edited an special issue of *Sexualities* devoted to Spain (2011), and is the author of *Pursuing Membership in the Polity: The Spanish Gay and Lesbian Movement in Comparative Perspective (1970–1997)* (2005).

**Richard Cleminson** is Reader in the History of Sexuality (Spanish, Portuguese and Latin American Studies) and Deputy Director of the Centre for Interdisciplinary Gender Studies at the University of Leeds (United Kingdom). His books include *Anarchism, Science and Sex: Eugenics in Eastern Spain, 1900–1937* (2000), *Anarchism and Sexuality: Ethics, Relationships and Power* (2011), edited with Jamie Heckert, as well as the co-authored volumes, with Francisco Vázquez García, *"Los Invisibles": A History of Male Homosexuality in Spain, 1850–1939* (2007) and *Hermaphroditism, Medical Science and Sexual Identity in Spain, 1850–1960* (2009), both translated into Spanish, and *Sex, Identity and Hermaphrodites in Iberia, 1508–1800* (2013).

**Óscar Guasch** is Associate Professor of Sociology at the Universitat de Barcelona (Spain). He has published extensively on sexuality and masculinity studies: *La sociedad rosa* (1991), *La crisis de la heterosexualidad* (2007), and *Héroes, científicos, heterosexuales y gays*

(2006). He has edited many books devoted to the sociology of sexuality and recently the volume entitled *Vidas de hombre(s)* (2012).

**Dieter Ingenschay** is Professor of Spanish and Latin-American Studies at Humboldt-Universität zu Berlin (Germany) and director of its Institut für Romanistik. Former president of the German Association of Hispanists, he has published extensively on gay, lesbian and masculinity studies in contemporary culture. He has edited a number of books devoted to Hispanic literatures, including: *Abriendo caminos. La literatura española desde 1975* (1993), *After-Images of the City* (2002), and *Desde aceras opuestas. Literatura/cultura gay y lesbiana en Latinoamérica* (2006).

**Elena Madrigal-Rodríguez** is Professor of Mexican Literature at the Universidad Autónoma Metropolitana-Azcapotzalco (Mexico). She is the author of *Del licántropo que aúlla con gran perfección. La poética de Julio Torri desde el Ateneo y el esteticismo* and *Julio Torri, De fusilamientos. Edición anotada* (2011 and 2013, respectively). She co-edited *Un juego que cabe entre nosotras. Acercamientos a la crítica y a la creación de la literatura sáfica* (2014). She has also published numerous articles and book chapters on women writers and lesbian literature. *Contarte en lésbico* (2010) is her first book of fiction.

**Alfredo Martínez-Expósito** was Professor of Spanish at the University of Queensland, Australia, until 2011, when he joined the University of Melbourne as Head of the School of Languages and Linguistics and Professor of Hispanic Studies. Between 2004 and 2006 he was president of the Association for Iberian and Latin American Studies of Australasia (AILASA). He has published *Los escribas furiosos: Configuraciones homoeróticas en la narrativa española actual* (1998), *Escrituras torcidas: Ensayos de crítica "queer"* (2004), and, in collaboration with Santiago Fouz-Hernández, *Live Flesh: The Male Body in Recent Spanish Cinema* (2007).

**Jordi Mas** is a doctoral student at the Universitat de Barcelona, after completing his studies in sociology and anthropology. His research interests include the analysis of medical discourses on transgender and transsexual peoples in Spain.

**Rafael M. Mérida-Jiménez** is Associate Professor of Hispanic Literatures at the Universitat de Lleida (Spain). He has published many academic works on

Spanish and Catalan literatures from the Middle Ages through the twentieth century, including the books *Fuera de la orden de natura* (2001), *El gran libro de las brujas* (2004), *La aventura de "Tirant lo Blanch" y de "Tirante el Blanco"* (2007), *Damas, santas y pecadoras* (2008), and *Cuerpos desordenados* (2009). He has also edited the first anthology of queer theory translated into Spanish: *Sexualidades transgresoras* (2002), as well as *Mujer y género en las letras hispánicas* (2008), *Manifiestos gays, lesbianos y queer* (2009), and *Minorías sexuales en España (1970–1995). Textos y representaciones* (2013).

**Alberto Mira** is Reader in Spanish and Film Studies at Oxford Brookes University (United Kingdom). He has edited and translated literary works from English into Spanish and has written two novels (*Londres para corazones solitarios*, 2005, and *Como la tentación*, 2007). He has published extensively on gender, gay, lesbian, film and masculinity studies: *Para entendernos. Diccionario de cultura homosexual, gay y lésbica* (1999), *De Sodoma a Chueca. Una historia cultural de la homosexualidad en España en el siglo XX* (2004), *Miradas insumisas. Gays y lesbianas en el cine* (2008), as well as the *Historical Dictionary of Spanish Cinema* (2010).

**Jorge Luis Peralta** studied Humanities at the Universidad Nacional de Cuyo (Mendoza, Argentina) and received his Ph.D. in Theory of Literature in 2013 from the Universitat Autònoma de Barcelona (Spain), with the dissertation *Espacios homoeróticos en la literatura argentina (1914–1964)*. He conducts his postdoctoral research at the Universidad Nacional de la Plata thanks to a CONICET fellowship. His research interests and publications include works on twentieth century Latin American and Spanish literatures, gender studies and queer theory.

**Carlos Pons** was born in Gran Canaria, Spain, and trained as a contemporary dancer at the Northern School of Contemporary Dance, Leeds, and the "María de Ávila" Royal Conservatoire for Dance in Madrid. Choreographically, his interests lie within the postmodern fields of pastiche and reconstruction, especially in relation to representations of queer identities through performance. He also obtained a B.A. (Hons) in English Literature from the Open University, and is a dance critic and translator for *Dance Europe/ Danza Europa*.

**Gracia Trujillo** holds a Ph.D. in sociology and is Doctora Miembro of the Juan March Institute, Madrid. Associate Professor of Sociology at the Universidad de Castilla-La Mancha and activist, she also teaches feminist and queer theories and practices in other postgraduate programmes. She has contributed to many collective works such as *El eje del mal es heterosexual. Figuraciones, movimientos y prácticas feministas queer* (2005), *Las lesbianas (no) somos mujeres. En torno a Monique Wittig* (2013), and *Feminismos lesbianos y queer* (2014). Her book *Deseo y resistencia. Treinta años de movilización lesbiana en el Estado español (1977–2007)* (2010) won the "Desayuno en Urano" award for the best essay on LGBT queer issues published in 2010, and the "Memoria necesaria" award in 2013.

# MASCULINITY STUDIES

## Literary and Cultural Representations

Josep M. Armengol and Àngels Carabí
*General Editors*

In line with the latest trends within masculinity scholarship, the books appearing in the Masculinity Studies series deal with representations of masculinities in culture, in general, and literature, in particular. The aim of this series is twofold. On the one hand, it focuses on studies that question traditionally normative representations of masculinities. On the other, it seeks to highlight new alternative representations of manhood, looking for more egalitarian models of manhood in and through literature and culture. Besides literary representations, the series is open to studies of masculinity in cinema, theatre, music, as well as all kinds of artistic and visual representations.

For further information about the series and submitting manuscripts, please contact:

Peter Lang Publishing, Inc.
Acquisitions Department
29 Broadway, 18th floor
New York, New York 10006

To order, please contact our Customer Service Department at:

800-770-LANG (within the U.S.)
212-647-7706 (outside the U.S.)
212-647-7707 FAX
CustomerService@plang.com

Or browse online by series at:

www.peterlang.com